D1195711

OHIO LANDS
AND THEIR HISTORY

OHIO LANDS

AND

THEIR HISTORY

WILLIAM E. PETERS

ARNO PRESS
A New York Times Company
New York • 1979

Editorial Supervision: ANDREA HICKS

———◆———

Reprint Edition 1979 by Arno Press Inc.

Reprinted from a copy in The Duke University
    Library

THE DEVELOPMENT OF PUBLIC LAND LAW
IN THE UNITED STATES
ISBN for complete set: 0-405-11363-3
See last pages of this volume for titles.

Publisher's Note: Frontispiece map of Ohio as
Originally Subdivided was deleted from this
edition.

Manufactured in the United States of America

———◆———

Library of Congress Cataloging in Publication Data

Peters, William Edwards, 1857-1952.
    Ohio lands and their history.

    (The Development of public land law in the
United States)
    Reprint of the 3d ed., 1930, published by the
author, Athens, Ohio.
    Bibliography: p.
    1. Ohio--Public lands. 2. Land subdivision--
Ohio. I. Title. II. Series.
HD243.03 P4 1979   333.1'09771   78-53541
ISBN 0-405-11383-8

OHIO LANDS

AND

THEIR HISTORY

By

WILLIAM E. PETERS of the Athens Bar

Author of "Legal History of the Ohio University";
Land Areas

———

THIRD EDITION

———

Published by
W.   E.   PETERS
Athens, Ohio

Printed by
THE LAWHEAD PRESS
Athens, Ohio

1 9 3 0

PREFACE

At the close of the revolutionary war many sought homes northwest of the Ohio river. Various reasons and purposes created different demands and caused many locations of land and settlements to be made in Ohio. Each has its own particular history. And to understand that history, which is basic, it is necessary to begin with the demand for homes and the different settlements of land itself, since the history of a new country often begins with that which made its settlement possible rather than with the settlement itself.

Some settlements were made because land could be obtained cheaply; some to satisfy army bounty warrants issued for services in the war, as in the United States and in the Virginia military tracts; some to recover money loaned the colonies, as the Symmes purchase; some to reimburse losses, as the French grants, the refugee and the fire lands; some to invite settlement, or as homesteads, as the donation tract; some to assure settlers their homes and for military purposes, as the twelve miles square reserve; some to satisfy colonial claims, as the Connecticut reserve and the Virginia military tract; some to recompense or reward some Indians and their white friends, as the Isaac Zane, Shane, Godfroy, Minor, Nevarre and other tracts; some to induce the opening of a roadway or "trace," as the Ebenezer Zane tracts at Zanesville, Lancaster and Chillicothe, while the endowments of universities, schools and religion and the protection of salt, likewise have made their impress.

In no other state is its fundamental history so varied or based so much upon subdivisions of land, grants, settlements and the laws which made such subdivisions of lands, grants and settlements possible, as is that in Ohio. And to understand the history which led to the adoption of the numerous methods applied, will enable one to comprehend more readily the wonderful and, in many instances, the romantic plan, system or purpose into which all these efforts culminated.

That Ohio's history may be more easily understood, endeavor has been made to classify these subdivisions of land, grants and settlements, and to refer under each respective subject, to the laws, colonial, federal, territorial or state, or to the other sources whence the titles to the various tracts of land or grants were derived, or the settlements were induced or were made possible.

Consequently all such laws, that they might be duly considered, were first compiled, in their entirety, into a code of land titles in Ohio, consisting of four thousand typewritten pages, arranged under the various subjects, that OHIO LANDS might be dependable for verification or for further research, alike to the courts, the historians or to the genealogists. And since "to know where to find is next best to know," the publications in which such laws or information may be found are referred to by footnotes.

Athens, Ohio.　　　　　　　　WILLIAM E. PETERS.
January 1, 1930.

CONTENTS

PLATS

REFERENCES

American Charters, Constitutions and Organic Laws,
    Thorp _____ A. C. C. O. L.
Archaeological and Historical Publications_____ Arch.
Charters and Constitutions of the United States_____ C. C. U. S.
General Assembly of the Territory_____ G. A. T.
Hening's Statutes of Virginia_____ H. S. V.
Howe's Historical Collections of Ohio_____ Howe
Land Laws for Ohio, 1825_____ L. L. O.
Laws of Ohio_____ L. O.
Laws of Ohio, Local_____ L. O. L.
Laws of the United States_____ L. U. S.
Legal History of the Ohio University, Peters_____ L. H. O. U.
Ohio Reports _____ O. R.
Ohio State Reports_____ O. S. R.
The Ohio Law Reporter_____ O. L. R.
United States Statutes at Large_____ U. S. S. L.
United States Supreme Court Reports_____ U. S. S. C. R.
United States Supreme Court Reports, Wheaton_____ Wheaton

CHAPTER 1

INDISCRIMINATE LOCATION

While it is said that in the beginning man was given dominion over all things, yet it soon became necessary, as man multiplied, to define the limits of the domain of each, and to have those limits or boundaries defined so plainly that all should know where the domain of one man ended and that of another began.

At first man could occupy whatsoever spot he wished without intruding upon that desired by another. Eventually as people increased in number there naturally came into existence families. These were called tribes, the members of which dwelt together and held property in common; and limitation of territory occupied by any individual was, therefore, unnecessary.

The first family, or tribe, of which history makes record as thus dwelling together in common, was that in which Abraham and Lot dwelt. But when members of that tribe had acquired tents and many flocks of sheep and herds of beasts, strife arose between the herdsmen, "and they could not dwell together." That there should be no quarrel between those two leaders it was agreed that one should go to the left hand and the other to the right. Whereupon Lot chose the country about Jordon and "Abraham dwelt in the land of Canaan." Thus began the subdivision of land by man into tracts small enough to meet the requirements of the individual family, and with such subdivision also began the recognized necessity of marking or defining the boundaries between such parcels and locating their several respective corners in such manner and so plainly that all might readily know them.

From the beginning of time, and quite naturally so, no plan of surveying, or subdividing, land seems to have been conceived, other than that of using as bases, the lines furnished by the sea, streams, mountain ranges, ridges, or some other visible, physical demarkations equally as arbitrary and unreliable, and all quite lacking in suggestion of relative location. The meridians or parallels of latitude, or some systematic plan, which, in the light of experience, would seem almost to have suggested itself, do not appear to have been thought of by any of the mathematicians of the many centuries passed, and it was not until the eighteenth century that any systematic method of subdividing land was conceived.

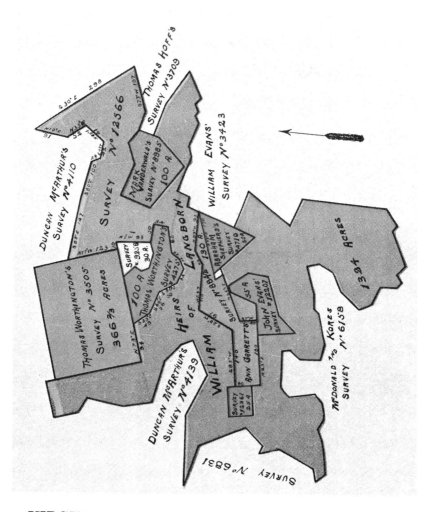

VIRGINIA MILITARY SURVEYS IN OHIO

INDISCRIMINATE
LOCATION PLAN
WEST VIRGINIA

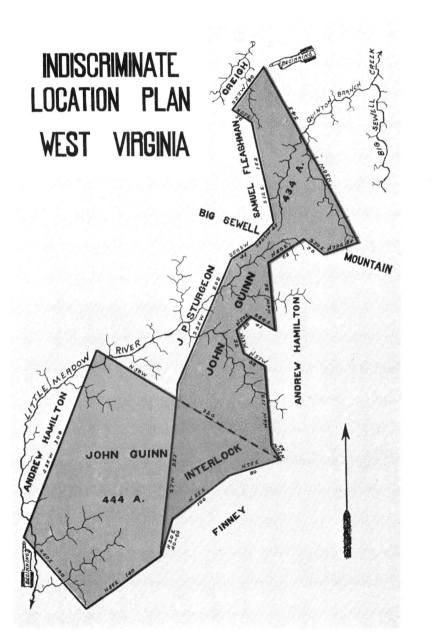

The earliest time of which any record is had of the separation of tracts of land and their boundaries, was when Abraham, who wished to procure a place in which to bury his wife, Sarah, purchased of Ephron, the Hittite and son of Zohar, "the cave of Machpelah which is in the end of his field, and all the trees that were in the borders round about," at Mamre which is in Hebron and in the land of Canaan, in the presence of the sons of Heth, for four hundred shekels of silver. And in the division of land among the tribes of Israel it was provided that "the west side also shall be the great sea from the border till a man come over against Hamath."

Thus, practically with no change, this indefinite method came down the centuries until 1606, when man becoming more acquainted with astronomy, the imaginary parallels of latitude were added to the physical boundaries of very large tracts of land in an effort to separate, distinguish and locate them.   Therefore, in that year King James I in his first charter of Virginia, endeavored to designate the limits or boundaries of the land thus given to the London Company, and divide it from that which he then also gave to the Plymouth Company, by combining the physical calls with those of the parallels of latitude.   To the former company he gave "that part of America commonly called Virginia and other parts and territories in America situate, lying, and

being all along the Sea Coasts, between four and
thirty degrees of Northerly Latitude from the
Equinoctial Line, and five and forty degrees of the
same latitude, and in the main land between the same
four and thirty and five and forty degress." (1)

In his second charter, in 1609, he also gave the
London company "all those Lands, Countries, and
Territories, situate, lying, and being in that part of
America, called Virginia, from the Point of Land,
called Cape or Point Comfort, all along the Sea Coast
to the northward, two hundred miles, and from the
Point of Cape Comfort, all along the Sea Coast to
the southward, two hundred miles, and all that space
and circuit of land, lying from the Sea Coast of the
Precinct aforesaid, up into the land throughout from
Sea to Sea, West and Northwest." (2)

As the subdivision of this land among individuals followed, and the various tracts necessarily
became more limited in area, the parallels of latitude
could not be used in bounding them, and, instead,
physical boundaries and corners were relied upon.
In the absence of constant, or reliable boundaries of
this character, less dependable objects such as trees,
buildings, stones, stakes, ownership of adjoining
lands, or other things of temporary existence only,
were employed quite generally, either to locate the

(1)   A. C. C. O. L., 3783; 5 Arch. 1.
(2)   A. C. C. O. L., 3790; 5 Arch. 5.

respective corners of tracts of land, or to witness the location of the corners; and the distances between the corners, either guessed at, or indifferently measured, and the directions of the lines connecting them, not always determined by the compass, were used to determine the areas of the tracts thus located, enclosed and bounded.

This plan, thus used from time immemorial, is known as the "Indiscriminate Location Plan." It is also sometimes called the "Southern" or "Virginia" plan because Virginia early became active in subdividing and disposing of her lands and employed that method of describing them.

Since the invention of the surveyor's compass the courses of the lines of many tracts of land have been run by that instrument; and the angles as thus ascertained, together with the measurements of the respective lines surrounding a tract of land, are used to determine its location and quantity of land. This method is known as that of "metes and bounds," and is used extensively. It must be depended upon almost entirely for such improvements as it may add to the subdivision, location and measurement of lands originally subdivided upon the indiscriminate location plan, while it is also used frequently in connection with the determination of the boundaries and areas of small or irregular tracts of land lying within land subdivided upon the rectangular plan.

Until the rectangular plan was adopted in 1785, all tracts of land in the United States were subdivided and described upon the indiscriminate location plan. Consequently, all lands in the states southeast of the Ohio river and east of the Mississippi, except in Alabama, Mississippi and Florida, have been subdivided and described in that manner. This plan has also been used in the subdivision of the land in Texas, between the Scioto and the Little Miami rivers in Ohio, and in many special grants in a number of other states. However, elsewhere thruout the United States the rectangular plan has been used instead. [3]

The maps of counties and townships in the states where the indiscriminate location plan has been used, all testify to the inefficiency and uncertainty of that plan; and the figures thus presented are so suggestive of the crazy quilt, that such manner of subdividing land may be termed very properly the "Crazy Quilt Plan." Two surveys of land in West Virginia, made for John Guinn, with their plats, will serve well to illustrate the uncertainty and confusion which that plan presents:

"434 acres of land lying in Fayette County on the top of Big Sewell Mountain joining the lands of David S. Creigh, Samuel Fleashman, J. P. Sturgeon and Andrew Hamilton, and bounded as follows, viz: Beginning at 4 chestnut oaks, sourwood and maple corner to Creigh and leaving S 37 W 80 poles to a chestnut and sugar tree corner to Fleashman and with S 55 E 36 poles to a chestnut, lynn and maple near a spring on a north hillside, S 12 E 152 poles to a white oak, locust and dogwood near the road S 42½ W 45 poles crossing the road to a stake on Fleashman and Sturgeon's line, and with the latter S 58½ W 41 poles to a small chestnut oak corner to Sturgeon and with S 25 W 202 poles to pointers on his line, and leaving S 7 W 253 poles to 2 Spanish oaks on the top of a ridge, corner to Finney N 20 E 60 poles to a double chestnut N 55 E 100 poles to a large black oak N 75 E 80 poles to a large black oak on a flat corner to Finney and leaving and with Hamilton N 30 W 25 poles to a spanish oak and hickory on a flat corner to same and with N 4 W 118 poles to a chestnut and white oak on a flat N 57 W 38 poles to a chestnut on the point of a ridge N 15 W 32 poles to a chestnut and dogwood on the point of a ridge N 50 E 28 poles to two beeches and two chestnuts on a flat S 64 E 41 poles to a chestnut and hickory on a flat N 4 W 95 poles to a white oak and gum on the point of a flat ridge N 58 E 62 poles to a black oak and chestnut sapling by the road S 50 E 38 poles crossing the road to three hickories on a flat N 72 E 54 poles to two chestnut and lynn on a flat ridge corner to same and leaving N 36 W 343 poles to the beginning." [4]

(3) See page 38.   (4) See page 19.

"444 acres of land lying in Fayette County, on the south side of Sewell Mountain on the head waters of Little Meadow River joining a survey made for Matthew Arbuckle and a survey of 1,000 acres made for Andrew Hamilton, and bounded as follows, to-wit: Beginning at a gum and two maples near the Little Meadow River corner to Arbuckle and with S 40 E 140 poles crossing the same to four chestnuts on a North hill side corner to Finney and with N 55 E 140 poles to two Spanish oaks and hickory on the top of a ridge N 20 E 40 poles to a double chestnut N 55 E 100 poles to a large black oak N 75 E 80 poles to a large black oak on a flat corner to Finney and leaving N 58 W 320 poles to a chestnut corner to Hamilton and with S 25 W 300 poles to the beginning." [4]

The confusion and uncertainty arising from locating land by this method, make it possible even for one person to confuse two surveys to himself, as was done by Mr. Guinn who located the 444 acre tract but four days after he had located the 434 acre tract, and yet a part of the latter overlaps a part of the former.

These surveys obviously depend for their location upon the knowledge of the relative location of Little Meadow River and Big Sewell Mountain; also upon the location of certain trees upon certain topog-

raphy. The uncertainty of the location of the corners of tracts of land described in this manner necessarily leads to much confusion; and many corners
are easily mistakenly relocated, or their identity
found to be uncertain and open to question. Consequently, gaps between tracts are frequent, while
overlaps, called "interlocks," similar to that caused
by the two surveys of Mr. Quinn, are often found.

Improvement was attempted in describing the
subdivisions of the tract of land reserved by Virginia between the Scioto and the Little Miami rivers,
in Ohio, by giving a number to each subdivision
thus indiscriminately described. This is known
as the survey number and denotes the order in
which the tract of land was surveyed. But as
these surveys could not be made continuously over
the entire tract or territory from any one side, but
rather in several different places thereof as the
settlement of the country and the location of the
various tracts of land required, no order or system
for the location of the consecutive numbers of such
surveys could be adopted. Therefore, as the indiscriminate location plan, theretofore employed in the
colonies, was continued to be used in the subdivision
of this tract, the designation of its various subdivisions, or surveys, by numbers did little, if anything, to simplify, or improve, the manner of describing its lands.

Two surveys of land in the western part of
Ross county will suffice to demonstrate their lack
of improvement over the indiscriminate location
method used elsewhere:

SURVEY No. 8842.

"Surveyed for Ann Garrett, 130 acres of land on
part of a Military Warrant No. 5901, on Upper Twin
Creek, a branch of Paint Creek.

"Beginning at two beeches, west corner to Abraham Shepherd's survey No. 4710; thence N. 73° E.
170 poles crossing the creek to a poplar, east corner
to said survey; thence N. 89° W. 93 poles to two
beeches; thence S. 55° W. 40 poles to a sugar tree,
hornbean and white oak; thence West 110 poles,
crossing the creek at 95 poles to two buckeyes and an
elm; thence S. 28° W. 97 poles to two poplars; thence
S. 83° W. 140 poles, crossing two branches to two
beeches; thence S. 7° E. 60 poles to a poplar and
buckeye; thence N. 83° E. 160 poles to an elm; thence
N. 7° W. 40 poles to two poplars and a beech; thence
N. 64½° E. 122 poles to a beech and sugar tree in the
line of Shepherd's survey; thence with said line, N.
45° W. 20 poles to the beginning. [5]

SURVEY No. 12566.

"Surveyed for the heirs of William Langborn,
deceased, 1324 acres of land on part of a Military

(5)   See page 18.

Warrant No. 6654, on the heads of Upper and Lower Twin Creeks, branches of Paint Creek.

"Beginning at a beech southwest corner of Thomas Worthington's survey No. 3505; thence N. 73° E. 94 poles to a poplar and sugar tree west corner of said Worthington's survey No. 4275; thence S. 35° E. 49 poles to a white oak; thence S. 68° E. 56 poles to two hickories; thence S. 30° E. 50 poles to a cherry tree; thence S. 75° E. 34 poles to a black oak; thence N. 59° E. 34 poles to a red oak; thence N. 36° E. 26 poles to a sugar tree; thence N. 80° E. 60 poles to two paw-paws, a sugar tree and lynn; thence N. 6° E. 34 poles to a sugar tree; thence N. 85° W. 50 poles to a sugar tree corner to Cadwallader Wallace's Survey No. 9258; thence N. 5° W. 83 poles to a walnut and dogwood; thence S. 73° W. 10 poles to four sugar trees and a mulberry southeast corner to Worthington's said survey No. 3505; thence N. 17° W. 123 poles to two lynns corner to Duncan McArthur survey No. 4110; thence S. 83° E. 147 poles to a sugar tree, mulberry and walnut; thence S. 80° E. 100 poles to two ashs and a black walnut; thence S. 20° E. 28 poles to a sugar tree; thence east 42 poles to three lines; thence N. 40° E. 61 poles to two sugar trees and a chestnut; thence N. 35° W. 52 poles to a chestnut and sugar tree; thence N. 10° E. 91 poles to a sugar tree and hickory; thence S. 30° E. 298 poles to a stake in the line of Thomas Hoff's survey No. 3709; thence S. 73° W. 107 poles to two sugar trees," etc. [5]

On account of its lack of order and arrangement, the indiscriminate location plan, unlike the rectangular plan, furnishes no suggestion of the relative location of the various tracts of land; and, but for the calls of physical objects and names, usually of streams, known locally only, there are no means of determining where any tract of land lies.

Since, under this old system, the calls are to and from physical objects, or, to and from points witnessed by trees or other common objects which soon cease to exist, or which are not readily apparent to the casual observer, it can be understood easily why the boundary lines and corners thus established can not be readily found. Besides, carelessness in measurement and the avarice of claimants ofttimes have led to fraud; and many surveys are found to have included much more acreage than claimed in the original entries. Consequently, the lapping of one claim upon another, or gaps between, have been unavoidable. By reason of these laps and gaps, and consequent uncertainty of boundary lines and corners, much contention has necessarily arisen between owners of adjoining tracts of land subdivided under the indiscriminate location plan, and it is, therefore, a matter of history that more litigation has been had concerning the boundaries and location of the tracts of land within the Virginia Military reservation in Ohio, thus subdivided, than in all the remainder of the land in the state.

CHAPTER 2

THE RECTANGULAR PLAN

The modern method of subdividing land is that of surveying it into well defined rectangular tracts, or districts, called townships, upon meridians of longitude and parallels of latitude as base lines. It is known as the "Rectangular Plan" to distinguish it from the so-called "Indiscriminate Location Plan" so universally used prior to its adoption. Because some features of it originated in the New England States, and many persons from that section were active in securing its adoption by the general government, it was first also called the "New England Plan" to distinguish it from the "Virginia Plan," which was that of indiscriminate location. Yet, as it can be compared, very properly, unto a checkerboard, with each block in turn further subdivided, the rectangular plan may also be termed the "Checkerboard Plan."

The simplicity and perfection of this new plan, followed by the United States government in the subdivision of all public lands, have added a stability to titles that nothing else could have added; and for more than one hundred years it has withstood every test of severe and exacting application, and is considered one of man's greatest conceptions.

It was first used in the subdivision of lands in eastern Ohio, and, after passing through its experimental stage, evolved itself into assuming, as bases, two lines: One, north and south, called a principal meridian; and the other, east and west, called a principal base, each crossing the other at right angles at some point in advance of the land already subdivided. The parallel of latitude at such point then becomes the base from which the townships are numbered, both to the north and to the south, while the longtitude of such point of intersection becomes the meridional base from which the ranges are numbered both to the east and to the west. Of these two bases that upon the meridian is the principal, or ruling base, while that along the parallel of latitude is secondary.

By reason of the rotundity of the earth, the townships are not perfect squares, but, in this north latitude, are shorter upon their northern boundary than they are upon their southern. Besides, notwithstanding however accurately they may have been surveyed, errors generally, necessarily result from inability to avoid them. However, on account of the convergence of meridians, these errors amount to more as progression is made to the north, or to the south, than either to the east or to the west.

To make provision for such errors, new bases, or sub-bases, called "Correction Lines," initiated from the principal bases, are established, astronomically, at intervals of twenty-four miles, north, east, south and west, respectively, from such principal bases. From these correction lines four more townships of six miles square each are surveyed; and thus the process is continued until surveys from other principal bases are met.

The correction lines thus established upon the parallels of latitude are called "standard parallels," while those along the meridians are called "guide meridians."

The plan of establishing correction lines every twenty-four miles was not adopted until after many of the early surveys had been completed. In those early surveys, therefore, such correction lines appear at very irregular intervals, and much farther apart than in the later surveys.

Townships and ranges are continued thus to be laid off from such principal meridian and parallel base lines until they meet other townships, or ranges, likewise established from other similar principal bases, or from new bases which circumstances or design may have established, according to a general plan. (5)

Each tract of land, subdivided upon the rectangular plan, constitutes an independent subdivision called an "Original Survey," because their respective boundaries were defined by the surveys as first made by the United States; and each range and each township is designated by a number. Each row of townships, running north or south from the adopted base, is called a range. These ranges are numbered consecutively from number one adjoining the ruling meridian, east or west to some other original survey; while the townships in each range are numbered consecutively, north or south, from number one adjoining the ruling base, to the respective north or south line of the survey. When the townships are numbered from a common regular, or lineal, base they constitute tiers.

By reason of this duplication of numbering, each township is, therefore, given two numbers by both of which it is known and should always be designated. One number is that of its township, and the other, that of its range. For instance: "A" upon the plan herein (5) is described as being "township number two, north, of range number three, west of the

(5) See page 35.

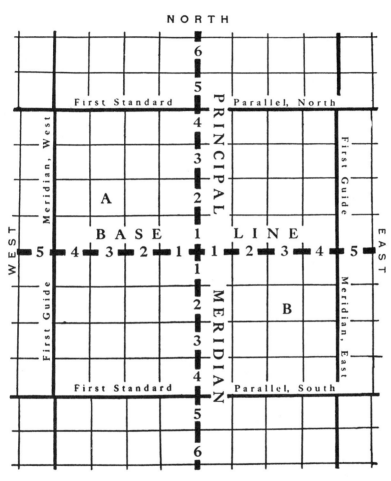

second principal meridian," while "B" is designated
as "township number two, south, of range number
three, east of the second principal meridian''; and
so on throughout the entire survey.

Therefore, to locate a township of land when
its number and that of its range are given,
it is necessary only to learn the meridian from which
it was established, and where its base line crosses
that meridian.   And in considering the principles
upon which this rectangular system are based, it
should be observed also that it suggests within itself
the relative location of any township, or of any section within any township; and that their respective
numbers indicate the direction and distance which
any one may be from another.

The relative importance of the words, north,
east, south and west, and the manner of punctuating
such descriptions should be noted and never neglect-
ed.   To describe "A" as "township number two,
north of range number three west of the second
principal meridian,'' would locate the township
north of, and entirely without, the survey of which it
is presumed to be a part, and is obviously so inconsistent as to suggest the absence of the comprehension of many of the simplest principles involved in
the subdivision of land, and other errors equally as
ridiculous may be expected.

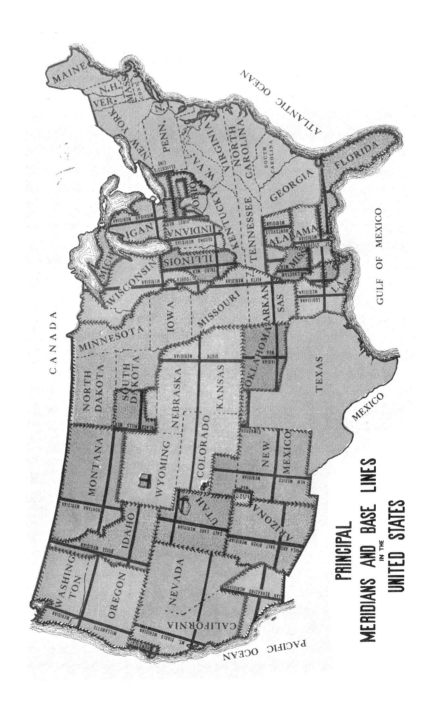

PRINCIPAL

MERIDIANS AND BASE LINES

IN THE

UNITED STATES

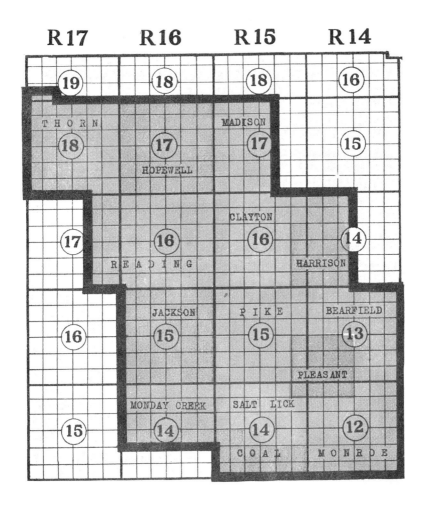

PERRY COUNTY

The errors within the township are taken care of in the north tier, and in the west range of sections, each of which is either more or less than a full section as the township may be more or less than six miles in either of its two directions. And the errors within these irregular sections are accounted for in their north and west sides. (6)

The township, therefore, is the unit. It is six miles square and consequently contains thirty-six square miles. As each square mile contains six hundred and forty acres, an entire township would, therefore, contain twenty-three thousand and forty acres. Variation of this amount, however, will arise necessarily from the mathematical and practical impossibility of the section being exactly one mile square; or, of the township being exactly six miles long on each of its four sides.

Early in the subdivision of public lands some few tracts were divided into townships of five miles square only, but this plan was soon abandoned for the six miles square township system.

By reason of circumstances and conditions inviting the early settlement of the country at widely separated places, the subdivision of the public lands throughout the United States could not be continued from any one point of beginning. The general grand subdivisions, therefore, have nothing within them-

(6) See page 63.

selves to suggest their relative locations. A few of the meridians upon which these grand divisions are based, are numbered, but the most of them have been given proper names, such as that of persons, tribes of Indians, or of towns, rivers or mountains through or near which they pass. Each general survey, however, has been given a distinctive name. In many instances these names are arbitrary but suggestive: such as "The Ohio River Survey," "The United States Military Survey," etc. Usually they have been given the names of their respective meridians: Such as "The First Principal Meridian Survey," "The Michigan Survey," etc. Therefore a tract of land in any general survey under the rectangular plan, is designated and located by its section or lot, township, range and survey. For instance: "The northwest quarter of section No. 1, town 3 north, range 8 east, of the first principal meridian survey" thus locates itself in Henry county, Ohio, without the necessity of stating it to be in that county, or even within Ohio. (7)

In the United States there are thirty-four meridians, called principal meridians, governing the surveys of public lands:

1. The Pennsylvania Line at longitude 80° 31' 17" west from Greenwich. This meridian was established in 1786 as the western boundary line of

(7) See page 5.   (8) 51 L. O. 554

Pennsylvania by a corps of surveyors of which Andrew Ellicott was chief engineer. It is, therefore, since known as "Ellicott's Line." It is, however, also referred to, sometimes as the "Washington Meridian," but this is improper as there is another meridian in Louisiana officially designated by that name. Ellicott's line governs the surveys of all the lands in the eastern side of Ohio. [8]

The townships of the lands subdivided from this meridian are numbered from two bases. Those in the land reserved by Connecticut are numbered north from the forty-first parallel of latitude, while the townships to the south of that parallel are numbered north from where each respective range intersects the Ohio river. To distinguish these two surveys, that north of the forty-first parallel of latitude is termed "The Connecticut Western Reserve Survey," while that to the south is termed "The Ohio River Survey."

2. The west line of the seventh range of townships first laid off in eastern Ohio, which governs the subdivision of the lands in the United States Military Survey. The ranges in this survey are numbered consecutively from the seventh range of the Ohio River survey, west to the Scioto river, while the townships are numbered from its southern boundary, north to the Greenville treaty line.

3. The Michigan meridian at longitude 84° 22' 24'' west from Greenwich. From this meridian, which runs near Lansing, all the lands in Michigan and those in the extreme northwest corner of Ohio have been surveyed. The ranges are numbered both east and west from such meridian, while the townships are numbered both north and south from a base which runs near Detroit at latitude 42° 26' 30''.

4. The Great Miami river in southwestern Ohio governing "Between the Miami Rivers Survey." Although this river does not, of course, coincide with any true meridian, yet it nevertheless serves that purpose in the survey and subdivision of the lands lying between the two Miami rivers, and should, no doubt, therefore, be treated as one of the principal meridional bases. The townships are numbered east from the Great Miami river, while the ranges are numbered north from the southern part of the tract.

5. The First principal meridian which divides the states of Ohio and Indiana at longitude 84° 48' 50'' west from Greenwich, and which runs north from the mouth of the Great Miami river.

This meridian governs the surveys of public lands in western Ohio and in that part of southeastern Indiana lying east of the Greenville treaty line. The ranges are numbered east and west from such meridian. The townships north of the Green-

ville treaty line are numbered both north and south
from the forty-first parallel of latitude, which runs
near Findlay, Ohio, while those south of that line are
numbered north from where the respective townships intersect the Ohio or the Great Miami rivers.
The ranges in Ohio, south of the treaty line, are
numbered east from this principal meridian to the
Great Miami river; while those in Indiana, lying east
of such treaty line, are numbered, from the principal
meridian, west, to that line.   To distinguish the surveys made from this meridian, that lying between
the Great Miami river, the Greenville treaty line and
Indiana is termed "The Miami River Survey"; that
lying between Ohio and that line in Indiana, "West
of the First Principal Meridian Survey," while that
part in northwestern Ohio lying north and south of
the 41st parallel of latitude is said to be "East of the
First Principal Meridian Survey."

6.   The Second principal meridian at longitude
86° 28' 00'' west from Greenwich which governs the
surveys of lands in the eastern part of Illinois and
all of Indiana except that lying east of the Greenville treaty line in the southeastern part of the state.
The ranges are numbered both east and west from
this meridian which runs just east of Paoli, Indiana,
while the townships are numbered both north and
south from the "Petersburg" base which runs some
six miles south of Paoli, at latitude 38° 28' 20''.

7. The Third principal meridian in central Illinois at longitude 89° 10' 15'' west from Greenwich, and from which the lands in central Illinois have been surveyed. The ranges are numbered both east and west from this meridian, running north from the mouth of the Ohio, while the townships are numbered both north and south from a base which runs near Centralia, Illinois, at latitude 38° 28' 20'', which is the same base from which the townships governed by the second principal meridian are numbered.

8. The Fourth principal meridian is at longitude 90° 28' 45'' west from Greenwich, and runs north from the mouth of the Illinois river. From this meridian all the lands in Wisconsin, in the northwest corner of Illinois, and in the extreme northeast corner of Minnesota have been surveyed. The ranges are numbered east and west from the meridian; while the townships are numbered from two bases: One of which runs near Beardstown, Illinois, at latitude 40° 00' 30'', from which the townships are numbered both north and south; and the other, along the line between the states of Illinois and Wisconsin at latitude 42° 30' 00'', and from which the townships are numbered north to the north line of Minnesota, or, to the Canadian line.

9. The Fifth principal meridian at longitude 91° 03' 42'' west from Greenwich, and running north

from the mouth of the Arkansas river. This meridian is extensive in the United States. It governs the surveys of lands in Arkansas, Missouri, Iowa, Minnesota, North Dakota and in the eastern half of South Dakota. The ranges are numbered east and west from the meridian, while the townships are numbered both north and south from a base running west from the mouth of the St. Francis river and a short distance south of Little Rock at latitude 34° 44' 00".

10.   The Sixth principal meridian at longitude 97° 23' 00" west from Greenwich. This meridian is located in the eastern part of Kansas and Nebraska and governs the surveys of lands in the south part of South Dakota, all the lands in Kansas and Nebraska, all in Wyoming, except a small tract in the northwest central part governed by the Wind River meridian, and all in Colorado, except the southwest onefourth part controlled by the New Mexico meridian, and a small tract in the extreme western side of the state governed by the Grand River, or Ute meridian. The ranges are numbered both east and west from the meridian, while the townships are numbered both north and south from the line between the states of Kansas and Nebraska extended through Colorado at latitude 40° 00' 00".

11.   The Tallahassee meridian at longitude 84° 16' 42" west from Greenwich, which governs the surveys of lands in Florida. The ranges are number-

ed east and west from the meridian which runs
through Tallahassee, while the townships are numbered north and south from a base also running
through Tallahassee, at latitude 30° 28' 00'', except
that west of the seventeenth range, to avoid several
large bays, the townships are numbered north and
south from a base one township, or six miles farther
north.

12.   The Saint Stephens meridian at longitude
88° 02' 00'' west from Greenwich.   The lands composing the south half of Alabama and about the southeast one-fourth of Mississippi have been surveyed
from this meridian.   The ranges are numbered east
and west from this meridian, while the townships
are numbered north and south from a base line forming the boundary between the states of Florida and
Alabama, and its westward continuation at latitude
31° 00' 00''.

13.   The Huntsville meridian at longitude 86°
34' 45'' west from Greenwich which governs the surveys of the lands in the north half of Alabama and in
a small tract in the northeast side of Mississippi.
The ranges are numbered east and west from this
meridian, while the townships are numbered south
from the north line of Alabama which is at latitude
35° 00' 00''.

14.   The Chickasaw meridian at longitude 89°
15' 00'' west from Greenwich which governs the sur-

veys of the lands in the north end of Mississippi.
The ranges are numbered east and west from the
meridian, while the townships are numbered south
from the old Tennessee boundary line at latitude
34° 59' 00".

15. The Choctaw meridian at longitude 90° 14'
45" west from Greenwich governing the surveys of
lands in central Mississippi. The ranges are numbered east and west from this meridian, while the townships are numbered north from a base which runs
near Hazelhurst at latitude 31° 54' 40".

16. The Washington meridian at longitude 91°
09' 15" west from Greenwich governing the surveys
of lands in the southwest corner of Mississippi. The
ranges are numbered east and west from this meridian, while the townships are numbered north from
the south line of Mississippi, at latitude 31° 00' 00",
which is a continuation of the same base that the
townships are numbered from in the tract governed
by the Saint Stephens meridian.

17. The Saint Helena meridian, also at longitude 91° 09' 15" west from Greenwich, controlling the
surveys of lands in Louisiana lying east of the
Mississippi river. This meridian is the continuation
of the Washington, and, of course, occupies the same
longitude. The ranges are numbered both east and
west from it, while the townships are numbered

south from the south line of Mississippi at latitude 31° 00' 00", and which is a continuation of the Saint Stephens base.

18. The Louisiana meridian at longitude 92° 24' 15" west from Greenwich which governs the surveys of all the lands in Louisiana lying west of the Mississippi river. The ranges are numbered east and west from this meridian, while the townships are numbered north and south from a base line in the central part of the state at latitude 31° 00' 00", which is a continuation of the Saint Stephens base.

19. The Indian meridian at longitude 97° 14' 30" west from Greenwich which controls the surveys of all the lands in Oklahoma, except those in the extreme west end governed by the Cimarron meridian. The ranges are numbered east and west from this meridian, and the townships north and south from a base which runs near Duncan, Oklahoma, at latitude 34° 30' 00".

20. The Cimarron meridian at longitude 103° 00' 00" west from Greenwich. This meridian is also the dividing line between New Mexico and Oklahoma and governs the surveys of the lands in the extreme western pan-handle of the latter state. The ranges are numbered east from the meridian, while the townships are numbered north from the Texas boundary line at latitude 36° 30' 00".

21. The Black Hills meridian at longitude 104°
03' 00'' west from Greenwich. This meridian coincides with the west boundary line of South Dakota
and governs the surveys of all the lands in the west
half of that state, except a small part in the south
side controlled by the sixth principal meridian. The
ranges are numbered east from the meridian, while
the townships are numbered both north and south
from the "Black Hills" base, which is in the south
central part of the state, near Rapid City, at latitude
44° 00' 00''.

22. The New Mexico meridian at longitude 106°
53' 40'' west from Greenwich. This meridian governs
the surveys of the lands composing the southwest
one-fourth of Colorado, and all the lands in New
Mexico, except a small part in the northwest corner
controlled by the Navajo meridian. The ranges are
numbered both east and west from the meridian,
while the townships are numbered both north and
south from a base line in the central part of New
Mexico which runs near Socorro, at latitude 34°
15' 25''.

23. The Navajo meridian at longitude 108°
32' 45'' west from Greenwich. This meridian is used
in subdividing the lands of the Navajo Indian reservation lying in the northwest corner of New Mexico
and in the northeast corner of Arizona. The ranges
are numbered west from the meridian, which is also

the east line of the tract, while the townships are numbered north from a base which forms the southern side of the tract, at latitude 35° 45' 00".

24.   The Grand River or Ute meridian at longitude 108° 33' 25" west from Greenwich and from which the lands allotted to the Ute Indians in the western part of Colorado have been surveyed.   The ranges are numbered east and west from the meridian, while the townships are numbered both north and south from a base line at latitude 39° 06' 40".

25.   The Wind River meridian at longitude 108° 48' 40" west from Greenwich governing the surveys of the lands constituting the Shoshone Indian Reservation in west central Wyoming.   The ranges are numbered east and west from the meridian, while the townships are numbered both north and south from a base line at latitude 43° 01' 20".

26.   The Uintah meridian at longitude 109° 57' 30" west from Greenwich, which governs the surveys of lands composing the Uintah Indian Reservation in northeastern Utah.   The ranges are numbered both east and west from the meridian, while the townships are numbered both north and south from a base line at latitude 40° 26' 20".

27.   The Montana meridian at longitude 111° 38' 50" west from Greenwich governing the surveys of lands in Montana.   The ranges are numbered both

east and west from the meridian, while the townships are numbered both north and south from a base
line in the southern part of the state, which runs
near Billings, at latitude 45° 46′ 48″.

28.   The Salt Lake meridian at longitude 111°
54′ 00″ west from Greenwich. This meridian governs
the surveys of all the lands in Utah, except a small
tract near the northeast corner controlled by the
Uintah meridian.   The ranges are numbered both
east and west from such meridian, while the townships are numbered both north and south from a
base line in the northern part of the state running
near Salt Lake City, at latitude 40° 46′ 04″.

29.   The Gila and Salt River meridian at longitude 112° 17′ 25″ west from Greenwich governing
the surveys of all the lands in Arizona, except a
small tract in the northeast corner surveyed from
the Navajo meridian.   The ranges are numbered
both east and west from this meridian, while the
townships are numbered both north and south from
a base line in the south central part of the state running near Phoenix, at latitude 33° 22′ 40″.

30.   The Boise meridian at longitude 116° 24′
15″ west from Greenwich governing the surveys of
lands in Idaho.   The ranges are numbered both east
and west from this meridian which is in the western
part of the state, while the townships are numbered

both north and south from a base line in the southern part of the state, near Idaho Falls, at latitude 43° 22' 31".

31.   The San Bernardino meridian at longitude 116° 56' 15" west from Greenwich which governs the surveys of the lands in southern California. The ranges are numbered both east and west from the meridian, while the townships are numbered both north and south from a base line which runs near San Bernardino, at latitude 34° 07' 10".

32.   The Mount Diablo meridian at longitude 121° 54' 48" west from Greenwich. This meridian governs the surveys of all the lands in Nevada, and all in California, except those in the southern part governed by the San Bernardino meridian, and those in the extreme northwest corner of the state controlled by the Humboldt meridian. The ranges are numbered both east and west from the meridian which runs near San Jose, California, while the townships are numbered both north and south from a base line, running near San Francisco, at latitude 37° 52' 49".

33.   The Willamette meridian at longitude 122° 44' 20" west from Greenwich. This meridian is located near the western boundaries of Oregon and Washington and controls the surveys of lands lying within those states. The ranges are numbered both

east and west from the meridian, while the townships are numbered both north and south from a
base line in the northern part of Oregon, running
near Portland, at latitude 45° 31' 00".

34. The Humboldt meridian at longitude 124°
08' 00" west from Greenwich controlling the surveys
of lands in the northwest corner of California. The
ranges are numbered both east and west from the
meridian, which is in the western part of the tract
thus governed, while the townships are numbered
both north and south from the "Humboldt" base,
which runs near Cape Mendicino, at latitude 40°
25' 12".

These meridians and base lines, and the surveys
which they respectively govern, are more fully
shown in colors, except green, by a map of the
"Principal Meridians and Base Lines in the United
States." (9) However, by reason of grants issued or
agreed to be, prior to the acquisition of the land by
the United States, or by occupancy on which special
grants have been issued by the United States since
acquiring title, there are many comparatively small
tracts of land within these rectangular surveys,
some times designated "Private Claims," that have
been surveyed or subdivided upon the indiscriminate
location plan.

(9) See page 38.

As the United States never owned the land in Texas, its subdivision never came within the jurisdiction of the general land office, or of the laws of the Federal government. Instead, that duty devolved upon the state of Texas which manages its lands through the "Commissioner of the General Land Office."

In consequence of the varied ownership and control of these lands, as well as the circumstances surrounding their settlement, their subdivision in harmony with the manner adopted by our general government for the subdivision of its lands was not possible. The indiscriminate location plan has, in effect, prevailed, although a rectangular system has been used by many railroad and other companies in the subdivision of their lands in the northern, central and southern parts of the state. It has, however, little in common with the rectangular system employed in the subdivision of lands controlled by the United States.

To call the rows of townships, ranges as progression is made east or west, was but logical when the first subdivision of land, lying to the west, was based upon the west line of Pennsylvania. The term range has, therefore, ever since been used in the enumeration of the rows of townships in an eastern or a western direction. To this rule there is, however, one exception, and that is in the subdivision of the territory between the two Miami rivers from the Ohio river, north to the Greenville treaty line, where the process is reversed.

Just why these modern subdivisions are called townships, is, perhaps, not now definitely known. They are thought, however, to have been so denominated from the fact that in some of the New England states the people in a territory of the size eventually adopted for townships in the subdivision of land, governed themselves similarly in detail to the manner of those in towns, or villages, in which the inhabitants were more thickly settled. The compactly settled territory was called a "Village," or "Town," and its people were endowed with certain local and independent forms of government, while the more sparsely settled district or territory surrounding such town, and considered as belonging to it, was called a "Township," and its people likewise endowed with local, independent self government. From the very complete independence of the local government of the people within these townships, they have been referred to, at times, as "Little Republics."

The etymology of the term township is not very clear, nor is it easy to trace. It is, however, presumed to have been constructed from the Anglo-Saxon word "tun," from "tynan," to enclose, and the Old English word "scipe," denoting state or condition,

and the two Anglicized into the word "Township."
The word "tun" seems also to have been applied first
in Germany early in the tenth century to farm buildings enclosed by hedges, and to villages surrounded
by walls, earthwork or ditches.

The meaning of the word "Township" in the
United States, however, has two applications: One
applying to a certain defined political territorial
subdivision of a county for the purposes of local self
government; and the other to the unit of the original
subdivision of extensive tracts of land, usually as
made by the general government.

To distinguish these two kinds of townships, it
may be said that those subdivisions made for governmental purposes only, are termed "Civil Townships,"
while those pertaining to the subdivision of land, are
properly called "Original Surveyed Townships."
They are, therefore, not the same, and the terms are
not interchangeable, although in many instances
their boundaries coincide, and either may, and often
does, include within its bounds all or parts of several
of the others.

Perry county is typical of these several conditions.   In that county, it will be observed, but two
civil townships, Jackson and Hopewell, coincide with
their respective original surveyed townships, numbers fifteen and seventeen of the sixteenth range of

the Ohio River Survey. The civil townships of Reading and Thorn respectively, contain one original surveyed township, and also a part of another. Harrison township contains but the west half of original surveyed township fourteen of the fourteenth range and four sections of original surveyed township sixteen of the fifteenth range; while Pleasant township, one of the smallest civil townships in the county, consists of parts of four original surveyed townships, twelve and thirteen of the fourteenth range, and fourteen and fifteen of the fifteenth range. Original surveyed township fourteen of the fifteenth range contains two civil townships, Coal and Salt Lick, and part of a third, Pleasant. [10]

The term "Original Surveyed Township" is used, therefore, to denote a unit of measurement in the subdivision of land; and such township is legally designated by numbers instead of by a name. For instance, "township number fifteen of range number sixteen of the Ohio River Survey."

Confusion may be avoided easily if it is remembered that the townships of land, properly designated by numbers, are the "original surveyed" townships, and that such name is as distinctly proper as is the given name of an individual to designate him from several others possessing the same sur-name. And

[10] See page 39.

to refer to a township of land only by the name of a
civil township lying within it, or partly within it, or
within which it may lie, is as erroneous as to refer to
the wrong given name of an individual.

As the increased population along the New England coast moved westward to the more fertile valleys of the Connécticut and Merrimac rivers, it became necessary to adopt some orderly plan of settlement. In this the colony of Massachusetts led, and
in 1634, its General Court granted to groups of people tracts of land suitable in size for plantations.
These grants were known as "towns," and were settled, surveyed and recorded as colonies with definite
forms of local government. Where the topography
permitted, they were about equal in size but not uniform in shape. Communication, limited by the difficulties of travel as well as the necessity of mutual
community protection, suggested the six miles
square "town" to be the most desirable. That size,
therefore, grew in favor as settlements advanced to
the west and soon became the popular unit of land
grants throughout the New England colonies.

The first "town" of this size, rectangular but not
square, was Chelmsford on the Merrimac river, incorporated in 1652 by the General Court of Massachusetts, while the first grant in the form of a square
of six miles to the side, was Marlborough incorporated in 1656. It was not, however, until 1749, when

Bennington, New Hampshire (now Vermont) was authorized by Governor Wentworth, that the first standard six miles square "town," with its boundary lines corresponding with the cardinal points of the compass, was established by official order.

These tracts of land, however, as thus designated, constituted units for local governmental purposes only. They were in no way integral parts, nor units of a subdivision of extensive territory, and therefore, did not, at that time, become any part of a system for subdividing land. The application, in those instances of the basic principles involved, however, seems to have furnished the first suggestion of a rectangular system of which there is any record.

The New England plan attracted the attention of prominent men of other colonies, particularly Jefferson who vainly urged its adoption by Virginia in the settlement of her western lands. However, Jefferson, strongly favoring a decimal system, proposed to have the "towns" ten miles square, divided into "hundreds" and the whole northwest territory divided into ten states, each in squares of one hundred miles to the side.

The rectangular system met with much opposition. Many favored the indiscriminate location plan as it permitted settlements to be made at once and the purchase money to be receivel by the government without awaiting the time and incurring the expense necessary to subdivide extensive territory, while others, who wished to profit by choosing the good land to the exclusion of the poor, also joined in opposing the adoption of the new plan.

With the enactment of the land ordinance of 1785, attempt was made for the first time to connect coordinately the several tracts or "town" units, into a general plan or survey. The ordinance, however, adopted no base lines or meridians, since found so essential, and many of the details of subdivision were left to the judgment of the geographer, or the surveyor. Besides, the necessity of early surveys was urgent, and little time could be devoted to working out any uniform order of detailed procedure. Consequently, while the rows or ranges of townships first surveyed were directed to be numbered west from the Pennsylvania line, and the townships in each range, north from the Ohio river, there was absent the conception of ruling bases coordinating with, or being governed by astronomical bases scientifically established, although Colonel Thomas Hutchins, the Geographer, then suggested the baneful influence of the convergence of meridians.

With the act of 1796, [11] under which Rufus Putnam was appointed the first Surveyor General, marked improvements were made in surveys. The mile square "lots" were then first officially termed

(11)   2 L. U. S. 533; 1 U. S. S. L. 464

"sections," to be numbered consecutively west from the northeast section which should be No. 1, and the corners witnessed by trees or other monuments, while General Putnam introduced the plan of throwing the excess or deficiency of measurement into the sections on the north and west sides of the townships; and that in each section into the north and west sides of the section.

6	5	4	3	2	1
7	8	9	10	11	12
18	17	16	15	14	13
19	20	21	22	23	24
30	29	28	27	26	25
31	32	33	34	35	36

SUBDIVISION OF TOWNSHIPS

Putnam was succeeded as surveyor general in 1803 by Jared Mansfield who introduced the use of principal meridians and parallels of latitude, established according to scientific principles, to control surveys, and which are like unto the steel framework of the modern "skyscraper" around which all else is built. Mansfield first applied it in the newly created territory of Indiana where less complication of personal interests and purposes prevailed than in Ohio. He adopted the line between Ohio and Indiana, established by Ludlow, for a principal or ruling meridian for the land east of that line, called it the "First Principal Meridian," and then proceeded to establish a "Second Principal Meridian" a short distance west of the middle of the new territory; and since the Indians still retained possession of the northern part of such territory till 1818, a latitudinal base line was established near the southern part. Later this base line was extended west to the Mississippi river near which a "Third Principal Meridian" was established for a new general survey.

The act of 1812 (12) created the General Land Office and provided for the appointment of a Land Commissioner. Edward Tiffin, the first governor of Ohio, was the first to be appointed to that office, and, to correct or offset the errors occasioned by the convergence of meridians, mathematical inaccuracies, etc., and to keep the basic plan adopted by Mansfield

(12)   4 L. U. S. 418; 2 U. S. S. L. 716

within workable limits, introduced guide meridians east and west of the principal meridians and standard parallels of latitude north and south of the principal base lines.

Thus the development and perfection of the rectangular plan of subdividing land, as known today, have, therefore, been the outgrowth of the process of evolution with many suggestions from many persons, and may be divided into five epochs: (1) The New England "town" or community plan of settlement, suggested in whole by no one in particular; (2) the land ordinance of 1785 grouping such towns, with which Hutchins, Putnam, Jefferson, and Pelatiah Webster had much to do; (3) the act of 1796 under which Putnam limited the excess or deficiency to the township and section respectively; (4) the establishment of the basing meridians and parallels of latitude upon scientific principles by Mansfield, and (5) the adoption of the guide meridians and standard parallels of latitude by Tiffin.

In his report of the expedition of Bouquet against the Indians in Ohio, in 1764, which he accompanied as captain of engineers, Col. Hutchins outlined a plan of settling the country in reservations of six miles square each. Under date of June 16, 1783, General Putnam wrote to General Washington advising the sale, by congress, of its western lands, and stating that, as some feared a monopoly might be acquired in such lands, he would suggest that no grants be made of them "except by townships of six miles square."

As the result of these recommendations of the sale and settlement of those lands, thus initiated, the ordinance of May 20, 1785, [1] was adopted by the Continental Congress. This ordinance is considered to have been the foundation upon which all subsequent acts of congress for the subdivision and sale of all public lands, is based. It is known as the "Land Ordinance," and should be classed with the few important state papers upon which the fundamental rights of mankind are founded.

The importance of the adoption of this ordinance and its aid in the settlement of the public lands cannot be over-estimated, as the system which it provided assured safety of title to lands much more completely than ever could have been done under the "indiscriminate location" plan then in vogue. Moreover, its entire lack of complication was so apparent that many sought lands so subdivided in preference to others equally as good, and even in more congenial climates, but subdivided under the old system.

This ordinance provided for the subdivision of the territory into units, or townships, of six miles square, and the subdivision of those townships into

(1)   1 L. U. S. 563; 3 U. S. S. L. 502

thirty-six equal parts, or sections, of six hundred and forty acres each.

On the 7th day of May, 1784, when this ordinance was first reported to the Continental Congress, it provided for the subdivision of public lands into tracts of ten miles square called "hundreds." These were to have been subdivided into one hundred lots of one square mile each. The mile was to have been six thousand and eighty-six feet in length, or 92.212 chains. Each lot, therefore, would have contained eight hundred and fifty acres, or rather 850.28 acres. The lots were to have been numbered from one to one hundred by beginning at the northwest corner of the "hundred" and numbering to the east; and thence from the east to the west, and so on, and ending with number one hundred in the southwest corner.

As this plan was not agreed to, it was then proposed, in a report made to Congress April 26, 1785, to make the township seven miles square, each mile to be fifty-two hundred and eighty feet, or eighty chains in length; and to divide the township into forty-nine lots, or sections of six hundred and forty acres each. And it was in this report that the terms "township" and "section," were used for the first time of which there is any history. But after much discussion, the plan as incorporated in the ordinance, was finally adopted.

Although the ordinance provided for the division of all such lands into general tracts or units, of seven ranges each, and each of these units to be subdivided within itself, the plan was not further carried out. The remaining lands then owned by the general government, as well as those since acquired by it, as independent and isolated tracts have been sub-

36	30	24	18	12	6
35	29	23	17	11	5
34	28	22	16	10	4
33	27	21	15	9	3
32	26	20	14	8	2
31	25	19	13	7	1

SUBDIVISION
OF
ORIGINAL SURVEYED TOWNSHIPS
UNDER
THE ORDINANCE OF MAY 20, 1785.

divided from various and several bases in such manner and at such times as their sale and demand, and the circumstances surrounding them, suggested.

The office of geographer was not filled after the death of Col. Hutchins, and the duty of having the public lands surveyed thereafter devolved upon the colonial board of treasury until some time after the

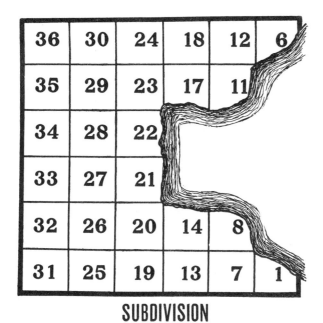

SUBDIVISION
OF
FRACTIONAL ORIGINAL SURVEYED TOWNSHIPS
UNDER
THE ORDINANCE OF MAY 20, 1785.

passage of the act of congress of May 18, 1796, when
the office of Surveyor General was created. To the absence, therefore, of an efficient head is due undoubtedly, the failure to continue the rectangular system
of subdividing land as initiated by the ordinance of
1785, and first put into practice by Col. Hutchins
who conceived its great value. The conditions then
prevailing undoubtedly also account for the many
different plans and base lines with which some
of the tracts of lands, particularly in Ohio, are
blessed. In 1799, Gen. Rufus Putnam was appointed
the first surveyor general, and more uniformity in
the division of lands and accuracy in their surveys
were at once required.

While the ordinance of 1785 directed the townships, or fractional parts of townships, to be numbered "progressively from south to north," and the
ranges, beginning with No. 1, by "progressive numbers to the westward," it failed to state the manner
of numbering the mile square lots, except that the
townships respectively, should be marked by subdivisions, into lots of one mile square, or 640 acres, in
the same direction as the external lines, and numbered from 1 to 36, always beginning the succeeding
range of the lots with the number next to that with
which the preceding one concluded. This requirement obviously suggested, by analogy, that the lots
in each row be numbered to the north and that the

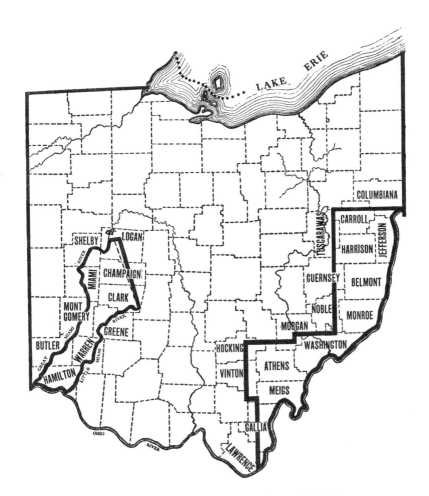

SECTIONS NUMBERED
UNDER
THE LAND ORDINANCE OF MAY 20, 1785

rows be numbered to the west. Consequently Colonel Hutchins, the geographer under whose directions the ordinance required the surveyors to act,
and who originated this plan of numbering the lots,
began with lot No. 1 in the southeast corner of the
township and numbered them north to No. 6 in the
northeast corner of the township, the next range of
lots to the west with No. 7 on the south line of the

6	5	4	3	2	1
7	8	9	10	11	12
18	17	16	15	14	13
19	20	21	22	23	24
30	29	28	27	26	25
31	32	33	34	35	36

SUBDIVISION
OF
ORIGINAL SURVEYED TOWNSHIPS
UNDER
THE ACT OF MAY 18, 1796.

township, and again numbered them to the north, and so on, terminating with lot No. 36 in the northwest corner of the township; and where the irregular boundaries of the tract, occasioned by rivers or junction with other tracts, caused fractions of townships, the lots in such fractional township were required to "bear the same numbers as if the township had been entire." (1)

4	3	2	1
9	10	11	12
16	15	14	13
19	20	21	22	23	24
30	29	28	27	26	25
33	34	35	36

SUBDIVISION

FRACTIONAL ORIGINAL OF SURVEYED TOWNSHIPS

THE ACT OF MAY 18. 1796. UNDER

This method of subdividing the land into township of six miles square each, and of so numbering the sections therein, was adopted in laying out the earliest tracts of land which the government first attempted to dispose of.   It is, therefore, found in the state of Ohio only; and in that state it was applied only to the land within the original seven ranges and the land purchased by the Ohio Company of Associates in the southeastern part of the state, and to the land lying between the two Miami rivers in the southwestern part.

The plan was changed in detail, but not in basic principles, by the act of May 18, 1796, [2] which required the sections to be "numbered, respectively, beginning with the number one, in the northeast section, and proceeding west and east alternately, through the township, with progressive numbers, till the thirty-sixth be completed"; and the fractional parts of townships to be "divided into sections in the manner aforesaid."

No good reason is known for changing the plan of numbering sections adopted by the ordinance of 1785, which was evidently analogous to the manner of numbering the townships and ranges, to the plan adopted by the act of 1796, as neither has any advantage over the other, unless it be that the latter follows more nearly the plan of our horizontal sys-

(2)   2 L. U. S., 533; 1 U. S. S. L., 464.   (3)   1 L. U. S., 564.

tem of printing, writing, etc. By coincidence, however, sections eleven, twenty-one and thirty-one occupy the same relative positions in each plan.

The ordinance of 1785, [1] required all lines to be run "by the true meridian," but as it was deemed that requirement would "too greatly delay the survey," it was repealed in May of 1786. [3] The act of

31	32	33	34	35	36
30	29	28	27	26	25
19	20	21	22	23	24
18	17	16	15	14	13
7	8	9	10	11	12
6	5	4	3	2	1

SUBDIVISION
OF
ORIGINAL SURVEYED TOWNSHIPS
IN
CANADA.

1796, [2] however, required all lines to be "run according to the true meridian."

Neither the ordinance of 1785 [1] nor the act of 1796 [2] provided for the subdivision of land into less quantities than sections or mile square lots. But as many were unable to purchase so much land, the act of May 10, 1800 [13] provided for its subdivision into half sections; that of February 11, 1805 [14] into quarter sections; that of April 24, 1820 [15] into half quarter sections and that of April 5, 1832 [16] into quarter quarter sections.

In Canada, the Dominion, or public, lands which lie in the western part, are "laid off in quadrilateral townships, each containing thirty-six sections of as nearly one mile square as the convergence of meridians permits." The sections are numbered inversely to the plan adopted in the United States, by beginning with section number one in the southeast corner of the township and numbering west, thence east, etc., and ending with section number thirty-six in the northeast corner of the township.

The townships are numbered, in regular order, northerly from the forty-ninth parallel of latitude which constitutes the international boundary line between Canada and the United States. In the province of Manitoba the ranges are numbered east and west from the principal meridian established in

1869; while at various points east and west from this meridian other initial meridians numbered the second, the third, the fourth, and so on, have, from time to time, been established by the Minister of the Interior. The land in the eastern part of the dominion, having been settled and its titles acquired by individuals many years prior to the adoption of the rectangular plan, is, of course, subdivided under the indiscriminate location plan.

(13)   3 L. U. S. 385; 2 U. S. S. L. 73
(14)   3 L. U. S. 637; 2 U. S. S. L. 313
(15)   6 L. U. S. 486; 3 U. S. S. L. 566
(16)   8 L. U. S. 536; 4 U. S. S. L. 503

CHAPTER 3

THE SEVEN RANGES

The first application in the United States, or elsewhere, of the township, or rectangular plan of subdividing land as provided for by the land ordinance of 1785, [1] was made in southeastern Ohio where seven ranges of townships were so subdivided. This tract, therefore, has become historical, and the ranges of which it is composed are referred to as "The Seven Ranges." It constitutes all the counties of Monroe, Belmont, Harrison and Jefferson, and parts of Washington, Noble, Guernsey, Tuscarawas, Carroll and Columbiana.

The adoption of the unit seven, doubtless by reason of its prevalent use in ancient times, for the number of ranges first to be laid out in the establishment of the rectangular system of subdividing land, instead of some other number, is believed to be due

(1)   1 L. U. S. 563;   3 U. S. S. L. 502.   (2)   See page 67.

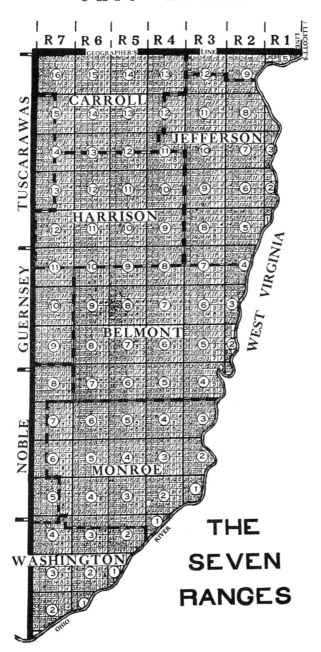

THE
SEVEN
RANGES

to the fact that at one time it was proposed to make
the township seven miles square,[2] but in changing
the township to six miles square the number of the
ranges first to be laid out was not likewise changed.

As the land lying immediately northwest of the
Ohio river was the most accessible of any owned by
the United States, it was the first to be desired by
settlers, and, of course, was the first land which the
United States endeavored to sell.   The land ordinance, [1] therefore, required that whenever seven
ranges should be surveyed, plats of the ranges should
be returned to the board of treasury so that the land
might be disposed of as readily as possible.

The officer in charge of surveys under the Continental Congress was called the Geographer of the
United States.   Colonel Thomas Hutchins was the
only person to hold that office which he held till his
death in April of 1789.   The duty of surveying these
ranges, therefore, devolved upon the geographer;
and, since Colonel Hutchins had taken such an active
part in developing the rectangular plan, it was quite
fitting that he should have had the honor and privilege of making the first survey under that system.

In compliance with the ordinance, Colonel
Hutchins, in the spring of 1786, attended, personally,
to running the first east and west line which was required to "begin on the Ohio river, at a point that

shall be found to be due north from the western termination of a line which has been run as the southern boundary of the state of Pennsylvania." [1] He ran this line west seven ranges, each six miles wide, or a total distance of forty-two miles, and numbered the ranges by progressive numbers to the west. This line is at 40° 38' 02" north latitude and is known as the "Geographer's Line." From it as a base, the respective ranges, south to the Ohio river, were subdivided into townships of six miles square, the west line of the seventh range being ninety-one miles in length and intersecting the Ohio river a short distance above the mouth of the Muskingum.

On account of the hostilities of the Indians the survey of the boundaries of the townships was not completed until the following year. The townships were afterwards subdivided into two-mile blocks and these blocks, in 1805-6, subdivided into sections.

CHAPTER 4

SUBDIVISION OF LAND IN OHIO

The land of which Ohio is composed was the first to be sold by the general government, and, of course, was the first land which that government had occasion to subdivide into parcels small enough to meet the requirements of individual ownership. In Ohio then, there thus became established the experimental station from which the United States government worked out a system for the subdivision of its lands. And, as the result of the initiation in such state of a new and, ultimately, a well defined and simple principle, or method, for the division and subdivision of lands, there is found within the borders of that state all plans and modifications of plans conceivable for such purpose, from the original "Indiscriminate Location" plan, with all its faults, as found within the Virginia Military tract, to the perfected "Rectangular," or "Checkerboard" system of the present day.

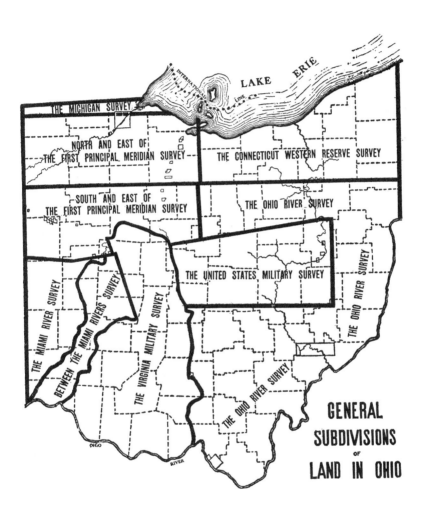

GENERAL
SUBDIVISIONS
OF
LAND IN OHIO

Ohio, consequently, is rich in real estate history. Within her borders may be found presented subdivisions of land in all their many and interesting phases. Nowhere else is there to be found such variety of plans dealing with that subject; and to understand the manner of subdividing the many tracts within her borders, and the history which led to the adoption of the numerous methods applied, will enable one to comprehend more readily the wonderful plan, or system, into which all these efforts finally culminated.

The land ordinance of 1785 [1] directed that as soon as seven ranges of townships and fractional parts of townships should be surveyed, the geographer should make and transmit plats of them to the board of treasury, where the plats and a report of the proceedings should be recorded. Virtually the same procedure for the return of the survey and plat of each tract of seven ranges of townships, was also contemplated by the act of 1796. [2]

The purpose of requiring this particular unit of subdivision to be made, and its survey and plat returned, was evidently to enable the federal government to place the lands on sale at the earliest possible date and thus to satisfy the demand of settlers for land. Besides, it was obviously impossible, as well

(1)   1 L. U. S. 563;   3 U. S. S. L. 502.
(2)   2 L. U. S., 533;   1 U. S. S. L., 464.

as inexpedinet, to attempt to survey and subdivide all public lands before placing any of them upon the market. Moreover, the demand for land at that time did not require extensive surveys. Therefore, subdividing a limited portion of the territory and placing its lands on sale, enabled settlements to be made at once, the people to acquire homes and the government to receive the much needed funds, without unnecessary delay.

Evidently it was the intent of the federal government thus to continue the subdivision of all public lands by general units of seven ranges each, but the demand of settlers for land at widely separated places made such procedure impractical. Besides, after the death of Colonel Hutchins, the personal desires of would-be purchasers, and the ideas of statesmen who did not grasp, or comprehend, the fundamental principles of the rectangular plan, prevailed; and many tracts in Ohio were permitted to be variously subdivided, much to their confusion ever since.

With the exception, however, of the large tract of land lying between the Scioto and the Little Miami rivers, which Virginia had reserved and afterwards caused to be subdivided under the indiscriminate location method, by and according to the avaricious whims of each individual purchaser, and known as the "Virginia Military Survey," all the land within the state has been subdivided upon some rectangular plan, but with many modifications of details.

Five of the meridians upon which the surveys of the public lands in the United States are based, are used in the subdivision of the lands within the state of Ohio, viz: (1) the west line of Pennsylvania; (2) the west line of the seventh range of townships of the Ohio River survey; (3) the Great Miami River; (4) the Michigan meridian, and (5) the First Principal meridian. The lands within the French grants, the Ebenezer Zane tracts, the Donation tract and in the Twelve and the Two Miles Square reserves, however, have no meridians, and their respective subdivisions have been made and numbered upon a plan limited to each.

In determining the absolute, or relative, location of townships in Ohio, much difficulty arises from the confusion occasioned by the many base lines from which the respective townships and ranges are numbered.

Excepting the townships lying between the Miami rivers and those within the Twelve Miles Square reserve, all "original surveyed townships" in Ohio are numbered north or south from some parallel of latitude, or other line, however irregular, as a base; and, together with the sections, are designated by a simple and uniform system of numbering. And

all ranges, except those between the Miami rivers,
are numbered east or west from some meridional line,
or base, called a "principal meridian."

Otherwise the manner of numbering the ranges
in Ohio is comparatively simple. Those in the eastern
part of the state are numbered from the Pennsylvania line west to the Scioto river, and to the western
limits of the Connecticut Western reserve, except,
however, that the ranges within the United States
Military tract are numbered from its eastern side,
while the lands in the Ebenezer Zane tracts and the
French grants are not included within any range.
The ranges in the western part of the state are numbered east from the Indiana line, except as to the
land between the two Miami rivers, the small strip
once claimed by Michigan, and that within the twelve
and the two miles square reserves.

By reason of the respective claims of Virginia
under the charter of King James I, and of Connecticut under that of King Charles II, the land in Ohio
became divided into two general, or grand,
divisions. That to the south of the forty-first parallel
of latitude was, therefore, thus claimed by the
former colony, while that to the north of such line
was claimed by the latter. However, on account of
its more congenial climate and lying in the trend of
travel to the western country, as well as the absence
of conflicting colonial claims of title, the land in that

part of Ohio thus claimed by Virginia was the first
to be subdivided and settled.

The principal and most important east and west
base line, or parallel of latitude, from which the
greatest number of original surveyed townships in
Ohio are numbered, is, therefore, the forty-first
which thus divided those two colonial claims. It was
first established by surveyors employed by the purchasers of the land reserved by Connecticut. But
some uncertainty soon arose as to the correctness of
this line as thus located, and Jared Mansfield was
appointed by the general government to determine
its proper location. He found the errors slight, and,
deeming it unwise to disturb the titles then acquired
by the settlers based upon the original survey,
recommended its adoption.

Immediately west of the reserve, along the
eastern side of Seneca county, lies a triangular
range (number eighteen, east) of three townships,
numbered one, two and three, north, with its apex to
the north and its base of fifty-two chains and seven
links resting on the forty-first parallel of latitude. It
is known as the "GORE" and was caused by the
failure to run the western line of the reserve parallel
with that of Pennsylvania. History and tradition
seem to suggest that it was the result of circumstances and design, and that the divergence was pur-
posely made to include the Castalia Springs.

The western line of the reserve was first fixed by United States Engineer, Maxfield Ludlow, under a contract made in 1805, with the Connecticut Land Company. With a company of twelve surveyors Ludlow began the work of locating the fire lands, but on account of errors in his calculation, he located the western line about one mile too far west, and his survey was rejected by the government.

In 1807, a new contract was made with Almon Ruggles who was to locate the southwest corner of the reservation and make an entirely new survey of the fire lands, which he accordingly did. But on account of the extensive swamps then existing in that vicinity, the last few miles of the southern boundary of the reserve were run with much difficulty. At a point one hundred and seventeen miles west of the Pennsylvania line, Ruggles, in his note book, states that "we are in danger of our lives"; and, one mile farther, that he had "traveled the woods for seven years, but never saw so hideous a place as this."

The western line of the reserve was run from its southwest corner to the lake, but evidently with the knowledge that it was not parallel with the Pennsylvania line, since Ruggles, in his field notes, shows the line to have been deliberately run with a divergence of 4° 40' to the west. It, therefore, could not have been through mistake or oversight. No reason is given for doing so and the conclusion must necessarily be that it was intentional.

In Ohio there are nine subdivisions of land which might be classed as general surveys. Within many of these are also other surveys which are no part of the system employed in the subdivision of the larger tracts by which such respective subsurveys are surrounded. These general surveys and subsurveys are:

1. The Ohio River Survey
    a. Ebenezer Zane's Muskingum River Survey. (Part)
    b. Ebenezer Zane's Hocking River Survey.
    c. Ebenezer Zane's Scioto River Survey.
    d. The Donation Tract Survey.
    e. The First French Grant Survey.
    f. The Second French Grant Survey.
    g. The Kimberly Survey.

2. The United States Military Survey.
    a. The Salem Tract Survey.
    b. The Gnadenhutten Tract Survey.
    c. The Schoenbrun Tract Survey.
    d. Ebenezer Zane's Muskingum River Survey. (Part)

3. The Virginia Military Survey.

4. Between the Miami Rivers Survey.

5. The Miami River Survey.

6. The Connecticut Western Reserve Survey.

7. South and East of the First Principal Meridian Survey.
   a. The Cherokee Boy Survey.
   b. The Upper Sandusky Town Survey.
   c. The Richardville Survey.
   d. The Labadie Survey.
   e. The Charley Survey.
   f. The Black Loon Crescent Survey.
   g. The Shane Surveys. (two)
   h. The Godfroy Survey.
   i. The Logan Survey.
   j. The Dochoquet, or Stoddard, Survey.
   k. The James McPherson Survey.
   l. The Stewart Survey.
   m. The Henry H. McPherson Survey.

8. North and East of the First Principal Meridian Survey.
   a. The Vanmeter Survey.
   b. The Walker Survey.
   c. The Armstrong and M'Collock Survey.
   d. The Spicer Survey.
   e. The Two Miles Square Reserve Survey.
   f. The Whitaker Survey.
   g. The Williams Survey.
   h. The Minor Survey.
   i. The Thebeault Survey.
   j. The McNabb Survey.
   k. The Twelve Miles Square Reserve Survey. (Part)

9. The Michigan Survey.
   a. The Twelve Miles Square Reserve Survey. (Part)
   b. The Aushcush and Ketuckkee Survey.
   c. The Lamarre Survey.
   d. The Wausaonoquet Survey.
   e. The Guoin Survey.

f. The Forsythe Survey.
g. The Hunt Survey.
h. The Autokee Survey.
i. The Petau Survey.
j. The Navarre Survey.
k. The Waysayon Survey.
l. The Ranjard Survey.
m. The Cheno Survey.

In 1846, after the completion of the surveys of land in Ohio, the surveyor general delivered all original field notes, maps, records and other papers pertaining to all land within the state, (except that within the Virginia military survey, of which copies only were given [3]) to the secretary of state of Ohio [4] who was directed to take charge of and care for the same, issuing certified copies thereof which should be received as legal evidence in all courts within the state. [5]   In 1877, [6] such records were delivered to the auditor of state who was made their custodian [7] with the duty to care for them and the authority to certify copies thereof, as had been given to the secretary of state.

(3)   See Chapter 8; 8 L. U. S., 184; 4 U. S. S. L., 355.
(4)   10 U. S. L. 33; 5 U. S. S. L. 384.
(5)   44 L. O. 65.
(6)   67 L. O. 164;   74 L. O. 217.
(7)   29 L. O. 500, Sec. 13;   82 L. O. 215.

CHAPTER 5

CONGRESS LANDS.

"Congress Lands" is a general term applied to all lands disposed of by the Federal government under general acts of congress, passed from time to time, whereby certain designated officials were authorized to sell and convey the lands belonging to the government in small parcels, to whomsoever might apply and would pay the stipulated price thus designated. Its application, therefore pertains to the manner by which the lands were sold by the general government and their title conveyed to purchasers, and has no reference whatever to the method of their subdivision. But as the Continental Congress had no power to execute any of its ordinances, no titles to land were conveyed by that body; and the first general act of the Federal Congress empowering executive officers to sell and convey "Congress Land," was that of May 18, 1796. [1]

(1)   2 L. U. S. 533; 1 U. S. S. L. 464.
(2)   19 U. S. S. L., 121.   (3)   10 L. U. S. 33.

The tracts of land which circumstances required
the general government to treat of first, particularly
in Ohio, were the reservations of Virginia and Connecticut, and the sales to the Ohio Company of Associates and John Cleves Symmes. The first two
tracts were reservations by the respective states of
Virginia and Connecticut, and the latter two were
sales of large tracts of land as a whole, made under
special acts of congress; and the purchasers were
permitted to subdivide them into parcels small
enough to suit the individual settler.

Besides these, many other grants of land were
made by special acts of congress for various reasons
and purposes, such as the "French Grants," the
"Dohrman Tract," the "Refugee Lands," the lands
of the United States Military Survey set aside to
satisfy army bounty warrants, etc. But as the disposition of the lands in these tracts by the general
government was provided for by special acts of congress, their conveyance did not come within any
general act; and the lands in such tracts are, therefore, not deemed "Congress Lands."

However, any lands reserved by the general
government within any special grant, as, for instance, sections eight, eleven and twenty-six in the
tracts sold to the Ohio Company of Associates and
John Cleves Symmes; or any part of any lands set
aside for a special purpose, such as those within the

refugee tract and not used to satisfy the claims of
the refugees; or, those within the United States Military tract, and not needed to satisfy army bounty
warrants; or any other lands which may have reverted to the general government and were afterwards sold by it under general acts of congress,—
all became "Congress Lands" upon being placed
upon sale under such general acts.   The anomaly,
therefore, is presented of "Congress Lands" being
within many tracts disposed of by special acts of
congress.

Land offices for the sale of "Congress Lands" in
Ohio, with a "Register of the Land Office" in charge,
were established at places convenient for prospective
settlers.   The first offices were located at Pittsburg
and Cincinnati, in 1796, [1] but as the lands were surveyed and the country became settled, other offices
were established, from time to time, elsewhere thruout the territory to be sold.   Those located within
Ohio were at Canton, Cincinnati, Chillicothe, Columbus, Delaware, Lima, Marietta, Piqua, Steubenville,
Upper Sandusky, Wapakoneta, Wooster and Zanesville.   And whenever the public land in any district
was reduced to less than one hundred thousand
acres, the secretary of the treasury discontinued
the office in any such district and placed such unsold
land for sale in the most convenient district. [3]   Finally, about 1876, [2] all land offices in Ohio were dis-

pensed with and sales of public lands have since been made through "The Commissioner of the General Land Office" at Washington.

The first attempt of the United States government to sell land was under the "Land Ordinance" of May 20, 1785. [4] However, but three tracts were contracted to be sold under it [5] and no sales were completed until after the adoption of the federal constitution, for the lack of effective executive means of transferring the title.

The first act enabling title to land to be acquired by individuals was that of August 10, 1790, [6] permitting holders of bounty land warrants from Virginia for military services rendered in the Revolutionary war, to obtain land between the Scioto and the Little Miami rivers. The next was that of April 21, 1792, [7] granting to each actual settler, without price, one hundred acres of land in the donation tract. Then followed the general acts of 1796 [1]; 1800 [8]; 1805 [9]; 1812 [10]; 1820 [11]; and 1832 [12]. Besides these, many special acts were also passed providing for private grants.

In the original description of the several tracts of land thus disposed of, they were designated, often, as being within one of these land districts; as, for in-

(4)   1 L. U. S. 563.   (5)   1 L. U. S. 456.
(6)   2 L. U. S. 179, 400; 1 U. S. S. L. 182, 394.
(7)   2 L. U. S. 276; 1 U. S. S. L. 257; 6 U. S. S. L. 8.

stance, "section eleven, town six, of range twelve, in the district of land subject to sale at Marietta," but, as the location of the agency for the sale of the lands had nothing to do with their system of subdivision, nor with the respective tracts of which they were a part, the names of such districts should not be referred to in descriptions of these lands.   Instead, however, the respective surveys of which they may be a part, should be used, as, for instance, "section eleven, town six, of range twelve of the Ohio River Survey."

(8)   3 L. U. S. 314, 385;   2 U. S. S. L. 14, 73.
(9)   3 L. U. S. 637;   2 U. S. S. L. 313.
(10)   4 L. U. S. 418;   2 U. S. S. L. 716.
(11)   6 L. U. S. 480; 3 U. S. S. L. 566.
(12)   8 L. U. S. 536;   4 U. S. S. L. 503.

CHAPTER 6

DESCRIPTION OF LAND

By the adoption of the rectangular system of subdividing land our ancestors builded wiser, if possible, than they knew; and, had subsequent generations adhered to the very wise foundation thus laid, all would have been well. Such, however, has not been the case, and some of the most grievous blunders in subdividing and describing land, imaginable, have been made. And, unfortunately, blunders are still being made by the continued failure to be guided by the few simple, fundamental principles upon which that system is based.

The method of describing land, used quite commonly, is, unfortunately, to employ physical boundaries, such as rivers, creeks, roads, crests of hills, or fences; or, by running from object to object, such as stones, stakes, trees, stumps, posts, buildings, etc. Oftentimes only the names of owners of adjoining lands are used. Many of these calls have but a temporary, or passing existence, and, after a few years, can not be found. Descriptions are also frequently given without measurements of any kind; sometimes, without even designating the number of the original surveyed subdivision within which the land may lie.

Moreover, many draughtsmen of descriptions of land fail to bear in mind the full purpose of the description; and, therefore, frequently describe, as one tract, a parcel of land consisting of parts of two or more original or legal subdivisions, or lying within two or more separate taxing districts. And by doing so they leave to the taxing officers, inexperienced in such work, the task of guessing the respective proportions of a tract which may lie within each of two or more original, or legal, subdivisions; or in two or more taxing districts; or, as to whether all the land is accounted for or not.

It is, therefore, often the abuse, and not the use, of our rectangular system of dealing with lands that has brought about much of the confusion now prevalent.

Adherence to a few general propositions will avoid many errors and much uncertainty, as well as also enable surveys and descriptions of land both to be made and understood more easily. It is, therefore, suggested that the following elementary and fundamental principles be considered:

1. The land itself is the principal subject for description, and should have preference, at all times, over whomsoever may have owned it. The land is the primary object under consideration, while its ownership is secondary; or, at best, is but an incident to the land which never should be required to depend upon its ownership for identification.

For instance, as the lands purchased by the Ohio Company of Associates, and those given to the refugees, are all parts of the Ohio River Survey, they should be referred to as being of that survey, and not designated as a part of "the Ohio Company's Purchase," or, of "the Refugee Lands," any more than should any section of land anywhere, purchased of the government by John Smith, for example, be referred to as "John Smith's Purchase," or "The John Smith Lands." These are purchases and not surveys, and they should never be referred to nor used as surveys.

2. Practical and consistent accuracy, rather than strict technicality, or absolute exactness, should be observed in making surveys or drawing description. [1]

It is mechanically impossible to determine the

(1) 45 O. S. R. 368.   (2) See page 104.

boundaries of a tract of land with strict mathematical exactness. So, when measurements of any considerable length are given in half links, or in hundredths of feet; or, when angles or bearings are given in minutes, and the description is not found to be connected with the lines of the original or legal subdivision within which the land intended to be described, may lie, or, perhaps, the number of the original or legal subdivision is omitted, it is evident that the fundamental principles pertaining to the subdivision of land have not been guiding factors.

3. Subdivisions of land may be of either (a) "the original surveyed," or (b) "the legal."

(a) The original surveyed subdivisions of land consist of sections, fractions or lots into which the original surveyed township has been subdivided, or, of the number of the survey, if in the Virginia Military tract. These are the subdivisions made usually by the general government when disposing of the land to individual purchasers; or, when sold in considerable tracts, are those made by such purchaser in accordance with the national law upon that subject.

(b) The legal subdivisions are those of the original subdivisions made in accordance with the legislative provisions of the state within which such lands may lie, as, for instance, the plat of a village or a city. Such subdivisions are called lots. They are given consecutive numbers and should be so described and conveyed when all the necessary legal formalities have been complied with, and the plat has been duly recorded. And these "legal" subdivisions, when subdivided, in turn, become, in effect, "original" subdivisions, as well.

4. Each part of an original, or legal, subdivision of land intended to be described should constitute a separate description, and be a numbered parcel of the numbered lot of which it may be a part. For instance: Lot No. 5 of the east half of the southeast quarter of section 4, town 5, range 14 of the Ohio River Survey. While the subdivision of lot No. 5, should be "Lot No. 1 of lot No. 5, of the east half of the southeast quarter of section 4, town 5, range 14 of the Ohio River Survey; and so on as to any number of successive subdivisions. Thus each deed will contain the proper description in all previous deeds and enable the land easily to be identified at any successive subdivision.

To describe a tract of land located in several original surveyed, or legal, subdivisions by using its outside boundary lines only, is to destroy its rectangular simplicity and resolve its description into the confusion of the indiscriminate location plan.

5. Descriptions of tracts of land should re-

fer to the general survey of which they are a part; as, for instance, section six, town tén, of range fourteen of the Ohio River Survey; or, Survey No. 8842 of the Virginia Military Survey.

6. The description of a tract of land may be by any one of four methods:

(a) As the whole of an original, or legal, subdivision.

(b) As an aliquot, or fractional, part of the whole original, or legal, subdivision.

(c) As a specified quantity of the whole original, or legal, subdivision, or,

(d) By boundary lines of which the bearings, or angles, and measurements, and, perhaps, calls, are employed.

7. The whole of an original or legal subdivision is properly described by giving its number, location and, probably, its area as, for instance, "section five, town six, range twelve of the Ohio River Survey, and containing six hundred and forty acres, more or less," or, as "Lot No. 50 in the city of Athens, Athens county, Ohio."

8. If the tract of land is an aliquot, or fractional, part of the whole original, or legal subdivision, such as a half, or a quarter, or a half quarter, or a quarter quarter of such original or legal subdivision, or is the north, east, south or west half or part thereof, it should be described as such,

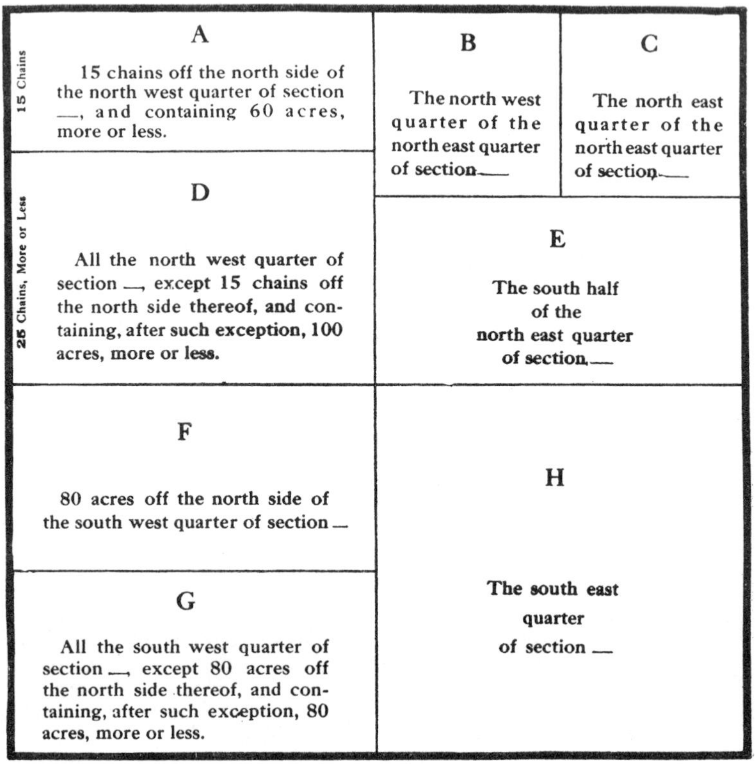

A		B	C
A 15 chains off the north side of the north west quarter of section ___, and containing 60 acres, more or less.	15 Chains	**B** The north west quarter of the north east quarter of section___	**C** The north east quarter of the north east quarter of section___

(left margin, vertical: 15 Chains)

(left margin, vertical: 25 Chains, More or Less)

D

All the north west quarter of section ___, except 15 chains off the north side thereof, and containing, after such exception, 100 acres, more or less.

E

The south half
of the
north east quarter
of section___

F

80 acres off the north side of the south west quarter of section ___

H

G

All the south west quarter of section ___, except 80 acres off the north side thereof, and containing, after such exception, 80 acres, more or less.

The south east
quarter
of section ___

as, for instance "B," "C," "E" and "H" in the plan
herein given. (2)

9. If a specified quantity is to be measured off
one side of an original, or legal, subdivision, or from
an aliquot or fractional part thereof, it should be so
designated.   For instance, eighty acres off the
north, east, south, or west side thereof, as at "F" in
the plan herein; or, as so many feet or chains off
such side as at "A."   And, in such cases, the balance
of the original, or legal, subdivision, or part thereof, should be described thereafter as a whole, and
except so many acres as at "G," or so many chains
or feet as at "D," as the case may be, off the side
from which any such part may have been so taken,
thereby conveying all the overplus, and guarding
against overlapping in case of shortage.

10. The description and the plat of a tract of
land should refer to the original survey, or to the
legal subdivision of which it may be a part; and be
connected with some corner thereof in such manner,
and contain such angles, bearings and measurements,
as will enable one skilled in such work, to calculate
the area of the tract and to plat it in its proper
relative location within its respective original or legal subdivision.

11. In the preparation and record of plats or
other instruments for the transfer of land, the

figures, writing and other characters should be made so plainly, and of such size, as to obviate any doubt as to what they are intended to be, and thus avoid any uncertainty of their being readily and correctly read by the layman. Let the characters be so plain and clear cut that "he who runs may read."

12. In describing lands the lines of civil townships, municipal corporations, special school districts, or other subdivisions made for civil governmental purposes only, should not be depended upon nor used. Such lines are temporary and are subject to arbitrary changes at any time, while the lines of original surveyed townships or of legal subdivisions will always remain and be permanent, as originally intended.

13. Locate the boundaries of civil townships, municipal corporations, special school districts or of any special or taxing district, along the lines of the original or legal subdivisions of land whenever possible, and thus enable the taxing officers to levy and distribute the various funds with convenience and certainty.

14. Various tracts of land were surveyed under different circumstances and under different instructions issued at various times. And to restore lost or obliterated corners, the manner in which they were originally established should be ascertained. [3]

(3)   8 O. R. 147.

Surveys and descriptions of tracts of land should correspond with the record of those previously made, thus following the title; while the history of the general survey or grant of which it is a part should be ascertained as well as the necessity, reason and purpose of its subdivision. Thus to know the history of the Ohio Company's purchase enables one to understand why it was subdivided into 8 acre lots, 3 acre lots, house lots, 160 acre lots, 100 acre or "fifth division" lots and fractions or 262 acre lots as well as also sections, and what tract determined the number of the share, and why.

15. Until the corners of original surveys generally, are established in some permanent manner, and the importance of their preservation and use is well understood by the layman, so the corners may be depended upon to mark the bases from which to triangulate, it is not deemed practical, nor advisable, as a general rule, to attempt to describe land otherwise than by calls, bearings, and distances. And, until such corners are so established, traversing, or, the use of angles to the right, or to the left, should not be resorted to in describing land.

CHAPTER 7

THE GREENVILLE TREATY LINE. [1]

One of the most prominent and important lines separating several original surveys of land in Ohio and in southeastern Indiana, is that part of the Greenville Treaty Line from near Bolivar, a small town in the north part of Tuscarawas county, to its termination on the Ohio river in southeastern Indiana near Lamb, a small town in the southwest corner of Switzerland county. In Ohio the line is generally known as the "Greenville Treaty Line," while in Indiana it is referred to as the "Old Indian Boundary Line."

The right of the Indians to remain in possession of their lands and sell them only when they desired, was recognized by the United States, which, however, claimed the exclusive right of pre-emption and would permit the Indians to sell to no one else. The

(1) 7 Arch., 207; 14 Arch., 158; 1 Howe, 532.
(2) 1 L. U. S. 454.

THE GREENVILLE TREATY LINE

sales of land to the United States, nevertheless, were altogether voluntary, and the compensation paid was always more valuable to the Indians than the use of the land which they ceded. [2] These sales were effected by treaties of which several were made prior to 1790 for the land in Ohio. By the treaty of 1784 [3] the Iroquois or Six Nations who claimed to have conquered all the western Indians, released title to all that part of the state east and south of the Greenville treaty line. The claim of the Iroquois being found erronious, a treaty was made in 1785 [8] with the Delawares, Wyandots and other tribes. Understanding the claims of all Indians interested to have been satisfied, congress that year provided for the survey and sale of this land. [9] But when the survey of the seven ranges [10] was attempted, other tribes protested. Another treaty was entered into in 1786 [11] with the Shawnees and another again in 1789 [12] with the Delawares, Wyandots and other tribes. But as several tribes, who also claimed a right in the land, had not joined in the treaties, and others who had done so, were influenced by the English to violate their obligations, Indian depredations became more and more frequent as settlements

(3) At Fort Stanwix, now Rome, New York; 1 L. U. S. 307; 7 U. S. S. L. 15.   (4) 2 Howe, 137.

(8) At Fort McIntosh; 1 L. U. S. 390; 7 U. S. S. L. 16.

(9) 1 L. U. S. 563.   (10) See page 78.

(11) At Fort Finney, near the mouth of the Great Miami River; 1 L. U. S. 358; 7 U. S. S. L. 26.

(12) At Fort Harmar, now in Marietta; 1 L. U. S. 309, 393; 7 U. S. S. L. 28.

were made. This culminated in the Indian war of 1790 and led to the establishment of the Greenville Treaty Line.

The defeat of St. Clair, where the town of Fort Recovery now stands, on the 4th day of November, 1791, greatly encouraged the Indians who thereafter became such a menace to the frontiersmen as to require strenuous action on the part of the government. Gen. Anthony Wayne was selected to lead an expedition against the Indians and endeavor to re-establish peace. Vigorous and effective military action was necessary to pave the way. It was work for a fighting diplomat and Gen. Wayne proved himself equal to the task.

Their defeat at Fort Recovery June 30, 1794, followed by the decisive battle of "Fallen Timbers," [4] (so called because the ground was covered with fallen timbers, caused probably by a tornado) on the west side of the Maumee river, just south of the town of Maumee, in Lucas county, August 20, 1794, left the Indians disheartened. Their military spirit and power were broken and their leaders were unable to enthuse them with the hope of successfully resisting Gen. Wayne and his army. The chiefs and the nations became divided as to continuing the war or considering peace. The Shawnees and the Indians near Detroit were for continuing the war, while the Wyandots were especially anxious for peace. The

Delawares and Miamis were divided, while the Chippewas were much discouraged. The desire for peace, however, prevailed and soon became known to Gen. Wayne, then in winter quarters at Greenville. The Wyandots, expressing themselves as having "determined to bury the hatchet and scalping knife deep in the ground," became the most active and earnest in the movement.

General Wayne responded readily to their overtures and invited the Indians to meet him at Fort Greenville. They began arriving in the early part of June, and by the latter part of the month all had assembled. Eleven hundred and thirty chiefs and warriors, representing eleven of the most powerful Indian tribes, took part in making the treaty.[5] With the prudence and policy of a diplomat, General Wayne did not attempt to call the council together until the middle of July. He occupied the meantime, however, in cultivating the friendship of the Indians, gaining their confidence and impressing them with the advantage of a lasting peace. The terms were agreed upon and the treaty signed on the third day of August, 1795. [6]

A line marking the division between the land retained by the Indians and that to which they proposed to surrender title, was first to be determined. Little Turtle, chief of the Miamis, who had led the

(5) 1 Howe, 532.   (6) 1 L. U. S. 398; 7 U. S. S. L. 49.

Indians in St. Clair's defeat and afterwards took an active part in framing the treaty, desired to have the line run south from Fort Recovery, directly to Fort Hamilton on the Great Miami river. But to protect the possible navigation upon that river, General Wayne had it established farther west. The location of the entire line was agreed upon July 17, 1795. It began on Lake Erie at the mouth of the Cuyahoga river and ascended that river to its portage with the Tuscarawas; thence across the portage, following substantially along "Portage Path," now a well known street in Akron, for a distance of nine miles, to the "Grand Crossing" of the Tuscarawas River near Bolivar, which is about one mile up that river from Fort Laurens [13] in the north part of Tuscarawas county where the "Great Trail," followed by the Indians from time immemorial, crossed that stream; thence south 78° 50! west, 153 miles and 35 chains to where the portage began at Loramie's store on Loramie creek near the village of Loramie [14] in the northwestern part of Shelby county; thence [15] north 81° 10! west, 22 miles and 51.5 chains to Fort Recovery in the southwestern part of Mercer county, and thence [16] south 8° 30! west to the north side of the Ohio river in southeastern Indiana opposite the mouth of the Kentucky river.

(13) Improperly spelled "Lawrence" in official records.
(14) Known as "Berlin."   (15) Saturday, August 3, 1797.
(16) Thursday, August 8, 1797.

The line from Fort Laurens to Loramie creek was located under the personal direction of Israel Ludlow, Deputy Surveyor of the United States, who began its survey at the "Grand Crossing," Sunday, July 9, 1797, and completed it "at a sycamore tree four feet in diameter standing at the fork of that branch of the Great Miami river near which stood Loramie's store." This part of the line, however, is not located upon a direct course between those points, but swings or bows, instead, to the south of a straight line. Moreover, the line does not cross Loramie creek at a common point. The part of the line from the west intersects that creek about one-fourth of a mile south, or down the creek, from the termination of the line from the east.

Having agreed to this line as marking the boundary of the land to which the Indians were conceded to have superior title, the general government, of course, respected it, and no surveys were made to the north or west. But as it was desired to subdivide the lands adjoining the line to the south and east, and to which the United States had thus acquired title, their surveys were begun at once after the conclusion of the treaty.

The Greenville Treaty Line, therefore, marks the division between original surveys from Bolivar to its termination in southeastern Indiana, except

through the Virginia Military reservation in which
the settlement of the land and its survey were delayed until after subsequent treaties had been made
whereby the Indians released their claims to the land
to the north.

Since circumstances delayed the subdivision and
settlement of the territory between the mouth of the
Cuyahoga river and Bolivar, until after the Indians,
by the treaty of Fort Industry, July 4, 1805 [7] had
also released their claims to the land to the west, it
was not necessary to recognize this part of the treaty
line when surveying the land through which it ran.

As evidence of their friendship and confidence
in the United States government and their desire to
aid in maintaining friendly intercourse, the Indians
also ceded to it several small tracts of land lying
within that reserved by them.   But as it was not
necessary to survey or subdivide many of these
reservations until after the United States had acquired the Indian title to the lands surrounding
them, virtually all, in Ohio, lost their identity and
subsequently became merged into the general surveys within which they were respectively located.
By reason, however, of the desire to maintain forts
in the twelve and the two miles square reserves, as
well as also to secure to the occupants of some of the

(7)   1 L. U. S. 409; 7 U. S. S. L. 87.

tracts within them their title to the land they occupied, the government, at an early date, provided
for the survey and subdivision of these two reserves.
Each, therefore, constitutes an independent and
original survey.

The consideration paid the Indians for the
rights thus surrendered, was goods valued at twenty
thousand dollars.   The government also further
agreed to deliver to these Indians every year thereafter, forever, "at some convenient place northward
of the river Ohio, like useful goods, suited to their
circumstances, of the value of nine thousand five
hundred dollars." [6]   This latter arrangement,
however, was soon abrogated by subsequent treaties.

CHAPTER 8

THE VIRGINIA MILITARY SURVEY

The 5th day of May, 1496, when King Henry VII of England commissioned John Cabot of Venice, to make discoveries and explorations in the Atlantic Ocean and commanded him to take possession of all the land he might discover, marked the beginning of England's claim to any part of this continent, and the beginning of its title, by discovery, to Ohio. In June following, Cabot landed upon the coast of Labrador of which he took possession in the name of the English King, and while on his return home he was twice within sight of New Foundland. Cabot's son, Sebastian, following in 1498, explored the east coast as far south as the Chesapeake Bay, and thus endeavored to bestow on the crown of England the title to all the land as far south as that bay, and extending indefinitely to the west.

(1)   A. C. C. O. L. 49.   (2)   A. C. C. O. L., 53.

For many years after the discovery of America only voyages of discovery or adventure were made; and permanent settlements were not attempted by the English until June 11, 1578, when Sir Humphrey Gilbert obtained from Queen Elizabeth a patent [1] permitting him to make settlement on any six hundred square miles of territory "not actually possessed by any Christian prince or people." He was unable, however, to raise an expedition until 1583, when he lost his life returning on his first voyage.

A new expedition was organized at once by his step-brother, Sir Walter Raleigh, who March 25, 1584, [2] obtained a charter from Queen Elizabeth to settle upon the east coast of the United States between the 33d and 40th parallels of north latitude, which the queen named Virginia. Sir Walter made several voyages within the next few years but failed to establish a permanent settlement and sacrificed his own fortune in the attempt.

Enthused by the glowing accounts of those who had returned, a number of prominent people in London and Plymouth became interested and applied to King James I for a charter permitting them to establish settlements. Those with headquarters in the city of London constituted the "First Colony" and were known as the "London Company"; while those with headquarters at Plymouth constituted the

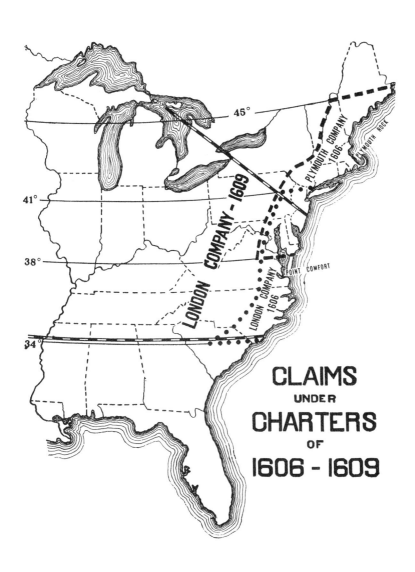

CLAIMS
UNDER
CHARTERS
OF
1606 - 1609

"Second Colony," and were known as the "Plymouth Company."

April 10, 1606, King James issued to these colonies a joint charter, [3] authorizing them to settle upon any land lying between the 34th and 45th parallels of north latitude "alongst the coasts of Virginia and America, as that coast lyeth," and "into the main land for the space of one hundred miles." To the first colony was given the right to settle upon the land lying between the 34th and 41st parallels of latitude, and to the second, the right to settle upon that lying between the 38th and 45th, except that neither colony should make settlement within one hundred miles of any begun by the other between the 38th and 41st parallels of latitude.

A new charter [4] was given May 3, 1609, to the London Company, constituting its members a corporation by the name of "The Treasurer and Company of Adventurers and Planters of the City of London for the first Colony in Virginia," and extending their right to include all the land "throughout from sea to sea, west and northwest"; and March 12, 1612, King James issued that company a third charter [5] enlarging its rights and including a number of islands.

(3)   A. C. C. O. L., 3783; 5 Arch., 1.
(4)   A. C. C. O. L., 3790; 5 Arch., 12.
(5)   A. C. C. O. L., 3802; 5 Arch., 33.

Proceeding under its charter of 1606, the London Company, in the spring of 1607, established the first permanent English settlement in America on an island in the James river and named it Jamestown; while the Plymouth Company, failing several times to effect a permanent settlement upon the land granted it, was succeeded by others with new charters which did not extend farther south than the 41st parallel The London Company, later assuming the name of Virginia, eventually broadened its claim to territory, under the charter of 1609, until it included all the land lying between the 34th parallel of latitude and a line running from a point on the coast of New Jersey two hundred miles from Point Comfort, north 45 degrees west, passing near Niagara Falls, "throughout from sea to sea." Consequently, under this construction of the 1609 charter, Virginia laid claim to all the territory as far west as the Mississippi river, except that now constituting the states of Maryland, Pennsylvania, Delaware, New Jersey and a part of New York, while the Plymouth Company and those holding under later issued charters for the territory to the north, made no claim to land south of the 41st parallel.

The claim of Virginia to the territory northwest of the Ohio river was based upon the charters of 1606 and 1609, and the expedition of George Rogers Clark, in 1779. But as those charters had been cancelled in 1624 by the Court of the King's Bench, the land in this territory, subject to the claims of France, became and continued to be "Crown Lands," till the treaty of 1783. [7] Besides, the treaty of 1763 released France's claim to England and the Quebec act of 1774 attached all the country north of the Ohio river to the Province of Quebec. The surrender, therefore, of the claim of Virginia was "One compromise of conflicting pretensions." [31]

However, as the efforts of the united colonies in fighting for their freedom, were considered by many colonies, especially those owning no western land, to be for the common good of all, it was early claimed that the unsettled western lands, particularly those acquired by England of France, should be held by the United States in trust for the union. [8] Whereupon the Continental Congress, September 6, 1780, [9] requested the several states "having claims to waste and unappropriated lands in the western country," to cede them to the United States "for the common benefit of the union."

Conceding the justice of the request, and also being anxious to have her frontier settled by English speaking people, Virginia led in endeavoring to comply, and in October of 1783, [10] authorized her

(7)   1 L. U. S., 202.   (31)   4 Arch. 91, 108, 123.
(8)   9 Wheaton 469; 22 U. S. S. C. R., 137; 2 Arch, 276.
(9)   1 L. U. S., 472, 475, note.
(10)   1 L. U. S., 472, 475, note, 572.

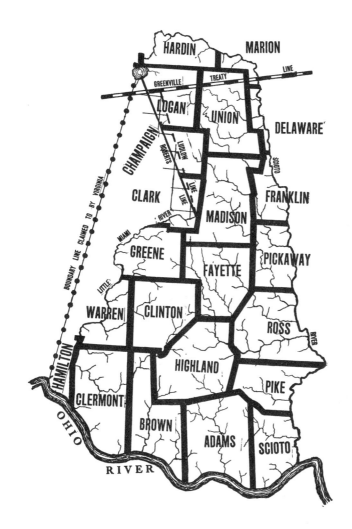

VIRGINIA MILITARY SURVEY

delegates in congress to convey to the United States all her right, including that to the soil and jurisdiction, to the territory northwest of the Ohio river, conditioned, however, that in case she did not have a sufficient quantity of good land on the southeast side of the Ohio river to satisfy her troops upon Continental establishment with army bounty warrants she had promised them, that such deficiency should be made up in land between the Scioto and the Little Miami rivers. The deed was executed by the delegates from Virginia and accepted by Congress in 1784. [11] This deed was modified, however, by Virginia in 1788, to comply with the fifth article of the ordinance of 1787. [12] And the title in fee to the land in this district, thus conveyed, is considered to have vested in the United States in trust for the officers and soldiers of Virginia to whom that colony had promised army bounty warrants for land.

As the Revolutionary war was conducted by the colonies as individual colonies as well as also by their united efforts, each colony sought to induce the enlistment of troops by whatever means it possessed. Virginia thus raised two kinds of troops: One for service at home, termed the "Virginia Establishment," or "State Line," including "Western" regiments; and the other for service with the Continental army, and termed the "Continental Establish-

(11)   1 L. U. S., 472.   (12)   1 L. U. S., 475; L. L. O., 258.

ment." That colony also established and maintained the most effective navy of any. [32] Virginia, consequently, had three regiments in the state line, two western regiments, sixteen for continental service and a navy of more than twenty vessels.

The plan of granting land for military service was first conceived by Virginia at the beginning of the French and Indian war, in 1754, when Governor Dinwiddie issued a proclamation promising two hundred thousand acres of land near the Ohio river to those who should enlist. [33] Consequently after the conclusion of that war and the completion of the 1763 treaty, King George III, desiring to reward the officers and soldiers of the army as well as also the officers who served on ships at the reduction of Louisbourg [34] and Quebec for their bravery, commanded and authorized, by proclamation of October 7, 1763, [35] the colonial governors to grant to such as should apply in person, and without further consideration, the following respective quantities of land:

Field Officers _____5000 Acres
Captains _____3000 Acres
Subalterns or Staff Officers ___2000 Acres
Non-commissioned Officers ____ 200 Acres
Privates _____ 50 Acres

For the lack of a unity with delegated powers sufficient to bind all for the expense of raising,

equipping, and supporting an army during the Revolutionary war, each respective colony necessarily
assumed that obligation; and as her land of which
she claimed an abundance west of the mountains,
was her most available resource, Virginia in 1779 [37]
promised land in that territory to all who should enlist. However, the quantity which each should receive was not definitely determined until in the
months of October of the respective years of 1779
and 1780, [13] when that colony proposed to give to
each officer, soldier or sailor, who should serve in
the army or navy to the end of the war, or to the
heirs or legal representatives of any slain, or their
heirs or assigns, the following amounts of unappropriated land:

Major General	15,000 Acres
Brigadier General	10,000 Acres
Colonel	5,000 Acres
Lieutenant Colonel	4,500 Acres
Major	4,000 Acres
Captain	3,000 Acres
Subaltern	2,000 Acres
Non-commissioned officer	400 Acres
Non-commissioned officer serving less than three years	200 Acres
Soldier or sailor serving three years	200 Acres
Soldier or sailor serving less than three years	100 Acres

To every person acting as chaplain, surgeon or surgeon's mate, the same quantity of land allowed commissioned officers receiving the same pay and rations.

With the exception of the major general and the brigadier general, all officers were allowed, by the act of October, 1780, [14] "an additional bounty in lands in the proportion of one-third of any former bounty granted them." By another act of the same month, Virginia proposed to give to each soldier serving to the end of the war, "a healthy sound negro, between the ages of ten and thirty years, or sixty pounds in gold or silver," at his option, and also three hundred acres of land, in lieu of all bounties previously promised. However, as this act was carried into the statutes by title only, it was overlooked in practice. [14] And by the act of 1782 [38] every officer or soldier who should continue in service more than six years, should also be entitled to one-sixth in addition to the amount to which he was otherwise entitled, for each year thereafter.

(33) 10 H. S. V. 661.   (32) 10 H. S. V. 23, 51, 160.
(34) A small village on Gabarus Bay in the eastern end of Cape Breton Island, Nova Scotia, where the fort, captured June 17, 1745, commanded the principal entrance to the St. Lawrence River, and was regarded as the key to the Canadian provinces.   1 L. U. S., 443.
(35) 10 H. S. V. 663; 1 L. U. S. 443.
A number of warrants issued under this proclamation, including one to Washington for 3000 acres, were located on land between the Scioto and the Little Miami Rivers.
(37) 10 H. S. V. 23, 51, 141, 160.   (14) 10 H. S. V. 373.
(13) 10 H. S. V. 141, 159, 326, 373.   (38) 11 H. S. V. 83.

In October of 1783, the Virginia legislature [39] provided for the disposal of her western lands, created a board of twenty army officers and authorized them to appoint superintendents to regulate the surveying of lands appropriated as bounties for the officers and soldiers of both the state and continental establishments, and to appoint two principal surveyors who, in turn, should select their own deputies, to locate the claims and to survey the lands.

The first principal surveyor thus selected was General Richard C. Anderson who also acted as agent for the Virginia troops. Gen. Anderson opened an office at Louisville, Kentucky, July 20, 1784, and continued to serve as principal surveyor of the Virginia military district in Ohio, until his death in 1826. The control of the office then fell to his son-in-law, Allen Latham who served as his personal representative till October 12, 1838, when William M. Anderson, one of the sons of Gen. Anderson, was appointed. This Mr. Anderson held office until January of 1848 when he was succeeded by Eleazer P. Kendrick who died in 1885 and was succeeded by his son, Samuel. Samuel Kendrick served until his death in 1893, and was the last principal surveyor of the district.

A part of the time the land office was located at Louisville, and part of the time at Chillicothe, un-

(39)   11 H. S. V. 309.

til 1829 when congress created the office of "Survey-
or of the Virginia Military Land District in Ohio,"
authorized him to receive from the personal representatives of Colonel Richard C. Anderson all the
original books, records, warrants, plats, certificates
of surveys, assignments and other papers relating
exclusively to lands already entered and patented,
or to be surveyed, entered and patented, within the
Virginia Military District in Ohio, and required him
to keep his office at the latter place. [40]

As many field notes and records made by the
principal surveyor and his deputies, were considered
to be the private property of the principal surveyor,
those thus accumulated were purchased in 1899 of
the estate of Samuel Kendrick by congress for $15,-
000.00 [41] and placed in the General Land Office at
Washington. In the mean time, however, Ohio had
procured copies which are in the office of the auditor of state. [42]

The title to the land thus reserved by Virginia
was acquired by the officer or soldier, or his heirs,
procuring from his superior officer a certificate of
his services and making proof of such services before any court of record in that state, either upon
his own oath or upon other evidence satisfactory to
the court, which fact the clerk endorsed upon the

(40) 8 L. U. S. 184; 4 U. S. S. L. 335.
(41) 30 U. S. S. L. 1099. (42) 84 L. O. 88; 85 L. O. 573.

back of the certificate. [43] Upon depositing such endorsed certificate in the Virginia Land Office at Richmond, such officer, soldier, or his heirs or assigns, received a warrant specifying the amount of land to which they were respectively entitled, and authorizing any lawfully qualified surveyor to survey and lay it off. The lands thus specified were then surveyed in the order in which the warrants were respectively delivered to the principal surveyor, except that those which had accumulated prior to March 15, 1784, were divided into classes according to acreage, and their respective priorities determined by lot. [39] Thus it happened that the first survey of land north of the Ohio river and later used, was No. 455 for 1000 acres of land adjoining the river in Niles Township, Scioto County, made November 16, 1787 by Deputy Surveyor John O'Bannon for Alexander Parker on warrant No. 771.

Upon receipt of the warrant the principal surveyor made in the books of his office an "entry" [44] that the person thus entitled to the land proposed to locate so many acres near a designated survey or more likely, upon a certain stream, endorsing upon the back of the warrant the number of surveys and quantity of land in each as designated by the holder: "Provided that a general officer was not to be al-

(43)   10 H. S. V. 50.
(44)   The record of the "entry" was notice to subsequent purchasers of such prior rights. U. S. S. R., 6 Cranch, 148; 6 Wheaton, 550.

lowed more than six surveys, a field officer five, a captain or subaltern four and the staff in proportion." [39] When the survey was completed it was reported to and recorded in the office which issued the order for the survey, and a copy certified to by the principal surveyor, together with the warrant or a certified copy, was forwarded to the general land office at Washington when a patent would be issued to the person entitled to it.

General Anderson began making and reporting surveys of land entered southeast of the Ohio river soon after his appointment. But it was not long until the lands northwest of that river were coveted by holders of warrants, and, notwithstanding such lands were to be used only in case a deficiency of good lands was found southeast of the river, surveys were soon being made and locations attempted upon the lands reserved in Ohio. However, congress in 1788 [16] stopped such procedure by declaring invalid all locations and surveys made between the Scioto and Little Miami rivers on account of the Virginia troops upon continental establishment, before a deficiency on the southeast side of the Ohio river had been determined according to the act of cession, [11] and requested information of the executive of Virginia as to the amount of such land, if any, yet required. Agents of the troops reporting a de-

(16)   1 L. U. S., 572.

ficiency of land to the southeast of that river, congress in 1790 (17) repealed the ordinance of 1788 and
directed the secretary of war to furnish the Virginia executive with the names of the officers and
soldiers entitled to such lands; that such officers and
soldiers might locate them between those rivers,
and, after the entries had been located and the surveys made, that the president of the United States
should issue letters patent for the lands to the persons originally entitled, or to the heirs or assigns,
who thus acquired title in fee simple, since the reservation of Virginia was only as to "the time within
which the lands thus appropriated should be separated from the mass." (46)   Virginia, however, protested against the act of 1790, because it considered
its vagueness rendered doubtful and possibly destroyed the rights of assignees of such warrants,
and also rendered uncertain whether those who did
not serve till the end of the war should receive
grants on the warrants they held. (60)   At first the
patents were sent by the secretary of state to the
executive of Virginia and by him delivered to the
grantee, but since 1794 (47) they were issued directly to the grantee.

In May of 1800 (18) congress authorized the ac-

(17)   2 L. U. S., 179, 440; 1 U. S. S. L., 182, 394; 9 Wheaton
        469; 22 U. S. S. C. R., 137.
(46)   U. S. S. C. R. 1 Peters, 634.
(47)   2 L. U. S. 440; 3 L. U. S. 582; 1 U. S. S. L. 394; 2 U.
        S. S. L. 274.   (60)   13 Hening, 236.
(18)   3 L. U. S., 393, 478; 2 U. S. S. L., 80, 155.

ceptance of any warrants for military services, since known as "resolution warrants," issued under any previous resolutions of the Virginia legislature, in favor of any one who had served in the Virginia line on the continental establishment: Provided the whole amount should not exceed sixty thousand acres, and that the surveys should be completed and the certificates deposited with the secretary of war before December 1, 1803.

As the privilege of locating army bounty warrants upon the land between the Scioto and Little Miami rivers was personal, congress could limit the time within which they could be made. [46] Consequently an act was passed in 1804 [24] requiring all locations to be made before March 23, 1807 and the surveys returned to the secretary of war before March 23, 1809. In 1807 [48] the time within which to complete such locations was further extended to March 23, 1810, and the time within which to return their surveys and warrants to the secretary of war, to March 23, 1812: "Provided, That no locations shall, after the passing of this act, be made on tracts of land for which patents had previously been issued, or which had been previously surveyed; and any patent which may, nevertheless, be obtained for land located contrary to the provisions of this section, shall be considered null and void."

(24)   3 L. U. S., 592; 2 U. S. S. L., 274.
(48)   4 L. U. S. 92; 2 U. S. S. L. 424.

By subsequent legislation [19] the time within which these lands could thus be entered and surveyed was extended from time to time until 1850, [49] when the time for doing so was limited to January 1, 1852, while the act of 1855 [50] permitted entries and surveys made prior to January 1, 1852, to be returned to the general land office by March 3, 1857. Therefore no entries or surveys of these lands could be made after December 31, 1851, nor the title thereto which was predicated upon service rendered in the revolutionary war, acquired in any manner after March 3, 1857. [51]

By the act of 1852, [52] and provided the legislature of Virginia released all further claims to such land, which was done December 6, 1852, and the governor authorized and required to execute a proper deed on behalf of the state, [53] all unsatisfied outstanding military land warrants issued or allowed by Virginia prior to March 1, 1852, could be surrendered to the Secretary of the Interior who should issue land scrip for such part as remained unsatisfied at the rate of $1.25 per acre and that such scrip should be received in payment for any land owned

(19)   4 L. U. S. 281, 714, 805;   6 L. U. S. 282, 549;   7 L. U. S. 171, 516;   8 L. U. S. 288, 379, 531, 677;   9 L. U. S. 829, 985;   10 L. U. S. 149;   2 U. S. S. L. 589;   3 U. S. S. L. 143, 212, 423, 612, 772;   4 U. S. S. L. 189, 395, 500, 578, 665; 5 U. S. S. L. 262, 329, 449;   9 U. S. S. L. 41, 244; 10 U. S. S. L. 98, 143, 701.   (49)   9 U. S. S. L. 421.
(50)   10 U. S. S. L. 701.   (51)   52 O. S. R. 567.
(52)   August 31, 10 U. S. S. L. 143.
(53)   Virginia Acts of 1852-53, page 357.

by the United States and subject to sale at private entry. Virginia issued land warrants for military and naval bounties to the amount of 6,146,950 acres. Of this Virginia satisfied much with land southeast of the river Ohio, while congress satisfied such bounties in land between the Scioto and Little Miami rivers to the amount of 4,334,800 acres and by land scrip for 1,041,916 acres elsewhere. [54]

By this time virtually all land warrants for services rendered upon continental establishment issued by Virginia had been located and satisfied. There yet remained, however, between the Scioto and Little Miami rivers, unlocated and unsurveyed, some 76,735.44 acres of which much was termed "vacant land." It was mostly wild and barren and valuable only for its timber which was being rapidly destroyed. The land was considered practically worthless and the government therefore did not desire to continue to be burdened with its care. Consequently congress by the act of 1871, [20] which was the equivalent of a patent, [55] ceded all this land remaining unsurveyed and unsold, to the state of Ohio, subject to the preemption of not exceeding 160 acres occupied by a boni fide settler, and to be disposed of in such manner as the legislature of the state might direct. The legislature accepted the land [56] and

(20)   16 U. S. S. L. 416;   52 O. S. R. 567.
(54)   19 Arch. 317.   (55)   52 O. S. R. 586.
(56)   68 L. O. 220;   69 L. O. 52, 204;   70 L. O. 107.

vested the title in the trustees of the Ohio Agricultural and Mechanical College, of which the Ohio State University is successor, [57] for its benefit, and authorized its trustees to deed to any occupant in actual possession at the time of the passage of the act of congress, forty acres upon his paying the cost of surveying and making the deed; and upon his paying one dollar per acre in excess of forty acres, to deed him such additional amount as he may have so occupied, not exceeding 160 acres in all. The balance of the land was to be surveyed and subdivided into tracts not exceeding 500 acres and numbered in consecutive order, called "Allotments," by commencing with the tracts in Adams county, and so continuing until all should be platted and numbered. The trustees also were authorized to sell the unoccupied lands at public or private sales at not less than their appraised value.

As the more desirable lands were selected by the earlier claimants, those coming later were neccessarily relegated to the rough and poor land. To make up this deficiency of "good lands" which the Virginia act of cession [11] promised, the later locators often took a much greater amount than their warrants called for by changing the actual distances between calls and monuments to such that when the

(21)   21 U. S. S. L., 142.   (27)   22 U. S. S. L., 348.

(57)   75 L. O. 126.   (58)   38 O. S. R. 156.

(59)   38 O. S. R. 156; 52 O. S. R. 567; 113 U. S. S. C. R. 550;
         123 U. S. S. C. R. 117.

contents were computed the survey would show but a small surplus, if any, over that to which it was entitled. And a survey embracing as much as sixteen hundred and eighty-two acres has been thus made on a warrant for but five hundred acres. [58] Trouble, of course, arose soon after the trustees began the survey. Whereupon proceedings were brought against those holding under patents thus covering such excess and also against the holders of unpatented surveys. The courts decided against the holders who, in 1880, [21] appealed to congress for relief, and again in 1882, [27] but without avail since the courts also held that congress was unable to modify afterwards its act of cession of February 18, 1871, which conveyed at the time of its passage, all the title the government had in the land. [59]

As much "unsurveyed land" remained, many occupants became alarmed concerning their holdings and appealed to the legislature for relief. Whereupon by the act of March, 1889, [22] approved June 20th following by the board of trustees of The Ohio State University, it was provided that that any person in possession of any unpatented lands in the Virginia military district for more than twenty-one years, under claim of title either through himself or through those under whom he claimed title, could pay to the board of trustees two dollars as the cost of preparing and executing the deed, and should receive a deed of conveyance from the board. Thus ended a controversy that vitally affected the title to many acres of land and the interest of many people.

While the lands between the Scioto and the Little Miami rivers were thus being located and surveyed, Congress in 1799 and also in 1800, [23] directed the surveyor general to complete the survey and subdivision of the land between the Miami rivers begun by Judge Symmes, to the Greenville treaty line; and in doing so it became necessary to determine the dividing line between that tract and the tract thus reserved to satisfy land warrants issued by Virginia. Thereupon, Israel Ludlow, deputy surveyor, located a line running from the source of the Little Miami river in the southwest quarter of section thirty, township seven, east, of range eight "Between the Miami Rivers," north twenty degrees west, a distance of forty miles, five chains and twenty-five links, to a point on the Greenville treaty line in the southeast quarter of section two, township two, east, of range fifteen which he assumed to be the source of the Scioto, and proceeded to subdivide all the land "Between the Miami Rivers" lying west of this line, since known as the "Ludlow Line," into ranges, townships and sections.

That the division line between these two tracts might be fixed, Congress in 1804, [24] accepted the

(22) 86 L. O., 92.   (25)   4 L. U. S., 455; 2 U. S. S. L., 264.
(23)   3 L. U. S., 264, 385; 1 U. S. S. L., 728; 2 U. S. S. L., 73.

Ludlow line and directed that it "be considered and held as the westerly boundary line, north of the source of the Little Miami, of the territory reserved by Virginia," provided Virginia within two years, should recognize it as the boundary.

While it was comparatively easy to locate the lands reserved by Virginia lying between the main channels of the Scioto and the Little Miami rivers, and also the source of the latter stream, yet it was not so easy to determine, within a large extent of swampy land, the "source of the Scioto," when any one of several widely separated places might, with equal reason, be so considered. Virginia, therefore, objected to the Ludlow line and Congress, in 1812, [25] provided for the appointment of three commissioners, who, with such commissioners as Virginia might appoint, should meet at Xenia in October of 1812, employ a surveyor and ascertain, survey and distinctly mark the westwardly boundary line according to the true intent and meaning of the act of cession. [11]

This commission met at Xenia in October of that year and employed Charles Roberts to survey and mark the line. The line began at the same headspring as the source of the Little Miami that the Ludlow line had been surveyed from, and was run north twenty degrees west to a point in the southeast quarter of section thirty-four, township five, south, of range eight east of the first principal meridian; thence north 75° 05' east, to a point in section thirty-six of the same township and range where the source of the Scioto river was assumed to be.   This line has since been known as the "Roberts Line."

While these lines, each having the same bearing, began at the same southern source they diverged about four degrees and the north end of the Roberts line is, therefore, some four miles west of that of the Ludlow line, thereby enclosing virtually one hundred square miles of territory which Virginia claimed. Why these lines, each with the same bearing, should diverge so much, is not explained by the records. Perhaps one survey may have been based upon the true meridian, while the other may have been upon the magnetic meridian at the time of the survey.

The Virginia commissioners, however, refused to agree to the Roberts line and even claimed a still larger tract by running from the **source** of the Scioto river straight to the **mouth** of the Little Miami. [15] This demand prevented an agreement establishing the division line between the tracts; and its settlement was deferred until in 1818, [26] when Congress confirmed the act of 1804 and established the line as run by Ludlow as the western boundary of the Virginia reservation lying south of the Greenville Treaty line, and the Roberts line as the boundary line of that part of the reservation lying north of that treaty line.

Meanwhile, land warrants, issued by Virginia, had been located between the Ludlow and the Roberts lines, and the right to do so was upheld, in 1824, by the supreme court of the United States in the case of Doddridge vs Thompson, [15] which virtually established the Roberts line as the proper division line, notwithstanding the act of 1818 [26] to which the court did not advert.

In 1824, Congress authorized the president to ascertain the number of acres, and their value exclusive of improvements, of all lands lying between the Ludlow and the Roberts lines according to the principles of the decision of the supreme court in the Doddridge case, and the terms by which the holders would relinquish their claims to the United States, and to report the facts to Congress. [28] Thereupon Congress in 1830, [29] authorized the president to pay to the Virginia military claimants of land between the Ludlow and the Roberts lines, located prior to June 26, 1812, the sum of $62,515.25, provided they relinquish their title to the United States.   In February of 1831, [30] Congress authorized the president to pay Phillip Doddridge $1,765.68 for military survey No. 6928 for seven hundred acres lying between the Ludlow and the Roberts lines, which he had already conveyed to the United States.   Thus while the supreme court seems to have recognized

(15)   22 U. S. S. C. R. 137;   9 Wheaton, 469;   13 Arch. 278.
(26)   6 L. U. S., 282; 3 U. S. S. L., 423.

the Ludlow line as the proper line, subsequent acts of congress seem to have conceded the title to the Roberts line and the commissioner of the general land office seems to have accepted the latter line as the proper one. [15]

Since the land warrants issued by Virginia determined the quantity of land to which each person was entitled, the indiscriminate location plan as applied in that state was used in subdividing the land between the Scioto and the Little Miami rivers, east of the Ludlow line; while that between the Ludlow and the Roberts lines, which is a part of the survey "Between the Miami Rivers," was subdivided upon the rectangular plan. As the surveys of the entries were made they were given numbers, known as survey numbers, but as the territory was settled at widely separated points, consecutive numbers are not contiguous. The tract lies in the southwestern part of the state and contains about 4,204,000 acres.

(28)   7 L. U. S., 320; 4 U. S. S. L., 70.
(29)   8 L. U. S., 318; 4 U. S. S. L., 405.
(30)   8 L. U. S., 411; 4 U. S. S. L., 440.

CHAPTER 9

THE OHIO RIVER SURVEY

The Ohio River Survey in the southeastern part of the state is the most extensive of any in Ohio. Within it lies the historic seven ranges where the rectangular system was first applied, and where the first line for the subdivision of land under the new system, known as the "geographer's line," was surveyed and established by Colonel Hutchins for the United States government.

This survey extends from the Pennsylvania line and the Ohio river west to the Scioto, and to the west line of the twenty-first range, north of the Greenville treaty line, and includes all the land lying between the forty-first parallel of latitude and the Ohio river, except that within the United States Military tract, the Ebenezer Zane tracts, the Donation tract the French grants and possibly two townships in the north end of the tenth range.

Its ranges, as begun under the ordinance of 1785 [1] are numbered west from the west line of Pennsylvania, and the townships in each range, except the eighteenth, are numbered north from where the ranges respectively intersect the Ohio river. The first township, or fraction of a township in each range thus bordering upon that river, is designated as township number one of such range, except in the eighteenth where the first fraction of township is called "fraction one." And the townships in each range are numbered thence consecutively from number one, north to the forty-first parallel of latitude. The townships or fractions of townships, lying north of the United States Military tract are each given such consecutive numbers in their respective ranges as they would have been given had that tract not intervened. Each range in this survey, therefore, contains as many numbered townships as there are full, or fractions of, townships within it. But, by reason of the irregularity of the Ohio river, few of these ranges are of the same length, and consequently instances are rare of adjacent townships in adjoining ranges having similar numbers. However, since the Ohio river is the base from which its townships are numbered, this survey very properly should be termed "The Ohio River Survey" [4]; and, except, as otherwise noted, the

(1)   See The Seven Ranges; 1 L. U. S., 563.
(4)   See Page 145.

THE
OHIO RIVER
SURVEY

land within it should be described as being in that survey, as, for instance, "The northeast quarter of section 26, town 5, range 13 of the Ohio River Survey."

The rule of numbering townships, or fractional parts of townships, in this survey, by beginning with number one on the Ohio river, has been departed from in the eighteenth range where the second fractional township from that river has been given number one, while the first, or most southern, fractional township is called "fraction township one," as shown by the plan of "Range 18" [5].

A rather remarkable coincidence, however, is that Fort Laurens, located, arbitrarily and by circumstances, in the wilderness, many years before, was virtually upon the continuation of the geographer's line—the first line directed to be surveyed by the new government——and further, that both, Fort Laurens and the geographer's line, should be substantially four full townships south of the forty-first parallel of latitude, which was the dividing line between original charter grants.

Except where the Ohio or the Scioto river, or the lines of other subdivisions cause fractions of townships, and in townships eleven and twelve of the thirteenth range, all townships in this survey are six miles square, and the sections, or mile square lots,

(5)   See Page 147.   (7)   See Page 152.

are numbered upon the plan adopted by the act of
1796, by beginning at the northeast corner of the
township and numbering west, east, etc., except as
to (1) the land south of the geographer's line in the
original seven ranges, and (2) that purchased by the
Ohio Company of Associates. In these two tracts

RANGE 18

the sections are numbered upon the plan required by the original land ordinance of 1785, by beginning in the southeast corner of the township and numbering north to the northeast corner, etc.

The ordinance of 1785 required the sections in fractional parts of townships to "bear the same numbers as if the township had been entire," [2] and the sections, or parts of sections, in fractional townships subdivided under that ordinance, have been numbered in that manner; but, while the act of 1796 [3] required "fractional parts of townships to be divided into sections, in the manner" provided by that act for the subdivision of entire townships, the rule of numbering sections, evidently required by that act, was not applied in townships eleven and twelve of the thirteenth range, in the fractional townships bordering the Ohio river in ranges sixteen, seventeen, eighteen, nineteen, twenty and twenty-one, or in the fractional townships bordering the Scioto river in the Langham and the Worthington surveys in range twenty-two.   In each of these fractions, section number one is in the northeast corner of the township, and the numbers thence proceed consecutively to the west, as provided for by that act.   But this process is thus carried only so far as there are sections, or parts of sections, within that tier of sections in the township, when the section, or

(2)   1 L. U. S., 563.
(3)   2 L. U. S., 533; 1 U. S. S. L., 464.

part of section in the tier of sections lying immediately to the south of the tier last so numbered, is given the next consecutive number. This process is continued thence to the east side of the township, thence west, and so on until each section, or part of section, within the fraction of township, is given a number, regardless of the plan evidently provided for by the act of 1796, [3] as may be seen by the plat of "Range 18" [5].

The method of numbering sections provided for by congress, has, therefore, been radically interfered with in these fractional townships and in townships eleven and twelve of the thirteenth range, [8] and no rule applies, since the order of the numbers of sections is seldom, if ever, alike in any two.

Much confusion arises from the manner of numbering the fractions of townships caused by the Scioto river in the twenty-second range. Three separate sets of numbers prevail. The first begins with township number one on the Ohio river, as the townships in the other ranges of such survey begin, and continues north for five townships until the trend of the Scioto river from the east cuts out the range entirely. This part of the range was surveyed in May of 1799, by Elias Langham, and was subdivided into sections, in 1805, by James Denny. It is known as the "Langham Survey." The next set

(8)   See Chapter 17.

of numbers begins with township number one immediately north of where the eastward trend of the Scioto crosses that range from the west, and continues north for four townships. This part of such range was surveyed in June of 1799, by Thomas Worthington, and subdivided, in 1805, by Jesse Spencer. It is known as the "Worthington Survey." That part of this range lying between Worthington's survey and the United States Military tract was surveyed in May of 1799, by John Matthews and Ebenezer Buckingham, and subdivided, in 1805, into sections, by Jesse Spencer. It is known as the "Matthews Survey." This latter survey consists of parts of four townships which are numbered two, three, four and five, respectively, but for some unknown reason the plan, however, did not begin with township number one, which is omitted.

Duplication of numbers of townships will be found also in range number twenty-one. Eleven townships from the Ohio river were first surveyed and numbered from one to the north, from that river, but the four townships composing the balance of the range, to the United States Military tract, were not given continuous numbers, but began with number nine immediately north of township number eleven of the first series.   Thus, townships numbers nine, ten and eleven, are duplicated in this range. The first or southern townships were surveyed in

1799, by Thomas Worthington and should be designated as of the "Worthington Survey," while the latter or northern townships, were surveyed in 1801, by Ebenezer Buckingham and John Matthews and should be referred to as the "Matthews Survey" [6].

To distinguish these five surveys and avoid confusion in describing the lands within them, they should be referred to, respectively, as "The Langham Survey," "The Worthington Survey," "The Matthews Survey," "The Worthington Survey," or "The Buckingham Survey." For instance, "Section number two of township number three of the Matthews Survey of range number twenty-two of the Ohio River Survey."

In 1800 when the tenth range immediately south of the 41st parallel was surveyed, the Indians had not released their title to the land west of the Tuscarawas river, and the two parts of townships were numbered 1 and 2. And to distinguish them from townships 1 and 2 on the Ohio river in that range they should be designated as town 1 or 2 of the Muskingum base, range 10 of the Ohio River Survey. [4]

To remedy defects occasioned by carrying the survey so far from its base, a "correction line," or true meridian, was established between ranges seventeen and eighteen; while the south line of township five of the eighth range, and continuing

(6) 1 L. O. 26; 3 L. O. 317.

west, was run by Israel Ludlow, under direction of the Federal government, to establish the north line of the one and one-half million acre tract contracted for by the Ohio Company of Associates.   This latter line is known as "Israel Ludlow's Survey."

Township eight of range sixteen of the Ohio River Survey, which also coincides with the civil

36	30	24	18	12	6
35	29	23	17	11	5
34	Fr. 35 / Fr. 34 / Fr. 33	Fr. 23 / Fr. 24 / Fr. 36	16	10	4
33	27	Fr. 30 / 21	15	9	3
32	26	20	14	8	2
6	5	4	3	2	1

THE OHIO COMPANY'S PURCHASE

WILKESVILLE   TOWNSHIP
VINTON   COUNTY

TOWN 8   *RANGE* 16

township of Wilkesville, Vinton county, has the unique distinction of possessing the plans of numbering sections provided for by both the ordinance of 1785 and the act of 1796. [7]

All of this township, except one mile off the south side, was included in the second purchase made by the Ohio Company of Associates, who subdivided their lands upon the general plan provided for by the ordinance of 1785, [2] but modified to suit their purposes; while the land composing the lowest tier of sections was within the lands retained by the general government which later subdivided it upon the plan provided by the act of 1796. [3] Sections one, seven, thirteen, nineteen, twenty-five and thirty-one were, therefore, omitted in the first survey. And when the surveyor general subdivided this remaining part of the township into sections, he was governed by the latter act, and so numbered the six sections thus composing such remainder, from one to six, and thereby duplicated sections two, three, four, five and.six in that township. Thus this is the only township in the United States in which sections are duplicated. And the land in these several respective duplicated sections should be described as, for instance, section 2 in the EAST side of town 8, range 16 of the Ohio River Survey; or, section 2 in the SOUTH side of town 8, range 16 of the Ohio River Survey.

CHAPTER 10

THE OHIO COMPANY

The first tract of land to be disposed of by the general government was that purchased by the Ohio Company of Associates in southeastern Ohio, and since known as "The Ohio Company's Purchase." This company, composed almost entirely of people from the New England states who effected the first permanent settlement in Ohio at Marietta in April of 1788, should not be confused with an earlier company known as "The Ohio Land Company," but frequently referred to as "The Ohio Company."

The Ohio Land Company was organized in 1748 by Governor Dinwiddie, Lawrence and August Washington and sixteen other persons prominent in London, Virginia and Maryland. A conditional grant of five hundred thousand acres lying between the Monongahela and Kanawha rivers, in what is now West Virginia, with the privilege of selecting a part on the north side of the Ohio, was obtained from the English crown in 1749. The conflicting claims of the French, Indians, English and the colonies, as well as also the the interference of the French and Indian and the Revolutionary wars, prevented substantial settlements being made in Ohio. A trading station, however, was established in 1749, in the northwest part of Shelby county where Peter Loramie later located his store; while Christopher Gist, in 1750, explored the land along the northern side of the Ohio river. This activity, among other things, led to the war between France and England being extended to the colonies, and in which the Indians sided with the French. At the conclusion of that war, France ceded England all her possessions east of the Mississippi river and north of the thirty-first parallel of latitude.

Several reasons have been given for the first settlement in Ohio, the star of hope to which the ragged army at Valley Forge looked for deliverance. That to which history is disposed, perhaps, to give the most credence is the efforts of the officers of the Revolutionary war to obtain lands promised them for services, and for which they held warrants.

At that time it was also apparent that about the only immediate resources of the general government, then in process of forming, were the lands west of the Allegheny mountains claimed by the Indians, as well as by some of the colonies; and it was with these lands that the Continental Congress had hoped to satisfy land warrants when provisions for their issuance were made. In April of 1783, Colonel Timothy Pickering, then quartermaster general, proposed to some of the officers of the army, then in army headquarters at Newburgh on the Hudson river, in Orange county, New York, that they petition congress to form a new state west of the Ohio river, and permit their land warrants to be satisfied from the land so set aside. This proposition was submitted "for consideration, amendment and suggestion" to General Rufus Putnam who recommended that a petition be presented to congress asking that lands, to which the holders of warrants were entitled, be located in the western territory, and that provision be made for selling other lands to them for public certificates.

Thereupon, in June of 1783, two hundred and eighty-five officers petitioned congress to procure from the Indians the land northwest of the Ohio river and cause it to be surveyed and given them for services in accordance with the provisions of the ordinances of congress of 1776 and 1780. Of this number one hundred and fifty-five were from Massachusetts, thirty-four from New Hampshire, forty-six from Connecticut, thirty-six from New Jersey, thirteen from Maryland and one from New York. [1]

(1) For copy of petition and list of petitioners see 1 Arch. 38.

Another reason assigned for this settlement was that, as the climate of the New England territory was more rigorous and the soil less fertile than in many other localities which had been explored, emigration had long been considered by many of its residents. In 1773, a number had migrated to west Florida, but finding that no title to the land could be had, they returned without effecting a settlement. This expedition, however, emphasized the necessity of stability of titles to land as well as also the assurance of a satisfactory government, to induce settlement. So, in 1787, when negotiating for land in the western territory, the Ohio Company of Associates insisted upon both good titles and good government. They, therefore, required not only the adoption of a contract for the purchase of the land in a manner they deemed reasonable, but also that satisfactory provisions first be made for the government of the country to which they should emigrate. Hence, it may be said that the contract [2] for the sale of the land in southeastern Ohio and the adoption of the ordinance of July 13, 1787, [3] were really one transaction, and that neither would have been satisfactory nor complete without the other.

The chaotic condition of the government during its creative period, prevented congress complying with the request of these officers for some years. In

[2]   L. H. O. U., 43.
[3]   1 L. U. S., 475.

the meantime, in 1784, Virginia had [4] ceded to the United States her claim to all the land in Ohio lying south of the forty-first parallel of north latitude; some of the Indian tribes, by the treaty of Fort M'Intosh in 1785, [5] had released their claims to that part of Ohio lying south and east of the line subsequently adopted at Greenville; [6] the land ordinance of 1785 [7] had been passed, and the seven ranges of townships surveyed. It was impossible, therefore, for the new government to consider selling any lands until about 1786.

However, while the French and Indian war was in progress, and Lord Dunmore marched thru the Hocking Valley to Pickaway county, many colonists, especially those from Virginia, had opportunity of seeing much of the Ohio country, and they were favorably impressed with its possibilities. During the Revolutionary war such good reports of this western country, to which General Washington added much from his own knowledge, were communicated from soldier to soldier, that, at the close of that war, many persons, particularly in the New England states, became much interested in this territory. General Rufus Putnam, a surveyor and a man of much ability and enterprise, became especially active in promoting its colonization. The very flattering

(4)   1 L. U. S. 472.
(5)   1 L. U. S., 390; 7 U. S. S. L., 16; 4 Arch. 6
(6)   1 L. U. S., 398; 7 U. S. S. L., 49.   (7) 1 L. U. S. 563.

report of Colonel Thomas Hutchins who had spent
many years northwest of the Ohio river, and the survey of the seven ranges, invited attention anew to
the Ohio country. About this time General Benjamin Tupper returned from Pittsburg enthused with
the reports of the Ohio country he had heard while
there. He spent the night of January 9, 1786, with
General Putnam, with whom he had been on intimate
terms for years, and they became so much interested
that they decided to organize a colony, purchase
lands and establish a settlement northwest of the
Ohio river. Accordingly, the next day they joined
in publishing a call for representatives of the officers
and soldiers of the Revolutionary war, and any
others who might wish to join in promoting the
scheme, to select representatives to meet at the
Bunch of Grapes tavern in Boston, on Wednesday,
March 1, 1786, to determine a plan for acquiring
land in the Ohio country and promoting its settlement.

Ten delegates were present at that meeting, and
it was agreed that the subscribers should constitute
an association known as the "Ohio Company;" that
one million dollars in continental specie certificates
should be used to purchase western lands and promote their settlement; that each one thousand dollars
subscribed should constitute one share, but that no
one person should hold more than five; that the
proprietors of twenty shares should constitute one

grand division of the company and appoint an agent to represent them, and that the agents should appoint five directors, a treasurer and a secretary. These directors were given the sole disposal of the funds and authorized to purchase land for the benefit of the company, either by themselves or by such other persons as they might intrust with the business; and, after the land had been purchased, they were required to subdivide it in such manner as the agents might direct, and execute deeds to the agents respectively for the proportions which should fall to their division, corresponding to the deeds the directors themselves might receive.

A full year was occupied in soliciting subscriptions and perfecting plans. The next meeting, therefore, was not held until March 8, 1787, when, at Brackett's tavern in Boston, a committee was appointed to apply to congress for the purchase of land upon such terms as the committee might deem adequate to the purposes of the company. Reverend Manasseh Cutler and Major Winthrop Sargent were selected to make the application.

For a while it was impossible to secure the attention of congress, and these agents, in despair, were about to abandon further efforts when arrangements were made with Colonel William Duer and others to join in attempting to acquire several

(11)   See The French Grants.   (8)   1 L. U. S. 573.

RESOLUTION OF JULY 23, 1787 ●●●●●
ONE AND ONE HALF MILLION ACRES ▬●▬●▬

million acres. [11]   Whereupon the Continental Congress, July 23, 1787, [8] empowered the board of treasury to contract for the sale of a tract of land bounded by the Ohio river from the mouth of the Scioto to the intersection of the western boundary of the seventh range of townships of the Ohio River Survey, by that boundary to the northern boundary of the tenth township from the Ohio river, by a due west line to the Scioto, and by that river to the place of beginning. [23]

It was required that the tract should be surveyed and its contents ascertained by the geographer or some other officer of the United States; that the purchasers, within seven years and at their own expense, should subdivide the tract into townships and fractional parts of townships, and the townships into lots according to the land ordinance of 1785; [7] that lot number sixteen in each township should be given for the maintenance of public schools within the township; lot number twenty-nine be given perpetually for the purposes of religion; lots numbers eight, eleven and twenty-six be reserved for the future disposition of congress, and not more than two complete townships be given perpetually for the purposes of a university, to be laid off by the purchasers as nearly the center of the tract as may be and applied to the intended object by the legislature of the state.

The price was not to be less than one dollar per

acre after excepting the reservations and gifts mentioned, payable in specie loan office certificates reduced to specie value, or certificates of liquidated debts of the United States, with a reduction of one-third of a dollar per acre for bad land, a privilege permitted in no other sales than that of 248, 450 acres in the southwestern part of the state to John Cleves Symmes. [9] Not less than five hundred thousand dollars were to be paid upon closing the contract and the remainder upon the completion of the work to be performed by the geographer or other officer on the part of the United States, when a grant should be made for whatever amount may have been paid for. [10]

The tract which this resolution permitted to be sold included all the land lying between the Scioto river and the seven ranges, extended as far north as the north line of Muskingum county and included many million acres more land than the Ohio Company of associates desired to purchase, which was the amount for which one million dollars would pay. The excess, however, was for the benefit of Colonel William Duer and others who were interested in the Scioto Purchase. [11]

The location of the land purchased by the Ohio Company was not determined by design, greed or

(9) 1 L. U. S. 456.   (23) See Page 161.
(10) 1 L. U. S. 491, 573, 574; 4 Arch. 11.

mercenary purposes, as some romancers would have believed, but by the very force of the fact that it was the most eastern land available for sale in large quantities. The seven ranges had been subdivided and directed to be sold in small parcels, while there was insufficient land in one body between those ranges and that reserved by Connecticut. Its purchase, therefore, was the nearest location in which the amount of land desired by the Ohio and the Scioto companies, could be obtained from the government.

Thereupon, October 27, 1787, Cutler and Sargent, as agents for the Ohio Company of Associates, contracted [2] with the board of treasury for one million five hundred thousand acres of land, besides the several townships, lots and parcels of land to be reserved or appropriated to specific purposes off the south ends of ranges eight, nine, ten, eleven, twelve, thirteen, fourteen, fifteen, sixteen and seventeen of the Ohio River Survey, for five hundred thousand dollars in Continental securities, then worth about twelve and one-half cents to the dollar, and a like amount after the tract had been surveyed by the geographer or some other officer of the United States authorized for that purpose. Having paid for half the amount of land contracted for, it was further agreed that the Ohio Company should have immediate possession of seven hundred and fifty thousand acres, besides the several lots and parcels of land reserved or appropriated to particular purposes, off the south ends of ranges eight, nine, ten, eleven, twelve, thirteen, fourteen and fifteen of the Ohio River Survey.

Having made the first payment at the time of entering into the contract and being unable to raise sufficient funds to purchase the whole amount contracted for, it was decided to obtain a deed for the amount for which such cash payment would pay, which, with the allowance for bad lands, was seven hundred and fifty thousand acres besides the several lots reserved or appropriated to particular purposes. Thereupon Congress in 1792, [12] confirmed the contract of 1787, and authorized the president to convey seven hundred and fifty thousand acres, after reserving the lots or parcels reserved or appropriated to particular purposes, as provided in that contract, off the south ends of ranges eight, nine, ten, eleven, twelve, thirteen, fourteen and fifteen of the Ohio River Survey, to "Rufus Putnam, Manasseh Cutler, Robert Oliver and Griffin Greene and to their heirs and assigns, in fee simple, in trust for the persons composing the Ohio Company of Associates, according to their several rights and interests, and for their

---

(12)   Annals of Congress, March 26, 1792, page 486; 2 L. U. S. 276; 1 U. S. S. L., 257; 6 U. S. S. L., 8.

(13)   1 L. U. S. 492.

(14)   Washington County Deed Book 1, page 115.

heirs and assigns, as tenants in common." [13] Accordingly, President Washington under date of May 10, 1792, executed a patent. [14]

This tract is located in Washington, Morgan, Athens, Hocking, Vinton, Meigs, Gallia and Lawrence counties. It contains, as computed, 913,883 acres, including the several lots or parcels of land reserved or appropriated to particular purposes, and is known as the Ohio Company's "First Purchase." [24]

Meanwhile the United States established the north boundary line of the one million five hundred thousand acre tract contracted for in 1787. [2] This line coincides with the south line of townships five of ranges eight and nine of the Ohio River Survey and the north line of the "Donation tract." It was surveyed by Israel Ludlow and has since been known as "Israel Ludlow's Survey."

Many associates of the Ohio Company held army bounty warrants for land, and, as the resolution of July 23, 1787, [8] permitted them to use these "rights for bounties of land in discharge of the contract, acre for acre," many availed themselves of the opportunity; and warrants sufficient to purchase 214,285 acres were presented to the secretary of the treasury. Thereupon, under the act of 1792, [12] President Washington under date of May 10, 1792,

[15] conveyed to Rufus Putnam, Manasseh Cutler, Robert Oliver and Griffin Greene and to their heirs and assigns the following described tract of land within the limits of the one million five hundred thousand acres contracted for, to-wit:

Beginning at the northwest corner of the Donation tract of 100,000 acres, on a line surveyed by Israel Ludlow as for the north boundary line of the tract of 1,500,000 acres contracted for October 27, 1787, [2] by the Ohio Company of Associates, and thence running west on the Ludlow line to the west line of the eleventh range; thence south to the intersection of the west continuation of the north line of the third township of the seventh range; thence west, along the continuation of the north line of the third township of the seventh range, to the west line of the sixteenth range; thence south, on the west line of the sixteenth range, to a point from which a line drawn east to the west line of a tract of 913,883 acres granted to Rufus Putnam and others by patent dated May 10, 1792, [14] will, with the other lines of this tract as herein specified and described, comprehend 214,285 acres; thence east to the west line of said tract of 913,883 acres; thence north on its west boundary to its northwest corner; thence east, on the north line of said tract, to the southwest corner of the 100,000 acre tract; thence north to the place of beginning. [13]

(15)   Washington County Deed Book 1, page 117.

This tract, in which no reservations for the benefit of schools, churches, or otherwise, were made, is located in Washington, Morgan, Athens, Hocking and Vinton counties, and is known as the Ohio Company's "Second Purchase."

For the purpose of subdivision among the shareholders the first and the second purchases were treated as one tract.   They amounted to 964,285 acres after excluding out of the first purchase the several parcels reserved, or appropriated, to special purposes.

However, since the subdivision of the land into sections of 640 acres each, as required by the land ordinance of 1785, or even into quarter sections, or other aliquot parts of a section, would not enable an equal division of the land to be made among one thousand subscribers, a special method of subdivision was necessary.

As it was assumed that one thousand shares would be taken, plans for the subdivision of the land upon that basis were formulated in Boston during the summer and fall of 1787.   Accordingly, months before any had seen the land, the directors provided for laying out 1008 house lots and 1000 eight-acre lots; while at their first meeting, held July 2, 1788, on the banks of the Muskingum river, they provided for laying out 1005 three-acre lots of which five were for public use.

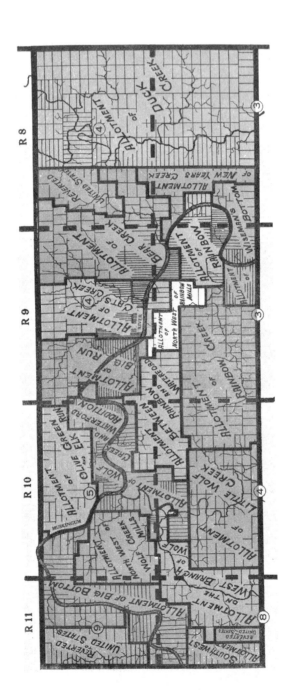

THE DONATION TRACT

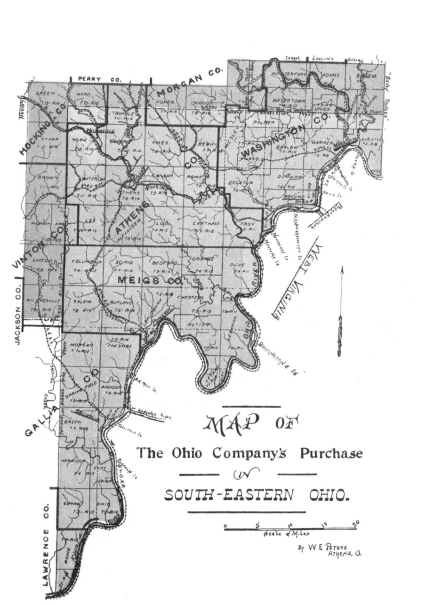

MAP OF
The Ohio Company's Purchase
IN
SOUTH-EASTERN OHIO.

Scale of Miles

By W. E. PETERS
ATHENS, O.

In 1792, when the patents were issued the whole number of shares was found to be 822 and each share entitled to about 1173 acres. Plans to divide the land upon that basis were accordingly adopted, and the amount to which each share was entitled, therefore, consisted of seven separate tracts, grouped in six divisions, as follows:

DIVISION		ACRES
First.	One eight acre lot..........	8.00
Second.	One three acre lot.........	3.00
Third.	One house lot of (about)...	.37
Fourth.	One one hundred and sixty acre lot	160.00
Fifth.	One one hundred acre lot...	100.00
Sixth.	One six hundred and forty acre lot or section.......	640.00
	One two hundred and sixty-two acre lot or fraction.	262.00
	Total	1173.37

To accomplish this purpose a general plan for the subdivision of the townships thruout these two tracts, into sections of 640 acres and fractions of 262 acres each, was adopted. And, to produce the necessary number of smaller tracts to complete the amount of land to which each share was entitled, a number of the sections and fractions were subdivided into the required number of eight acre lots, three acre lots, house lots, one hundred and sixty acre lots and one hundred acre lots. These latter lots, also termed "Fifth Division" lots because they

36 640 A	30 640 A	24 640 A	18 640 A	12 640 A	6 640 A
35 640 A	29 640 A	23 640 A	17 640 A	11 640 A	5 640 A
34 640A	Fr. 36 262 A / Fr. 34 162 A / Fr. 24 262 A	Fr. 23 262 A / Fr. 17 262 A / Fr. 18 262 A	16 640 A	Fr. 5 262 A / Fr. 4 262A / Fr. 12 262 A	4 640 A
33 640 A	Fr. 33 262 A / Fr. 32 262 A	Fr. 30 262 A / Fr. 31 262 A	Fr.36 262 A / Fr. 6 262 A / Fr. 1 262 A	Fr. 2 262 A / Fr. 3 262 A	3 640 A
32 640 A	26 640 A	Fr. 25 262 A / Fr. 19 262 A	Fr. 7 262 A / Fr. 13 262 A	8 640 A	2 640A
31 640 A	25 640 A	19 640 A	13 640A	7 640A	1 640 A

GENERAL PLAN
OF
SUBDIVISION OF TOWNSHIPS
IN THE
OHIO COMPANY'S PURCHASE

were the fifth parcels of land in the enumerated
order of tracts constituting one share, were made by
subdividing a section into six equal parts, or, in some
instances, two adjoining sections lengthwise into
twelve equal parts, each of which so called one hundred acre lots contain about 107 acres. [25]

To meet the requirements of the land ordinance,
and also to effect an equitable division of the land
among the shareholders, a number of townships
were variously subdivided.   This required modification of the general plan and many townships were
subdivided in a manner limited to each.

The number of the share was designated by the
number of its eight acre lot which was the first parcel
enumerated in the list of tracts constituting the
amount of land assigned to each share.

On account of the continuance of the Indian war,
the directors were unable to complete the survey or
to determine the tracts of land to which each share
was entitled, until December of 1795, when 817 shareholders were found entitled to participate in the
division.   Thereupon at a meeting held January 23,
1796, the land was directed to be partitioned among
that number of shareholders, and each assigned,

(25)   In 1868 the legislature authorized and directed the survey and resubdivision of the land in town 13, range 15 and
towns 12 and 13, range 16, in Hocking county.   This was
done by the surveyor assigning a number from one up to
the tracts of land within each section.   65 L. O. 258.

thru his respective agent, the several tracts of land falling to his share.   February 1, 1796, a deed in partition, or rather, a deed in allotment, [16] was accordingly executed by the directors, and the respective agents, in turn, conveyed to each proprietor the shares of the land thus assigned him; while on the day before partition was made, the directors conveyed all the tracts not disposed of, or assigned to some proprietor, to Rufus Putnam and Benjamin Ives Gilman "in trust to sell and dispose of for the benefit of the proprietors of the Ohio Company." [17]

The anomaly of there being two or more fractions with the same number in a township, as, for instance: four fractions 11 and two fractions 7, in town 10, range 14; and three fractions 8, two fractions 11 and three fractions 26 in town 12, range 15, is due to the fact that such respective fractions were so numbered to correspond with the section in the "Second Purchase" to which they were respectively attached as part of a share.

While it was the intention of the subscribers to obtain articles of incorporation from Congress or from some one of the states, they never did so. However, from the magnitude of the transaction, the complications involved and the great number of stockholders interested, it was impossible to carry

(16)   20 O. R. 231.
(17)   Washington County Deed Book 3, page 185.

out any plan of subdividing the land usually employed by joint tenants in making partition.   This duty, therefore, was performed by the directors and agents who "might almost be considered as holding a semi-official relation to the proprietors," [16] much after the manner of a board of directors of a corporation which represents the many stockholders.

The title acquired in this manner has been held good in the proprietor of each respective share by the supreme court, in the case of Blake vs. Davis [16] whether any conveyance was made by the agent or not.

The only meeting of the stockholders had since that in January of 1796 when partition of the land was made, was that held by representatives of 464 shares, at the Franklin House, in Providence, Rhode Island, September 18, 1835; [18] attempts in 1831 and 1832 to hold meetings having failed for the lack of a quorum.   At this meeting provision was made for the sale of "all the undivided lands in the Ohio Company's purchase, now remaining undisposed of, and especially the ten sections number sixteen located in the second purchase"; and Nahum Ward and Temple Cutler were appointed a committee to make the sale. An agent also was appointed to petition Congress "for the fair and just claim the company have on

(18)   Washington County Deed Book 40, page 531.
(19)   Washington County Deed Book 40, page 535.

Congress for ten sections of land in lieu of ten sections number twenty-nine (belonging to said company by contract) in the second purchase and disposed of otherwise by Congress.'' Adjournment
was had to meet the first Monday of April, 1837, at
the court house in Marietta. An adjourned meeting
was held in that city July 8, 1839. [19]

Acting under the authority thus given them,
Nahum Ward and Temple Cutler as agents of the
Ohio Company, in 1849, conveyed all the lands not
then disposed of, and especially sections sixteen in
the ten townships in the second purchase, to William
S. Ward and Charles R. Rhodes for two hundred dollars. [19]

Having acquired 353 shares, Nahum Ward filed
his bill in chancery in the Washington county, Ohio,
court of common pleas, [20] July 21, 1848, against
Temple Cutler, Ephriam Cutler, William R. Putnam,
Griffin Greene and the unknown heirs of Manasseh
Cutler, Robert Oliver, Rufus Putnam and Griffin
Greene, alleging that he was entitled, in equity, to
have conveyed to him the 353-817 parts of such lands
not then disposed of, including sections sixteen in
the ten townships in the second purchase. Whereupon, at the March, 1849, term, it was decreed that
the defendants convey to the complainant all their
estate, right, title and interest in and to such tracts
of land, and that upon default to execute deeds, the

decree should have the force and effect of such deeds. In December of 1849, Mr. Ward conveyed the interest he thus acquired to William S. Ward and Charles R. Rhodes for one hundred dollars. [21]

Copies of the record of the proceedings of the Ohio Company of Associates, made by Rufus Putnam, William Rufus Putnam or William S. Ward, for Washington, Athens, Meigs, Gallia, Morgan and Lawrence counties, are admissible as evidence in all courts. [22]

(20)   Chancery Records 2, page 589.
(21)   Washington County Deed Book 40, page 533.
(22)   16 L. O., 134; 17 L. O., 180; 18 L. O. L. 81; 54 L. O. 119.

CHAPTER 11

THE DONATION TRACT

To encourage settlements in different parts of the land in Ohio purchased by the Ohio Company of associates, and to protect those who might settle upon it, that company proposed to donate to each settler one hundred acres out of each share of the fund. Accordingly, the "Fifth division" was to have been used for that purpose; and each donee was required to have arms and ammunition and to maintain upon each tract thus donated a man able to bear arms during the term of five years when the donee was to receive a deed for the land.

The Indians, however, resented settlements being made at Marietta and Cincinnati as encroachments upon their rights, and the war of 1790 resulted. The slender protection of the garrison at Fort Harmar was impaired by the transfer of nearly all the troops to Fort Washington, to protect the settlers of the Miami valleys and in Kentucky, and to operate to better advantage against the great body of hostile Indians then assembling in western Ohio. The settlers at Marietta were required, therefore, to protect themselves; and the expense of doing so was borne by The Ohio Company. [9]

The hardship and injustice of thus being compelled to assume the responsibilities of the government were presented to congress in March of 1792. To relieve the company of the obligation of donating the land, and also to induce people with limited means to settle in Ohio, Congress, in April of that year, [1], with Vice-President John Adams casting the deciding vote, authorized the president to grant and convey to Rufus Putnam, Manasseh Cutler, Robert Oliver and Griffin Greene and to their heirs and assigns, in fee simple, in trust for the persons composing the Ohio Company of Associates, the following described tract of land, to-wit:

Beginning on the west line of the seventh range of the Ohio River Survey at the northeast corner of a tract containing 913,883 acres conveyed May 10, 1792, to Rufus Putnam and others, [2] and thence running north, on the west line of the seventh range, to the northeast corner of a tract of one million five hundred thousand acres contracted for, October 27,

(1)   Annals of Congress, March 26, 1792, Page 486; 2 L. U. S., 276; 1 U. S. S. L., 257; 6 U. S. S. L., 8.

(2)   Washington County Deed Book 1, page 115.

(8)   See Pages 161 and 171.   (9)   1 Arch. 283.

1787, [3] by the Ohio Company of Associates, and as established by Israel Ludlow; thence west along the north line of the one million five hundred thousand acre tract, as established by Israel Ludlow, to a point from which a line drawn south to the north line of the 913,883 acre tract would, with the other lines of this tract, include one hundred thousand acres; thence south to the north line of the 913,883 acre tract and thence to the place of beginning. [4]

This land was to be held for five years and conveyed in fee simple, as a bounty and free of expense, in tracts of one hundred acres to each male person not less than eighteen years of age who should become an actual settler upon the land at the time of such conveyance; and whatever part of the tract not thus conveyed to actual settlers within five years, was to revert to the United States.   A patent was issued accordingly, May 10, 1792. [5]

This tract is situated in Washington and Morgan counties, immediately south of "Israel Ludlow's Survey," in ranges eight, nine, ten and eleven of the Ohio River Survey, and is known as "The Donation Tract," altho it is sometimes referred to as the Ohio Company's "Third Purchase." [8]   It has the distinction of being the first land which the government authorized to be "homesteaded," that is acquired by

(3)   L. H. O. U., 43.   (4)   1 L. U. S., 494.
(5)   Washington County Deed Book 1, page 122.

occupancy alone, and the beginning of subsidizing the settlement of the land west of the Mississippi river which in later years was so extensively granted to encourage its development and provide people with homes without cost.

To accomplish the purpose for which this tract was set aside, it was necessary to subdivide it into parcels of one hundred acres each; but as its subdivision into townships and the townships into sections, as provided by the land ordinance, would not permit this to be done, some other plan of subdivision was necessary. Besides, settlements were desired to be made at different places before the entire tract could be subdivided upon any general plan. It was also necessary to subdivide the land immediately surrounding each proposed settlement into such number of one hundred acre lots as the demand required. Therefore, the entire tract was necessarily first subdivided into settlements, or "Allotments," and the allotments, in turn, were subdivided into one hundred acre lots, or, in some instances, into parcels of which two or more would equal one hundred acres. The lots in each allotment were numbered from one to the highest number within the allotment.

Whatever part of this tract that was not conveyed to actual settlers within five years by the Ohio Company, reverted to, or rather remained in the United States. (1) However, after the expiration of

that time nothing was done about its disposal until
1818, [6] when congress required Rufus Putnam and
the surviving patentees in trust, to report to the surveyor general the quantity and location of the land
conveyed by them to actual settlers, according to the
act of 1792; directed the surveyor general to subdivide the residue in the same manner as required of
other public lands, or, if he thought best, into tracts
of one hundred acres each, conforming to the plan
on which the lots granted to actual settlers had been
laid off, and provided that such part of the tract as
belonged to the United States, with the exception of
the usual proportions for the support of schools,
should be sold for not less than two dollars per acre
on the same terms and conditions as other "Congress
lands."

The subdivision of the allotments into one hundred acre lots as begun by the Ohio Company, was
continued thruout the remainder of the tract which
thereby became an independent, original survey, altho it is within the Ohio River Survey. The lots,
however, are also referred to as being within their
respective townships and ranges.

As this tract was not subdivided into sections, it
had no sections sixteen for the maintenance of
schools. However, in accordance with the act of

(6)   1 L. U. S., 261; 3 U. S. S. L., 409.
(7)   3 L. U. S., 541; 2 U. S. S. L., 225.

1803, [7] the secretary of the treasury, in 1805, selected for that purpose sections eight in each of the four
townships immediately to the south, and a small
quantity within the Donation tract itself.   In making the selections, the Donation tract was considered
as being subdivided into townships, and the tracts
thus selected were accordingly assigned to the support of the schools of the respective townships for
which they were each selected.

CHAPTER 12

THE OHIO UNIVERSITY LANDS

The Ohio University at Athens, established February 18, 1804, is the oldest collegiate institution northwest of the Ohio river. Its conception is credited to Reverend Manasseh Cutler, of Ipswich, now Hamilton, Massachusetts, a member of the New England clergy who considered religion, patriotism and good government as necessary elements for the foundation of homes of settled and contented peoples. But its actual fruition, however, should be credited rather to General Rufus Putnam who devoted the last twenty years of his life to its establishment and guidance.

The plan of setting aside one section of land in each township for the maintenance of schools and one for religion became a fixed principle in the minds of the people of the New England states; and that all who might aspire to a higher education than that

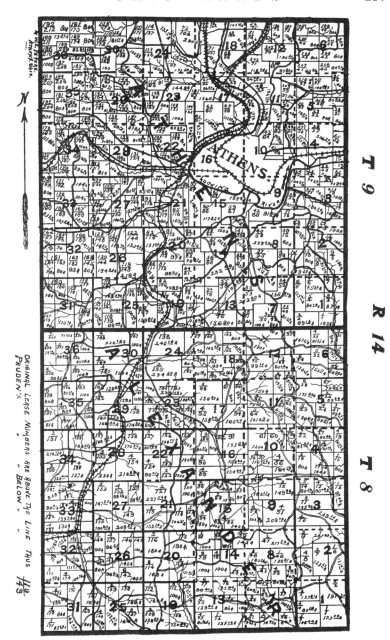

furnished by the common schools, should have the opportunity of acquiring such advanced education, the promoters of the first settlement of the territory northwest of the Ohio river planned for land for that purpose. So, in 1787, when Dr. Cutler, as agent of the Ohio Company, applied to congress for the purchase of land in Ohio, he insisted upon two townships of land being appropriated for the support of a university. Accordingly, the Continental Congress, by resolution of July 23, 1787, [1] provided that "not more than two complete townships should be given perpetually for the purpose of an university; that they be laid off by the purchasers as near the center of the tract as may be and applied to the intended object by the legislature of the state." Thereupon, two original surveyed townships of thirty-six square miles each, to be located by the directors of the Ohio Company, as nearly as possible in the center of the first tract paid for, were reserved for that purpose. [2]

As the 750,000 acre tract, known as the Ohio Company's first purchase, was the first tract paid for, these two townships were to be located within that tract [3]; and the directors of the company, at a meeting held December 16, 1795, designated town-

(1)   1 L. U. S., 573; L. H. O. U., 39.
(2)   1 L. U. S., 491, 574; 2 L. U. S., 276; 1 U. S. S. L.,
      257; L. H. O. U., 43.
(3)   L. H. O. U., 43; 2 L. U. S., 276; 1 U. S. S. L., 257;
      Washington County Deed Book 1, page 115; 6 U. S. S. L. 8.

ships eight and nine of the fourteenth range of the Ohio River Survey, which correspond with the civil townships of Alexander and Athens, respectively, in Athens county, for the maintenance of the proposed university. [4]

Nothing further was done toward establishing the university until 1802 when the territorial legislature [5] passed an act creating such institution under the name of the "American Western University," and provided for leasing the lands set aside for its support for a period of twenty-one years.

No attempt was made to establish the "American Western University," or to carry any of the provisions of the act of 1802 into effect, as no one could be induced to accept leases and improve the land for the short term it specified.

This act was never expressly repealed, [6] but is considered to have been superceded, by implication, by that of 1804, [7] by which the "Ohio University" was incorporated by the name and style of "The President and Trustees of the Ohio University;" vested with the two townships, and authorized to lease the land for the term of ninety years, renewable forever, on a yearly rental of six per centum on the

(4)   L. H. O. U., 64.
(5)   1 Sess. 2, G. A. T., 161; L. H. O. U., 92.
(6)   10 O. R., 235; L. H. O. U., 182.
(7)   2 L. O., 193; L. H. O. U., 99.

amount of the valuation, subject to a revaluation at
the end of thirty-five, sixty and ninety years from the
commencement of the term of each lease.   This act
is recognized as the charter of the institution.

There was as much objection to the act of 1804
as to that of 1802.   No leases were taken and much
dissatisfaction was manifested.   No one could be induced to settle upon and improve the land under a
title that was liable to be disturbed so frequently,
especially when land in the adjoining townships
could be bought outright for one dollar per acre, or
even less.   Persons who had been induced to settle
upon these lands by those interested in the establishment of the university, were discouraged; many,
whose improvements were little, left, while others
remained, hoping that some relief would be provided.

As nothing could be done with the land under
this act, Governor Edward Tiffin, in December of
1804, reported that fact to the legislature and suggested that "these lands ought to be valued at a
generous price once for all." [8]   Accordingly, in
February following, the legislature authorized the
trustees of the university to lease the lands "for the
term of ninety-nine years, renewable forever, with a
fixed annual rent of six per centum on the appraised
valuation." [9]

(8)   L. H. O. U., 128.   (9)   3 L. O., 79.

With the understanding that the act of 1805 repealed the revaluation clause of the act of 1804, leases of the lands were readily made. [10] The leases were signed by the treasurer who affixed the seal of the university, under a resolution adopted April 5, 1806, by the board of trustees. [11] In 1841, the supreme court held the lands to be subject to reappraisement under the act of 1804, notwithstanding the act of 1805. [12] However, in 1843, the legislature passed an act construing that of 1805 to mean that no revaluation of the lands thus leased should be made. [13] No reappraisement of these lands has been made, and the appraisements made at the time of issuing the original leases remain unchanged.

Meanwhile, provisions were made for the sale of the fee in the lands to the lessees. Accordingly, in 1826, [14] the university was authorized to sell and convey in fee simple any of these lands to the lessee upon his paying to the treasurer of the university such sum of money as would yield yearly, at six per cent, the sum reserved in his lease. This act was modified in 1854, [15] and again in 1883, [16] and is now sections 7932, 7933 and 7934 of the General Code. The title thus acquired by the lessee has been sustained by the supreme courts of Ohio, [17] and of the United

(11)   Trustees Record 1, Page 21; L. H. O. U., 160.
(10)   L. H. O. U., 125.
(12)   11 O. R., 134.
(13)   41 L. O. L., 144.
(14)   24 L. O., 52.
(15)   52 L. O.. 175.
(16)   80 L. O., 193.

States [18] in the case of Armstrong vs. Treasurer, which, in effect, held that the act of congress of itself, together with that of the legislature in 1826, was the equivalent of a patent to the Ohio university. [19]

The land within these townships is subdivided into lots called "Farm lots" which are of various sizes and shapes. They are numbered consecutively, but a different system is used in each township, neither of which was subdivided into sections. In the eighth township the lots are numbered in each assumed section from one to the highest number approximately within such assumed section; while in the ninth township they are numbered from one to the highest number within the township, by beginning with number one in the southeast corner of the township, and, with few exceptions, numbering those within the first row of sections to the north side of the township, and beginning again in the next row of sections to the west, and on the south side of the township, and numbering to the north, etc., until the northwest corner of the township is thus reached.

That the numbers of the lots might aid in determining their relative locations, Judge Samuel B. Pruden, who, for several years prior to 1835, was

(17)   10 O. R., 235.   (18)   16 Peters, (U. S.) 281.
(19)   52 O. S. R. 586.

county surveyor of Athens county, decided to re-number them. He began at the southeast corner of the respective townships and numbered the lots northward by assumed sections to the north line of the township. Then beginning again at the south line of the township and then numbering north by assumed sections, and so on throughout the township. In this way each lot was given duplicate numbers; one being the original farm lot number, and the other that thus given by Mr. Pruden, frequently referred to as "Pruden's numbers." These latter numbers should never be used since no legal or official action has ever been had making them valid.

No land was reserved in either township for the maintenance of schools or for the purposes of religion. The secretary of the treasury, however, set aside section eleven in the fourth township of the thirteenth range for the maintenance of schools in the eighth, or Alexander township, and section eleven in the twelfth township of the fifteenth range for the schools in the ninth, or Athens township.

CHAPTER 13

THE FRENCH GRANTS

The French Grants were the result of an effort upon the part of the general government to right a wrong suffered by a number of French people who endeavored to purchase and settle on lands within the present bounds of the state of Ohio.

The scheme which defrauded so many French people originated when overtures were first made to purchase land of the general government. Even then, people of honorable intentions found it difficult to obtain the attention of Congress without the intercession of persons too often of mercenary motives. So when representatives of the Ohio Company of Associates first proposed, in 1787, to purchase lands northwest of the Ohio river, of the Continental Congress, they found it impossible to accomplish their very laudable purposes without first associating themselves with persons of influence

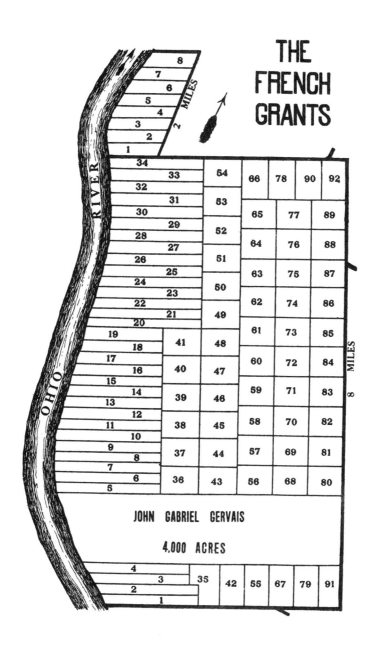

with Congress. Such influence in this instance, was used for selfish purposes, and it was due, undoubtedly, to the highly honorable character of Rev. Manasseh Cutler, one of the most active members of the Ohio Company, that their purchase was not involved in the scandal subsequently connected with the purchase proposed to be made by the Scioto Company.

Before their purchase could be made it became necessary, therefore, for the representatives of the Ohio Company to associate themselves with Col. William Duer of New York City, who, at that time, was Secretary of the Board of Treasury of the Continental Congress and, consequently, in position to influence legislation. Col. Duer was a man of much means, of a speculative turn of mind, and disposed to use his official influence for his personal gain. The representatives of the Ohio Company, therefore, could not command the attention of Congress until they had enlisted the aid of Col. Duer and his associates, for whom they agreed, secretly, to obtain an option on a large tract of land, estimated to be three and one-half million acres, [6] to be located immediately north and west of that which they themselves expected to purchase for the Ohio Company, and extending to the Scioto river. [7]

(6)   Subsequent surveys show it to contain 4,901,480 acres.
(7)   Resolution of July 23, 1787. 1 L. U. S. 573.

Upon securing this option a company was formed called the "Scioto Company," of which Col. Duer
was chosen President; and its stock, or "Scioto
Rights," as Duer called it, was divided into thirty
shares of which Cutler and Sargent had thirteen,
Duer thirteen and four were to have been sold
abroad. Each share then was assumed to represent
150,000 acres, or 163,382 2-3 acres according to subsequent surveys. Joel Barlow, a well known poet of
the Revolution, became interested in the company,
and, in May of 1788, was sent to France to sell the
land. At first he was unsuccessful, but in the summer of 1789, with the aid of William Playfair, an
Englishman, he organized the "Society of the
Scioto."

Extensive advertising was engaged in, based
upon the purported advantages found in this land
as set forth in an anonymous pamphlet which
grossly misrepresented the climate and the fertility
of the soil, and otherwise painted conditions entirely
too glowing and much beyond those which the facts
warranted. All these representations, however, were
endorsed by Colonel Thomas Hutchins, geographer
of the Continental Congress, who, as a surveyor, had
spent many years northwest of the Ohio river.
These extravagant statements were further em-
bellished by Playfair who was quite unscrupulous
and cared little whether the facts supported his
statements or not. Many French people of means

and influence, and who had never engaged in agriculture of any kind, were thus influenced to purchase much of the land for which they were, of course, promised good titles.

Two hundred and eighteen of these purchasers left France on February 19, 1791, and landed in Alexandria, D. C. on the third day of May following, when they learned that the Scioto Company owned no land anywhere. This situation was occasioned by Col. Duer, who seems to have been the moneyed man, meeting with financial reverses so serious as to cause him to be committed to prison for debt which prevented his making payment and acquiring the land as he had expected.

The failure of Col. Duer and his associates left the French settlers stranded and entirely dependent upon their own resources. Upon receiving some funds repaid them by the Scioto Company, they started for their destination and located upon the present site of Gallipolis, under the impression that it was within the territory for which they could eventually obtain title from the general government; but when the survey of the land acquired by the Ohio Company was completed, this settlement was found to be entirely within the bounds of that purchase.

In December of 1791, and as soon as it was possible for them to do so, the directors of the Ohio

Company arranged to sell to the people of Gallipolis
the land upon which they had thus settled and made
improvements, for $1.25 per acre, which was at that
time the price of government land, and thus enable
these settlers to retain their homes.

To relieve their distress, Congress, March 3,
1795, [1] granted these people twenty-four thousand
acres of land in what is now Scioto county, and opposite the mouth of Little Sandy creek. It constituted a tract eight miles long, with the Ohio river
which it joined on the east, and extended something
over four and one-half miles back from that river.
Four thousand acres in the southern part were conveyed to John Gabriel Gervais to compensate him for
his services in obtaining the grant; and the balance
was divided among all the male persons over eighteen
years of age, and widows, who were in the town, or
settlement, of Gallipolis on the first day of November, 1795. As ninety-two persons thus qualified
themselves, each, therefore, drew, by lot, a tract containing two hundred seventeen and two-fifths acres
for which the president was authorized to issue
patents. These lots were numbered from one to
ninety-two, and, with the tract given Mr. Gervais,
constitute the "First French Grant."

This act also provided that the patents should be
void and the title revest in the United States should
Mr. Gervais, or his heirs, personally, fail to settle

upon the land thus given him, within three years, and
continue to remain upon it for three years thereafter; or, should any of the other settlers fail to
settle upon his or her respective lot within five years,
and continue to remain upon it for five years thereafter. This limitation, however, was removed by
the act of 1806, [2] which provided that in every case
where a patent had been issued containing such
limitation, the limitation should be considered null
and void and the fee simple title should "vest, to all
intents and purposes, in the person to whom such
patent had been issued, his or her heirs or assigns."

As eight inhabitants of Gallipolis had been prevented from obtaining their proportion of the land
granted by the act of 1795, Congress, June 25, 1798,
[3] granted them, by name, each a lot containing one
hundred and fifty acres, and directed the surveyor
general to survey and subdivide twelve hundred
acres, beginning on the bank of the Ohio river at the
lower corner of the first tract, into eight lots of one
hundred and fifty acres each. The lots were numbered from one to eight and constitute the "Second
French Grant."

Many of these settlers were reluctant to lose
their labor expended at Gallipolis, and, therefore,
acquired land from the Ohio Company; while some
sold their shares in the grants, and others sent
tenants to live upon the land thus given them. A

large part of the original settlers, however, remained at Gallipolis, while comparatively few actually
settled upon the grants.

No reservation having been made of land within
these grants for the support of their schools, Congress, May 20, 1826, [4] authorized and directed the
secretary of the treasury to select one and one
quarter sections of land elsewhere for that purpose.
Accordingly the west half of section No. 26, the east
half of section No. 27 and the northeast quarter of
section No. 34, town 3, range 18 of the Ohio River
Survey, were selected. [5]

(1)   2 L. U. S. 503; 1 U. S. S. L. 442.
(2)   4 L. U. S. 4; 2 U. S. S. L. 350.
(3)   3 L. U. S. 68; 6 U. S. S. L. 35.
(4)   7 L. U. S. 491; 4 U. S. S. L. 179.
(5)   16 O. St. 11; 31 O. St. 301; 51 L. O. 528.

CHAPTER 14

THE EBENEZER ZANE TRACTS

In pioneer days road building was a proposition quite different from that of the present day. It then consisted usually of simply blazing or marking trees along the proposed roadway through the virgin forest, and thus only indicating a line of travel thereafter to be followed. It was known as a "Trail," or "Trace," and required few tools other than the faithful axe.

Among the early roads of this character was that known as "Zane's Trace." [1] It was about two hundred miles long and was opened, in 1797, by Colonel Ebenezer Zane, from Wheeling, West Virginia, through Ohio by the way of Zanesville, Lancaster and Chillicothe, to Maysville, Kentucky, then known as "Limestone," under a contract made by Col. Zane with the general government, whereby he

ZANE'S TRACE

was given the privilege of selecting, or, rather locating, three sections of land.

Col. Zane was a descendant of a Mr. Zane who came over with William Penn, and was of a long line of progressive pioneers who continually pressed developments westward. He was born October 7, 1747, in Berkeley county, Virginia, and died, in 1812, in Wheeling, where he had made the first permanent settlement on the Ohio river in 1770, and had since resided. He was one of a family of five brothers whom he led in all their enterprises. Being a man of wealth, general knowledge, initiative and much influence, he was naturally an originator of enterprises and a leader of men. His brother Jonathan, who had already traveled much over a considerable part of Ohio, however, was an able lieutenant.

Having, with keen foresight, settled on the Ohio river at a point so advantageous to travel from the east, Col. Zane naturally conceived the further advantage of also continuing his activities across the river westward through the new country, and thus making his original location at Wheeling, the junction for still other avenues of trade and travel beside that already upon the river. His enterprise and industry in endeavoring to open the new country for

(1)   13 Arch. 297.

settlement, and particularly his experience in blazing a roadway from Brownsville to Wheeling, eminently fitted him for the duty of locating a line of travel through the western country, and enabled him readily to command the attention of congress when he petitioned that body, in March of 1796, for permission to open the roadway. On the 6th of April following, the senate committee to which his petition had been referred, reported:

"That the petitioner sets forth that he hath at considerable expense, explored and in part opened a

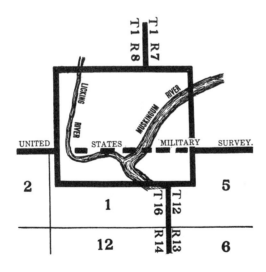

ZANE'S
MUSKINGUM RIVER SURVEY

road, northwest of the river Ohio, between Wheeling and Limestone, which when completed will greatly contribute to the accommodation of the public as well as individuals. But that several rivers intervening, the road proposed cannot be used with safety until ferries shall be established thereon.

"That the petitioner will engage to have such ferries erected provided he can obtain a right to the land which is now the property of the United States. And therefore prays that he may be authorized to locate and survey—at his own expense—military bounty warrants upon as much land at Muskingum, Hockhocking and Scioto rivers as may be sufficient to support the necessary establishments. And that the same be granted to him by the United States.

"That they having received satisfactory support of the above statement are of opinion that the proposed road will be of general utility, that the petitioner merits encouragement and that his petition being reasonable, ought to be granted.

"The committee therefore submit the following resolution:

"Resolved, That the petition of Ebenezer Zane is reasonable; that he be authorized to locate warrants granted by the U. S. for military services upon three tracts of land, not exceeding one mile square each, at Muskingum, Hockhocking and Scioto where the proposed road shall cross those rivers, for the purpose of establishing ferries thereon; and that leave be given to bring in a bill for that purpose." [4]

The proposition of Colonel Zane and the report of the committee recommending its acceptance, resulted in the act of May 17, 1796, [2] by which he was given three tracts of land of one square mile each: One on the Muskingum river, one on the Hockhocking and one on the Scioto, conditioned that he survey them at his own expense; return plats of them to the treasurer of the United States; deliver United States military land warrants to the amount of the number

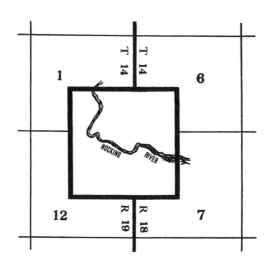

ZANE'S

HOCKING   RIVER   SURVEY

of acres; establish ferries at each of the three rivers; open the proposed roadway; produce satisfactory proof by the first day of January, 1797, that such road was opened and the ferries were established, and give security that the ferries would be maintained during the pleasure of Congress.

For the three tracts of land to which he was thus entitled, Col. Zane selected one on the Muskingum river, including the falls for its power of which he then saw the value, and on which tract he laid out the town of Zanesville, in 1799; one on the Hockhocking river on which he laid out the town of Lancaster in the fall of 1800; and, since the land on the west side of the Scioto river had been reserved by Virginia, he located the third tract on the east side of that river, opposite the city of Chillicothe.

As it was desired to select and locate these tracts before the surrounding lands were surveyed into sections, townships or ranges, they became no part of the rectangular system adjoining, and were necessarily surveyed and described upon the indiscriminate location plan.   Consequently each tract occupies parts of two or more sections, while that on the Muskingum is also within two extensive, original surveys.

(2)   2 L. U. S. 533 ; 6 U. S. S. L., 27.
(3)   Fairfield county Deed Book 52, page 471.
(4)   American State Papers, Miscellaneous. Vol. 1, page 145.

The tract at Zanesville lies in both the Ohio River and the United States Military surveys. It is in township twelve of range thirteen and township sixteen of range fourteen of the former survey, and in townships one of ranges seven and eight of the latter survey. That at Lancaster in Fairfield county lies in townships fourteen of ranges eighteen and nineteen of the Ohio River Survey, while that near Chillicothe in Ross county, lies on the east side of, and adjoins, the Scioto river in township eight of range twenty-one and township one of range twenty-

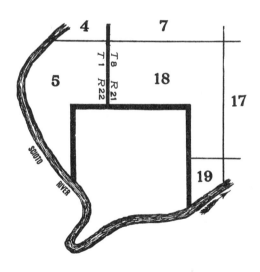

ZANE'S

SCIOTO   RIVER   SURVEY

two of Worthington's Survey of the Ohio River Survey. The patent was issued by President John Adams, February 14, 1800. [3]

While it would appear that Colonel Zane paid well for these lands, as land then sold, the important advantage he gained by the transaction was the privilege of selecting these tracts before the surrounding lands were surveyed and opened for general settlement. He did this, of course, to advantage to himself and thereby acquired, at each of the three important river crossings, a monopoly of the ferry business, which, in those early days, was a business of much consequence and one well worth controlling.

This "road," so-called, was hastily cut through the forest, but with no attempt to make it more than passable for horsemen. No survey of it is known to have been made and no record of its location is found in the general land office, except that a dotted line, indicating its general course, was made by the government surveyors upon the plats of the original subdivision of the land in much of the territory through which this trail ran.

As a highway, however, this trace was of much importance, and being used quite generally by emigrants bound for the west, readily diverted much of the travel which before then had been by land over the Cumberland mountains, through Crab Orchard, Kentucky, and by canoes and keel boats down the Ohio river. Settlements consequently began at once to spring up along this trail which soon proved itself a prominent factor in the development of the western country.

CHAPTER 15

THE REFUGEE TRACT.

During the revolutionary war many persons in Canada and Nova Scotia deeply sympathized with the colonists in their struggle for freedom. Some joined the unsuccessful expedition against Quebec and were forced to leave their homes and retire to the south with the American troops. Some joined the continental forces under General Hazen, while many others were so open in their endorsement of the attitude and demand of the colonists as to invite persecution. Their property was confiscated and many were obliged to flee their country and **seek** refuge in the colonies. In grateful recognition of their loyalty and sacrifices, the American colonies endeavored to care for these refugees as best they could. New York made them a number of grants of 500 or 1000 acres of land on Lake Champlain, while the United States government transported many of such refugees to these lands and provided them with rations for fifteen months, and the aged and infirm for a year thereafter. But being poor in every thing but land of which it had an abundance, the new government was unable to thus properly care for these stranded people otherwise than with land, its most available resource. In due time, therefore, all who had thus suffered were given, upon application, land in proportion to their respective losses.

The first step to that end was taken by the Continental Congress in 1783, [1] when it expressed its "lively sense of the services" of Brigadier General Hazen, his "officers and others Canadian refugees . . . for their virtuous sufferings in the cause of liberty," and promised to reward and compensate them with land as soon as it was possible to do so.

UNITED STATES MILITARY TRACT

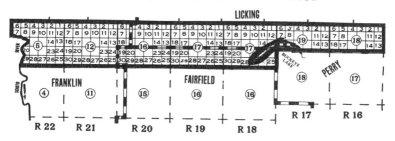

REFUGEE LANDS

A like promise was made also, in 1785, [1] to Jonathan Eddy and other refugees from Nova Scotia. In the land ordinance of 1785, [2] the Continental Congress endeavored to reserve "three townships adjacent to Lake Erie" for the use of these refugees, but as the land belonged to Connecticut it could not be appropriated for that purpose.

In 1798, [3] Congress, recognizing these obligations thus expressed by the Continental Congress, directed the secretary of war to give notice in newspapers published in Vermont, Massachusetts, New York, New Hampshire and Pennsylvania, to all persons claiming under those resolutions, to file with him an account of their claims within two years. All claimants were required to have been residents of one of the provinces of Canada prior to July 4, 1776, and to have had to abandon their settlements there in consequence of having given aid to the colonies during the Revolutionary War; or, with the intention of giving such aid, had remained in the colonies while that war lasted and had not returned to reside in the dominion of the King of Great Britain prior to November 25, 1783. In 1810 the provisions of this act were extended also to the widows and heirs of such persons as may have died within the United States, or in their service during that war. [4]

(1)   1 L. U. S., 577.   (3)   3 L. U. S., 37; 1 U. S. S. L., 547.
(2)   1 L. U. S. 568.   (4)   4 L. U. S., 246; 2 U. S. S. L., 556.

The secretaries of war and the treasury were directed to examine the testimony of all claimants and determine the quantity of land which each should be allowed "in proportion to the degree of their respective services, sacrifices and sufferings in consequence of their attachment to the cause of the United States." This proof later could be made also before the judge of any court. [4] No claim, however, was permitted to be assigned until after the land had been granted to the person found entitled to it.

By the act of February 18, 1801, [5] the claims were to be located by the secretary of the treasury, by lot, in those fractional townships of the sixteenth, seventeenth, eighteenth, nineteenth, twentieth, twenty-first and twenty-second ranges of the Ohio River Survey, adjoining the southern boundary line of the United States military survey. The surveyor general was required to subdivide those townships into half sections containing 320 acres each, but as John Matthews and Eben Buckingham had subdivided them into sections in May, 1799, it remained only to divide the sections into two parts which Elnathan Schofield did in 1801. The lots, made by dividing all sections, except 1 and 6, by a north and south line, were numbered from one in the northeast corner of each township, west, and thence east and

(5)   3 L. U. S., 420; 2 U. S. S. L., 100.

so on as the sections are numbered, and ending with Lot No. 30 in the southwest corner of the township, in ranges 16 and 17; with 55 in range 18; with 54 in ranges 19, 20 and 21, and with lot No. 43 in the southwest corner of the township in range 22.

These fractional townships, aggregating one hundred and three thousand, five hundred and twenty-seven acres, and located in Franklin, Fairfield, Perry and Licking counties, were thereupon set aside and reserved to satisfy the claims of these refugees; or, more properly, they constituted the tract within which the lands thus given were to be located. For that reason it has since been known as the "Refugee Tract."

By various acts of Congress [6] there was awarded land within this tract to sixty-seven claimants, to the amount of fifty-eight thousand and eighty acres, as follows:

Martha Walker, widow of Thomas Walker	2240 Acres
John Edgar	2240 Acres
Prince Francis Cazeau	2240 Acres
John Allen	2240 Acres
Seth Harding	2240 Acres
Samuel Rogers	2240 Acres
The heirs of James Boyd	2240 Acres
Jonathan Eddy	1280 Acres
Colonel James Livingston	1280 Acres

(6) 3 L. U. S., 420, 557, 587; 4 L. U. S., 414; 2 U. S. S. L., 242, 270, 712.

Parker Clark ....1280 Acres
The heirs of John Dodge.......1280 Acres
Thomas Faulkner .... 960 Acres
Edward Faulkner .... 960 Acres
David Gay .... 960 Acres
Martin Brooks .... 960 Acres
Lieutenant Colonel Bradford... 960 Acres
Noah Miller .... 960 Acres
Joshua Lamb .... 960 Acres
Atwood Fales .... 960 Acres
Charlotte Hazen, widow of Moses
   Hazen .... 960 Acres
Chloe Shannon, wife of James
   Noble Shannon and relict of
   Obadiah Ayer, deceased...... 960 Acres
The heirs of Elijah Ayer....... 960 Acres
The heirs of Israel Ruland...... 960 Acres
The heirs of Nathaniel Reynolds 960 Acres
The heirs of Edward Antill..... 960 Acres
Joshua Sprague .... 960 Acres
John Starr .... 960 Acres
William How .... 960 Acres
Ebenezer Gardner .... 960 Acres
Lewis F. Delesdernier .... 960 Acres
John McGown .... 960 Acres
Jonas C. Minot............... 960 Acres
The heirs of Simeon Chester.... 960 Acres
Jacob Vander Heyden......... 640 Acres
John Livingston .... 640 Acres
James Crawford .... 640 Acres
Isaac Danks .... 640 Acres
Major B. Von Heer........... 640 Acres
Benjamin Thompson .... 640 Acres
Joseph Bindon .... 640 Acres
Joseph Levittre .... 640 Acres
Lieutenant William Maxwell.... 640 Acres
John D. Mercier.............. 640 Acres
James Price .... 640 Acres

Seth Noble .... 640 Acres
Martha Bogart, relict of Abra-
ham Bogart and formerly
relict of Daniel Tucker....... 640 Acres
John Halsted .... 640 Acres
Robert Sharp .... 640 Acres
John Fulton .... 640 Acres
John Morrison .... 640 Acres
James Sprague .... 320 Acres
David Dickey .... 320 Acres
John Taylor .... 320 Acres
Heirs of Gilberts Seamans...... 320 Acres
The heirs of Anthony Burk.... 320 Acres
Elijah Ayer, Jun. .... 320 Acres
David Jenks .... 320 Acres
Ambrose Cole .... 320 Acres
James Cole .... 320 Acres
Adam Johnson .... 320 Acres
The widow and heirs of Colonel
Jeremiah Duggan .... 320 Acres
Daniel Earl, Junior .... 320 Acres
John Paskell .... 320 Acres
Edward Chinn .... 320 Acres
Joseph Cone .... 320 Acres
John Torreyre .... 320 Acres
Samuel Fales .... 160 Acres
        Total ....58,080 Acres

Since little more than one-half the land within
the tract was claimed by the refugees, their widows
or heirs, within the time allowed, Congress in 1816,
[7] at the request of the legislature of Ohio, [8] directed the remainder to be attached to the Chillicothe land district and sold by the register of that
land office to the highest bidder for not less than
$2.00 per acre on such day as the president should

designate; and that such part not so sold within six days, should be sold by the register of that office at private sale, in the same manner provided by law for the sale of other public lands in the district. These latter tracts when sold, therefore, became, in fact, "Congress Land," notwithstanding they were within the so called "Refugee Tract."

Several refugees failed to claim land before the privilege had been withdrawn and the balance of the tract had been placed on sale with other public lands. Congress, however, endeavored to care for such persons and, in 1827, extended the provisions of the several acts relating to the refugees, to the heirs of Gregory Strahan and permitted them to locate in Arkansas, the amount to which they should be entitled. [9] Andrew Wesbrook was granted a patent in 1828, for 1280 acres to be located on any unsold land; [10] while in 1834, the heirs of Lieutenant Colonel Richard Livingston were granted the privilege of locating the amount to which they should be entitled on any land subject to entry at private sale. [11] In 1831 the president was authorized to issue a patent to John Gough for a quarter section of land near Vincennes, Indiana, and the law for the correction of errors in the purchase of the public lands was made applicable to erroneous location of warrants by the refugees. [14]

(7)   6 L. U. S. 133; 3 U. S. S. L., 326.

In addition to endeavoring to compensate the Canadian friends of the colonies for their losses by reason of being such, congress also endeavored likewise to compensate those who would forsake the British service. So in August of 1776, that body passed a resolution [15] granting to a colonel 1,000 acres; a lieutenant colonel, 800 acres; a major, 600 acres; a captain, 400 acres; a lieutenant, 300 acres; an ensign, 200 acres; every non-commissioned, 100 acres, and to every other officer or person employed in such foreign corps, in like proportion to their rank or pay, who would change his allegiance to that of the Colonists. None, however, took advantage of this offer, except Nicholis Ferdinand Westfall who, in 1792, [16] was granted one hundred acres to be located in the western territory, and $336.00 in money.

No reservation was made of land in these fractional townships for the support of their schools. To provide them with their respective proportions of land for that purpose, the secretary of the treasury, under the act of 1803, [12] selected it in the adjoining townships in Perry, Fairfield and Franklin counties. Each fractional township was thus given section 15 in the township immediately south of it, except fractional township 5 of the 22nd range which was given section 21 of township 11 of the 21st range. [13]

(8)   14 O. L., 469.   (9)   7 L. U. S., 593.   (10)   8 L. U. S., 79.
(11)   6 U. S. S. L., 570.   (12)   3 L. U. S., 541; 2 U. S. S. L., 225.
(13)   L. L. O., 160.   (14)   8 L. U. S., 497; 6 U. S. S. L., 467.
(15)   1 L. U. S. 575.   (16)   2 L. U. S. 262.

CHAPTER 16

THE DOHRMAN TRACT. [1]

At the beginning of the Revolutionary war Arnold Henry Dohrman, a subject of the Netherlands, resided in Lisbon, Portugal. He was a prosperous merchant with an extensive trade, but his love of liberty for the colonists while that war progressed led to his financial failure.

During that war Mr. Dohrman supplied the United States with large amounts of clothing and other warlike material and furnished many American prisoners, carried into the ports of his adopted country, with money and other necessaries. Frequently his own house was the hospital and the home of whole crews of captive seamen whom he lodged and fed for considerable periods of time.

As early as 1780, Patrick Henry wrote the committee on foreign affairs in Congress of Mr. Dohr-

(1)   23 Arch. 227.   (2)   1 L. U. S. 578.

man's good work and great sacrifices, while Jefferson
also wrote him commending his valuable services to
the union. So, in June of that year, that committee
reported to Congress the many humane and bene-
volent acts thus extended by Mr. Dohrman. Whereupon a resolution was passed appointing him agent
for the United States in the Kingdom of Portugal
but without salary, authorizing him to extend to such
of our citizens as might apply whatever relief he
might deem proper and directing him to render a
bill for such expenditures. Congress also assured
him that it would take pleasure in refunding him
whatever amount he might thus expend at its
earliest opportunity.

July 19, 1786, Mr. Dohrman presented a statement to Congress and asked that body to reimburse
him the sum of $26,084.24 which he claimed to have
spent in behalf of the United States. However, as
satisfactory vouchers could be presented for but
$5,806.80, settlement was delayed until October 1,
1787 when he was paid that amount only. The
balance of $20,277.44 was not paid, but Congress,
desiring to acknowledge in the most honorable manner the eminent services rendered by Mr. Dohrman,
paid him a salary of sixteen hundred dollars per year,
computed from the time his expenditures began, and
also allowed him to make choice of any township of
land out of the last three ranges of the first seven

surveyed in Ohio. [3]   This obligation to Mr. Dohrman was the only revolutionary war debt, assumed
by the government, to be paid with land.

Without having seen the land and acting upon
the advice of others, Mr. Dohrman selected the
thirteenth township of the seventh range of the Ohio
River Survey and of which one-half is in Harrison
county and the other in Tuscarawas.

By act of February 27, 1801 [3] the president was
authorized to issue a patent for this land to Mr.
Dohrman, "or his legal representatives," in accordance with the ordinance of October 1, 1787, [2] granting it to him, and also with the land ordinance of May
20, 1785, [4] which reserved section sixteen "for the
maintenance of public schools within the township."
But as this latter ordinance had also reserved sections eight, eleven, twenty-six and twenty-nine "for
future sale," doubt arose as to whether Mr. Dohrman had acquired their title.   To remove this doubt,
Congress, in June of 1834, [5] passed an act relin-
quishing "to the heirs at law of said Arnold Henry
Dohrman, and not to any other person whatever,"
any claim to said sections which the United States
might have reserved by the ordinances of 1785 and
1787.

(3)   3 L. U. S. 423; 6 U. S. S. L. 43.
(4)   1 L. U. S. 563.
(5)   9 L. U. S. 92; 6 U. S. S. L. 573.
(6)   6 L. U. S., 223; American State Papers, Claims. Page 508.

For many years Mr. Dohrman lived in New York City where he engaged in business, but his dwelling being twice destroyed by fire, and other misfortunes befalling him, he was obliged to abandon business and mortgage his land to his creditors. This prevented his subdividing and selling it to advantage, and caused it to become a burden, rather than a help, to him in his declining years.

After his failure in New York, Mr. Dohrman moved to Steubenville that he might be near his land. He died in the latter city, in 1813, when about to depart for Washington to appeal to Congress for that charity which he himself, in better days, had been so free to bestow upon others. Four years later, however, Congress granted his widow, Rachel Dohrman, an annuity of four hundred dollars and one hundred dollars to each of his children until of the age of twenty-one. [6]

CHAPTER 17

SALT RESERVATION.

One of the necessities for which the early settler felt the most need was salt. With his gun and an abundance of game at hand, he could easily stay hunger, but he could not so readily provide himself with salt which seems so necessary to the animal kingdom that its members ofttimes jeopardized their lives that they might obtain that article found at the few springs of water containing it, even in a weak solution. With the unlimited sources of supply of the present day, it is difficult now to conceive how precious salt was but a few generations ago.

Long prior to the advent of the white man in Ohio, the wild animals and the Indians, and, undoubtedly, the mound builders as well, had located many salt springs called "Deer Licks," where friend and foe alike met, notwithstanding the mutual danger thus invited. That no one should obtain

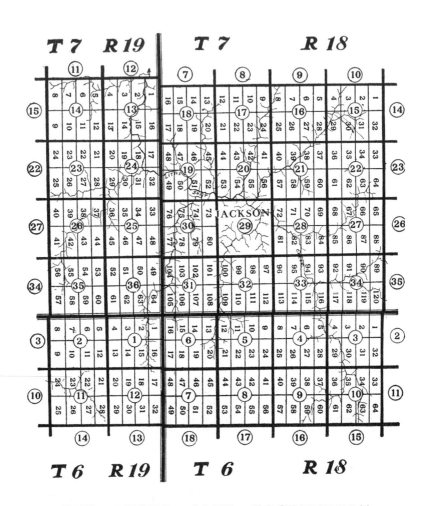

THE SCIOTO SALT RESERVATION

the land upon which such springs were located, and thus acquire a monopoly of a necessity, the national government adopted the precaution of reserving from sale all land upon which salt bearing springs of water might be found. [1]   And to encourage its production and protect the industry the government for a number of years levied a duty on all salt imported.   In 1797 [17] it was twenty cents per bushel. However, as the country became settled and developed, and salt bearing water was found to be general, it became evident that the production of salt could not be monopolized, and the government thereupon ceased reserving from sale the land upon which such springs were found, and repealed all import duties.

The first salt springs in Ohio, discovered by the white people, were in Muskingum, Delaware and Jackson counties; those in Jackson county being known to the English as early as 1755.   So, when admitting Ohio into the union, Congress, therefore, reserved from sale four tracts of land in those counties, two in Muskingum and one each in the other two, and granted their use to the people of the state under such terms as the legislature might prescribe, providing the land should never be sold nor leased for a longer period than ten years. [2]

The two reservations in Muskingum county con-

(1)   2 L. U. S., 533, 565; 3 L. U. S., 596; 1 U. S. S. L., 464, 490.
(2)   3 L. U. S., 496; 2 U. S. S. L., 173.   (17)   3 L. U. S. 17.

sisted of section thirteen in the thirteenth township of the twelfth range, and section nine in the
eleventh township of the thirteenth range of the
Ohio River Survey, and each, respectively, contained
six hundred and forty acres. [3] The reservation in
Delaware county consisted of lot one, or the northeast quarter, of the fifth township of the eighteenth
range of the United States Military Survey, and
contained four thousand acres; while that in Jackson county was the equivalent of one six miles square
township of 23,040 acres. [4]

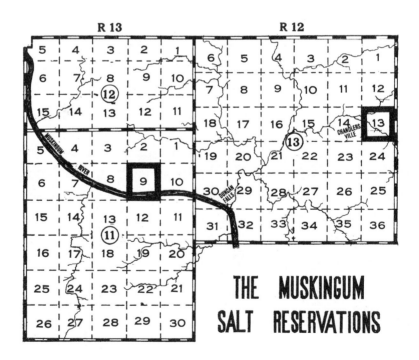

THE MUSKINGUM
SALT RESERVATIONS

The Jackson county reservation did not coincide with any one original surveyed township, but was located in parts of four: The sixth and seventh townships of the eighteenth and nineteenth ranges of the Ohio River Survey. Its boundaries, however, corresponded with the lines of the sections, all of which, except the twenty-ninth of the sixth township of the eighteenth range set aside for the town of Jackson, were subdivided into eighty acre lots by a north and south line dividing each quarter section into an east half and a west half. These lots were numbered from one to the highest number of lots within the respective original surveyed townships, by beginning with number one at the northeast corner of that part of the reservation lying within any original surveyed township, and numbering west, thence east, and so on to the southeast corner of each part of the reservation lying within any such township. This reservation also included section 16, town 7, range 18 and section 10, town 8, range 18, was selected instead for the support of schools in that township.

As early as possible the legislature provided for leasing these lands for the manufacture of salt. They were cared for by agents, [5] and a rental was

(3) Town 11 of range 13 is but five sections wide, and consequently contains but thirty sections. These sections have been numbered continuously from one to thirty, and, after the fifth section, none occupy the location provided for by the act of 1796, which was applied to the sections in adjoining townships.

(4) 2 L. U. S., 533; 3 L. U. S., 496; 1 U. S. S. L., 464.

charged for the privilege of making salt. In 1803
the rental was three cents per gallon per annum for
the capacity of the kettles or other vessels used. [6]
This rental was reduced from time to time until
1810, when it was but five mills. [7]

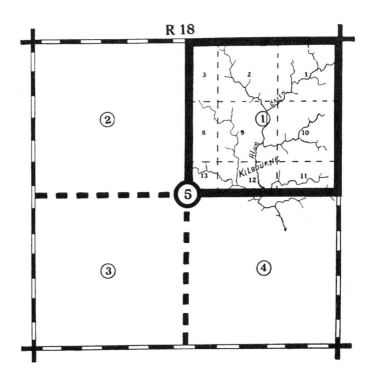

THE   DELAWARE
SALT   RESERVATION

The springs in Jackson county, called the "Scioto Salt Springs," were the most extensive and important of any. Consequently, they were the first to be operated and soon became the most famous. Wells about thirty feet deep were sunk, but, as the water was low in saline matter, it required ten or fifteen gallons to make one pound of salt. The salt was carried upon pack horses to the various settlements and sold, in 1801, for as much as eight dollars per hundred pounds.

Meanwhile, the salt springs in Muskingum county were also operated somewhat extensively, but those in Delaware county, being limited in their supply of water, invited but little attention.

When Jackson county was organized in 1816, it was desired to locate a town within the salt reservation, and the legislature requested congress to permit it to sell so much of the land as might be necessary for that purpose. [8] Thereupon congress authorized the legislature to select and sell one section of land and apply the proceeds to the erection of a court house, or other public buildings, for the use of the county. [9] Section twenty-nine in the seventh township of the eighteenth range was accordingly selected, and was sold for $7,196.00.

(5) 1 L. O., 121, 153; 2 L. O., 104.   (6) 1 L. O., 121.
(7) 2 L. O., 104; 3 L. O., 233; 6 L. O., 111; 8 L. O., 228.

In 1824, when appealing to congress for permission to sell the school lands, the legislature also requested permission to sell the salt lands. [10] Whereupon congress authorized that body to sell and convey all the lands thus reserved in Ohio and apply the proceeds to such literary purposes as it might direct ,but "to no other use, intent or purpose whatsoever." [11]   Accordingly, several acts [12] were passed, providing for the sale of these lands, and, in due time all were sold. [13]

The fund thus realized from the sale of these lands accumulated until 1849, when it amounted to $41,024.05. [14]   This sum appeared each year thereafter as a part of the irreducible debt of the state until 1870, since when it ceased to be accounted for [15] notwithstanding the state, by the act of 1873,

(8)   14 L. O., 459.

(9)   6 L. U. S., 63; 6 U. S. S. L., 161.

(10)   22 L. O. L., 153.

(11)   7 L. U. S., 334; 4 U. S. S. L., 79.

(12)   23 L. O., 32; 24 L. O., 41; 25 L. O., 39; 25 L. O. L., 34; 26 L. O., 19; 29 L. O. L., 52; 31 L. O. L., 171; 58 L. O., 33.

(13)   Acts not specifically referred to in the text, concerning, the Jackson county reservation: 5 L. O... 68; 10 L. O., 110; 11 L. O., 78; 12 L. O., 88; 13 L. O., 293; 14 L. O., 290; 15 L. O., 57; 16 L. O., 196; 18 L. O. L., 48, 60; 20 L. O., 33; 21 L. O. L., 30; 23 L. O., 32; 27 L. O., 61; 35 L. O. L., 203; 37 L. O. L., 198; 41 L. O. L., 18; 48 L. O. L., 671; 58 L. O., 33. The Muskingum county reservations: 7 L. O., 143, 213; 8 L. O., 215; 10 L. O., 126; 12 L. O., 173; 16 L. O., 99; 17 L. O., 130; 18 L. O. L., 69. The Delaware county reservation: 5 L. O., 93; 10 L. O., 94; 15 L. O., 157; 27 L. O. L., 97; 29 L. O. L., 52; 31 L. O. L., 171. All reservations: 9 L. O., 76; 33 L. O., 10.

(14)   Report of Auditor of State for 1849, page 15.

(15)   Report of Auditor of State for 1913, page 56.

(16)   70 L. O., 232; G. C., 7577.

was to have distributed annually the interest arising from the fund "in the same manner as is provided for the distribution of the state tax for the support of common schools." [16]

CHAPTER 18

THE CONNECTICUT WESTERN RESERVE

In 1606, King James I gave the Plymouth Company, or the "Second Colony," as it was sometimes called, [1] a charter or license, to make settlement upon any part of North America lying between the 38th and 45th parallels of north latitude. This company made several attempts to establish a settlement, but all resulted in failure. Its first vessel carrying settlers, sent in August, 1606, was captured by the Spaniards, while other vessels sent later were so badly damaged by storms as to be compelled to return. Other difficulties, of which many were properly attributed to the jealousy of its rival, the London Company, also beset the Plymouth Company, both at home and in America.

Much time was spent in making and unmaking plans for colonization, and the name of the company

[1] The Virginia Military Tract; A. C. C. O. L., 3783; 5 Arch 1.

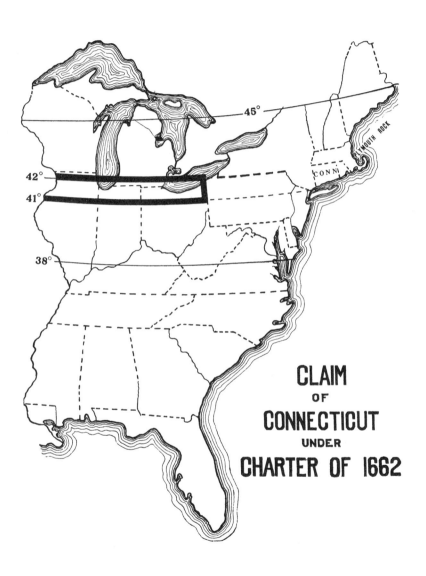

CLAIM
OF
CONNECTICUT
UNDER
CHARTER OF 1662

was changed, in 1618, to "The Council of Plymouth," which consisted of forty of the most wealthy and influential men in England. In 1620, King James granted this new organization a charter [2] for all the land lying between the 40th and 48th parallels of north latitude and extending from ocean to ocean, to be held in fee simple, and conferred almost unlimited power in the forty persons to whom the charter was issued. However, while plans for colonization were being made in England by the members of the new company, a permanent settlement upon the territory granted that company was made by the Pilgrims, who, in 1620, landed upon Plymouth Rock without the consent, or even the knowledge, of the king or of the members of the companies to which these charters had been given.

The history of Connecticut proper, however, began, in 1630, when the Council of Plymouth granted territory, including that state, to the Earl of Warwick, who, in March of the following year, transferred it to Lord Say-and-Seal and others. [3] Settlements were made at Hartford, Windsor and Wethersfield by colonists from Massachusetts, and provisional government was established under a commission granted, in 1635, by the General Court of that state. [4] In 1638, these settlers formed a voluntary compact, or constitution, and chose a governor. [5] Civil government was begun shortly thereafter at

Hartford, and was known as the "Hartford Colony."
Meanwhile, a settlement had been made also at New
Haven where a "Fundamental Agreement," or constitution, was adopted, in 1639, [6] and civil government established. This latter settlement was known
as the "New Haven Colony." These colonies maintained separate governments until 1665, when they
joined in the acceptance of the charter of 1662 and
became united into one colony. [7]

The war of 1651 between England and Holland,
however, left the people of Connecticut in doubt as
to their charter rights. A charter was prepared
and taken to England by John Winthrop (the
younger) and King Charles II signed it, in April,
1662, [8] without change or modification. This
charter constituted Mr. Winthrop and others a body
corporate by "The Name of Governor and Company
of the English Colony of Government in New
England in America," with perpetual succession, and
gave them all that part of New England "bounded on
the east by the Narragansett river commonly called
Narragansett Bay where said river falleth into the
sea; on the north by the line of the Massachusetts
Plantation; on the south by the sea; and in longitude
as the line of Massachusetts Colony ran from the

(2) A. C. C. O. L., 1827   (5) C. C. U. S., 249
(3) 1 L. U. S., 464, note   (6) A. C. C. O. L., 523
(4) A. C. C. O. L., 519   (7) A. C. C. O. L., 529
(8) A. C. C. O. L., 529; 1 L. U. S., 464; 10 Arch., 105

east to the west, that is to say from Narragansett
Bay on the east to the south sea on the west.''   In
1687 King James II. attempted to recall this charter
but the colonists refused to surrender it and hid it in
the hollow of an oak tree, called the "Charter Oak."
The charter was recognized again in 1689, after the
accession of William and Mary.   In 1776, the people
of Connecticut based their declaration of rights upon the charter of 1662 and continued it in force as
the organic law of the state. [9]

As the south and the north boundary lines of the
tract, as described in the charter of 1662, correspond
virtually with the 41st and 42nd parallels of north
latitude, respectively, Connecticut claimed all the
land lying between those parallels, west to the

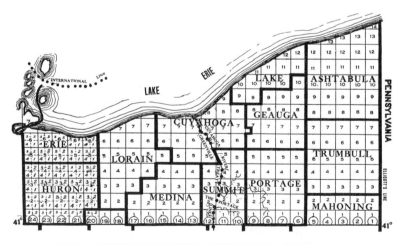

THE CONNECTICUT WESTERN RESERVE

Mississippi river, except that part granted to the Duke of York. Pennsylvania, however, in 1782, contested this claim as to the land lying between the Delaware river and her western boundary, and was sustained by a federal court sitting at Trenton, New Jersey. [10]

In accordance with the recommendation of the Continental Congress of September 6, 1780, [11] (act not found in journals) that all colonies owning waste land cede them to the United States, Connecticut, in October of that year, agreed to relinquish that part of such land claimed by her under the charter of 1662, [12] but exacted conditions which Congress failed to accept, and the proposition was withdrawn in January 1783. [13]

By authority of a resolution of Connecticut of May 26, 1786, [14] the delegates in congress from that state, in September of that year executed to the United States a deed of release and cession of the right of Connecticut to all the land lying west of one hundred and twenty miles west of the west line of Pennsylvania, and north of the 41st parallel of latitude. Congress accepted the deed the following day. [14]

As the jurisdiction of Connecticut over her

(10)   2 Arch., 475; 11 O. R. 475; 13 O. R., 430.
(11)   1 L. U. S., 472; 2 Arch., 285
(9)   C. C. U. S., 257   (13)   2 Arch., 288
(12)   2 Arch., 287   (14)   1 L. U. S., 484

western reserve, as well as her title to the land itself, was as complete as that over her own state, it was evident that the reserve could not become a part of the new state then expected to be established northwest of the Ohio river.   It, therefore, soon became desirable that the jurisdiction be released to the United States.   Besides, question arose as to the title of the United States to the land within the reserve acquired by the treaty with Great Britain and the deeds from New York and Massachusetts.   Few, therefore, cared to buy the land thus reserved by Connecticut.   Whereupon the president was authorized by the act of April, 1800, [15] to convey to Connecticut all the right, title and interest of the United States to the soil of the reservation, provided that state, within eight months, should renounce all claims under any grant or charter, to its jurisdiction and also to the soil and jurisdiction of that lying to the west.   Connecticut promptly agreed to this, and the governor accordingly executed a deed to the United States under date of May 30, 1800. [16]

New York and Massachusetts also claimed some right to this western land.   The claim of New York seems to have been based upon the extension of the rights granted James Duke of York by his brother, King Charles II, by the charter of 1664, [17] to include jurisdiction over the territory of the "Six Nations"

(15)   3 L. U. S., 364   (16)   1 L. U. S., 485
(17)   A. C. C. O. L., 1637; 1 L. U. S., 464

which that state assumed to assert after the com-
mercial treaty with the Indians at Albany in 1722;
while the claim of Massachusetts was based upon the
charter of 1691, [18] given by William and Mary to
the Massachusetts Bay Colony. By act of the legislature of February 19, 1780, the delegates in congress
from New York were authorized to convey to the
United States all the claim of that state to this
western land, and a deed was accordingly executed
March 1, 1801. [19] By act of the General Court of
Massachusetts of 1784, the delegates in congress
from that state were empowered to release to the
United States all the rights of Massachusetts to the
land lying between the Hudson and the Mississippi
rivers. A deed was accordingly executed and accepted April 19, 1785. [20]

Meanwhile, Connecticut endeavored to sell her
western land thus reserved. In 1786, the legislature
provided for its survey into townships of six miles
square and appointed a committee to sell it. No attempt, however, was made to carry out this plan or to
sell the land, until after the "Sufferers' Lands,"
known as the "Fire Lands," had been set off. [10] In
May 1793, the legislature appointed a committee of
eight, one from each county in the state, to sell all
the reserve, except the five ranges set off the west
end to compensate those who had suffered loss by fire,

(18) A. C. C. O. L., 1870; 1 L. U. S., 454 note, 462
(19) 1 L. U. S, 467   (20) 1 L. U. S., 482

and provided that the money "arising from the sale, should constitute a perpetual fund of which the interest should be appropriated to the use of the several ecclesiastical societies, churches or congregations of all denominations in the state, and to be applied by them to the support of their respective ministers and schools of education under such regulations as should be adopted by the general assembly. [10]

The attempt to make the churches trustees of the fund, precipitated much discussion and nothing was accomplished until May 1795, when the legislature repealed the act of 1793, appointed a committee to sell all this land except that part given the "Fire Sufferers," and provided that the proceeds should constitute a perpetual fund of which the interest should be applied to the support of the schools of Connecticut. [10]

The land was sold August 12, 1795, for $1,200,-000.00 to seven persons, who, as agents, represented a large number of the inhabitants of Connecticut, and who were known as the "Connecticut Land Company." [10]

In 1843, the legislature of Ohio [21] requested the legislature of Connecticut to deliver to the recorder of Trumbull county all original, or certified copies of, papers connected with the business of the Connecticut Land Company and deposited with the secretary of that state by the legal representatives of Ephraim Root, formerly clerk of that company. Accordingly, the original draft book is to be found at Warren, in the office of the recorder of Trumbull county.

That part of the reserve lying east of the Cuyahoga river was cleared of the Indian title by the treaty of Greenville in 1795; [22] while that to the west was cleared by the treaty of Fort Industry, in 1805. [23] The United States compensated the Indians for their title released under the former treaty, but the Connecticut Land Company and the Proprietors of the Sufferers' Land, joined in the latter treaty and paid the Indians four thousand dollars in cash, and agreed to pay the further sum of twelve thousand dollars in six annual installments of two thousand dollars each, and an annuity of one hundred and seventy-five dollars.

By reason of its being west of Connecticut, this reserve was naturally referred to by the inhabitants of that state, as "New Connecticut," "The Western Reserve," "The Western Reserve of Connecticut," and, "The Connecticut Western Reserve." [10] It is, however, now referred to, usually, by the latter name. It is located in the northeast corner of Ohio

(21)   41 L. O. L., 260   (24)   7 O. R. 456.
(22)   1 L. U. S., 398; 7 U. S. S. L., 49.
(23)   1 L. U. S., 409; 7 U. S. S. L., 87.

and contains about 3,840,000 acres, including the "Fire Lands."

All the reserve, including the "Fire Lands," constitutes one original survey known as "The Connecticut Western Reserve Survey," and has been subdivided into townships of five miles square, each containing sixteen thousand acres, except those bordering along Lake Erie.   The ranges are numbered west from the Pennsylvania, or Ellicott's line, from range number one to twenty-four, while the townships are each numbered north from the forty first parallel of north latitude, or from the south line of the reserve.

The townships have been variously subdivided. No one plan seems to have been followed very generally, except in ranges twenty, twenty-one, twenty-two, twenty-three and twenty-four, known as the "Fire Lands," where they have been subdivided into quarter townships of two and one-half miles square,

containing four thousand acres each, and numbered from one to four by beginning with number one in the southeast corner of the township and numbering north, west and south to number four in the southwest corner. These quarter townships are usually designated as the "first," "second," "third" and "fourth" quarters, respectively.

However, a number of townships, outside the Fire lands, denominated "equalizing townships," were subdivided into smaller tracts and one of these called an "annexation" was added to a five mile square township when it was not considered of average value. (24)

CHAPTER 19

THE FIRE LANDS

While no great battles were fought on the soil of Connecticut during the Revolutionary war, yet the British made several raids upon different towns in that state and did much damage to property owned by its inhabitants. This damage was so extensive that those who suffered losses felt they should be compensated, and therefore, petitioned the legislature for relief. For a while the state abated their taxes but that fell short of compensation. In May of 1787, the legislature was again appealed to, and the committee to which the application was referred, reported, a few months later, the many losses suffered by these petitioners and advised that they be reimbursed by the state. The committee also reported that the only resource possessed by the state with which to pay these losses was its western land. [1] This report was approved, but no further action was taken until 1791, when the legislature appointed a

(1) See The Connecticut Western Reserve.

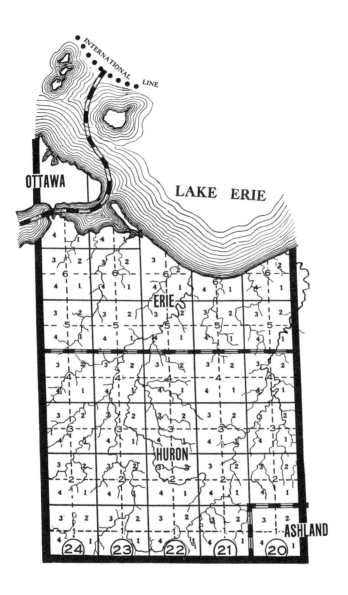

THE FIRE LANDS

committee of three to ascertain and report the losses. The task was a difficult one and required about one year to complete it. According to the report [2] about eighteen hundred and seventy persons residing in nine towns, were found to have suffered losses. Of these, 289 resided in Norwalk; 283 in Greenwich; 269 in Fairfield; 186 in Danbury; 410 in New Haven and East Haven combined; 275 in New London; 65 in Ridgefield and 93 in Groton. The greatest number were of the town of Norwalk, while those of New London lost the most in value. The total loss reported, however, amounted to $602,265.75 and varied, in individual amounts, from $13,792.88 lost by Nathaniel and Thomas Shaw, of New London, to 49 cents lost by Michael Judah, of Norwalk; or an average of about $322.00 to each claimant. [3]

Thereupon the legislature of Connecticut, May 10, 1792, granted to these sufferers, their heirs and assigns forever, or, if dead, to their legal representatives, five hundred thousand acres off the west side of the land belonging to that state lying west of the state of Pennsylvania, to be divided among them in proportion to their respective losses. [4]

The tract thus set aside consisted of ranges twenty, twenty-one, twenty-two, twenty-three and twenty-four of the Connecticut Western Reserve, ex-

(2) For list of names and losses, see L. L. O., 81.
(4) L. L. O., 81.   (5) L. L. O., 101, 105.
(3) 2 Arch., 475; 10 Arch., 435.   (6) 1 L. O., 106.

tended north into Lake Erie to the International boundary line and included about 781 square miles. It also includes all the present county of Huron, nearly all of Erie, one township in Ashland, and a small part of Ottawa.

The grant of the land, however, did not complete the settlement of the claims. Many problems had to be solved before the beneficiaries could avail themselves of its use. It was located many hundreds of miles away, in territory to which the Indian title had not been obtained, and where it was unsafe for the white man to settle. Besides, the many persons interested in the land and the varied interests possessed by each, presented many further difficulties; and it was not until October of 1796, and after the Indians, by the treaty of Greenville, had released their claim to that part of the reserve lying east of the Cuyahoga river, that any plan of subdividing and settling the land could be completed.

The great number of persons interested, residing in many different places, prevented united action. So, in October of 1796, [5] the legislature of Connecticut constituted the proprietors, or owners, of the land a corporation by the name of "The Proprietors of the Half Million Acres of Land, lying south of Lake Erie," and authorized that corporation to hold the land for its proprietors and their heirs and assigns. The proprietors of each respective town were authorized to select one agent for each ten thousand pounds, or fractional part thereof, of losses suffered by its inhabitants, to represent them in the corporation; and in voting for such agent each person who had suffered loss had one vote for each one hundred pounds, or fractional part, lost by him, but no person was entitled to cast more than ten votes.

The board of agents of this corporation had full power to extinguish the Indian title, to survey and locate the land, to partition it into townships, or otherwise, and to do whatever else should appear necessary, or proper, for the interests of the proprietors.

However, since the land was located in Ohio, it was deemed desirable to incorporate also under the laws of that state.   Accordingly, the legislature in 1803, [6] constituted these owners and proprietors a body corporate by the name of "The proprietors of the half million acres of land lying south of Lake Erie, called Sufferers' Land."   The board of directors consisted of nine persons of whom one was selected by the proprietors of the respective towns where losses had been suffered.   These directors had the same power to extinguish the Indian title, to survey, locate and partition the land that had been given the agents by the Connecticut corporation. The record of the proceedings of these companies and the survey of the land are on file with the recorder of Huron county. [7]

(7)   10 L. O., 163; 10 Arch., 220; 13 O. R., 430.

CHAPTER 20

THE UNITED STATES MILITARY SURVEY.

For many years following the earliest settlements in America, separate governments prevailed. "The colonies had different governors, different laws, different forms of government, different interests; and so much jealousy existed that they were unable to unite even for their common defense against the Indians."

Their experience with the Indians, their knowledge of the country and their bravery during the French and Indian war, made the colonists indispensable to the English; and, while their participation in that war taught them the art of war, it also taught them the value of united and concerted action and inspired them with self confidence. Drawn together by mutual necessities, prompted by community of interests and strengthened by confidence in their own independence, the colonists were moulded gradually into a union of common thought and purpose. This led eventually to the "American Association," composed of delegates from the colonies, held in Philadelphia in 1774. [1] Other conventions followed until 1777 [2] when articles of confederation and perpetual union between the colonies, styled "The United States of America," were adopted. These articles provided a national organization which conducted the war and governed the colonies until the present constitution went into effect in 1789.

The business of this union was carried on by delegates from the several colonies acting in conventions as the "Continental Congress"; but, lacking conclusive authority, or executive power, this congress was advisory only, and could enforce none of its resolutions. Any contract, or obligation, proposed by it, involving the united colonies, became effective only when approved subsequently by the congress under the present constitution. [13] Meanwhile, however, these resolutions were acquiesced in quite generally by the colonies, and their union was thus preserved until the present form of government became effective.

The Continental Congress had no money, or other resources. It had no national credit upon which to draw, and but little else to offer. Even the unsettled western lands, of which there was an abundance, were claimed by some of the individual

(1)   1 L. U. S., 1.   (2)   November 15; 1 L. U. S., 135.
(13)   Clause 1, Article 6; 1 L. U. S., 69.

colonies under the charters by which they themselves existed.   In its extremity, however, the Continental Congress assumed that these lands would be
given, eventually, to the union; or that arrangements would be made, ultimately, whereby they
could be used for the common benefit of all.   It
thereupon acted accordingly and promised bounties

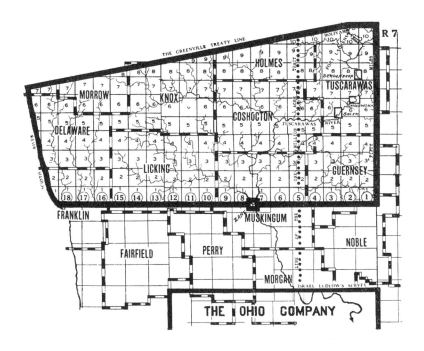

THE UNITED STATES
MILITARY TRACT

in land to induce enlistment in the army.   By resolutions of September 16 and 18, 1776; August 12, September 22, and October 3, 1780, [3] this congress proposed to give to each officer or private continuing to serve in the United States army until the close of the war, or until discharged, or to the representatives of those "slain by the enemy," the following respective amounts:

Major General	1,100 Acres
Brigadier General, or Director	850 Acres
Colonel, Chief Physician or Purveyor	500 Acres
Lieutenant Colonel, Physician, Surgeon or Apothecary	450 Acres
Major, Regimental Surgeon or Assistant Apothecary	400 Acres
Captain, or Hospital, or Regimental Surgeons' Mate	300 Acres
Lieutenant	200 Acres
Ensign	150 Acres
Non-commissioned officer or soldier	100 Acres

Originally the certificates for land thus awarded, were not assignable, as congress, among its early acts, [4] provided that no grant of land should be made to any person claiming under an assignment from an officer or a soldier.   This provision, however, was modified in 1788, [5] when the secretary of

(3)   1 L. U. S., 567.   (5)   1 L. U. S,. 570.
(4)   September 20, 1776; 1 L. U. S., 570, note.

war was authorized to issue land warrants to such officers or soldiers, "or to their respective assigns or legal representatives." But, while assignments of certificates were thus permitted, they could be used by the assignees only in the purchase of full quarter townships in the military tract prior to January of 1800; [6] and, by the act of March of that year, [7] no locations were allowed, or patents permitted to be issued, for any of the one hundred acre lots, except to the persons originally entitled to the warrants, or to their respective heirs.

While the war progressed, the Continental Congress endeavored to shape affairs to meet its obligations. Therefore, on September 6, 1780, [8] it recommended that each colony, having waste or unappropriated land in the western country, cede it to the United States for the common benefit of the union. Virginia was the first to comply, but did not do so until March of 1784 when her delegates in congress conveyed to the United States [8] all her claim to the land lying northwest of the Ohio river and south of the forty-first parallel of north latitude, reserving, however, the right to use so much of the land lying between the Scioto and the Little Miami rivers as might be necessary to satisfy such army bounty warrants issued by that state as could not be satisfied with land southeast of the Ohio river.

(6) 2 L. U. S., 565; 1 U. S. S. L., 490.
(7) 3 L. U. S., 314; 2 U. S. S. L., 14.   (8) 1 L. U. S., 472.

This title to the land in Ohio, lying south of the forty-first parallel of latitude, has been approved by the supreme court of the United States which held that "It has been very truly observed that the government of the union is to be considered as holding the territory ceded by Virginia in trust for the nation." [9]

Congress first attempted, in 1785, [3] to carry out its promises to grant land to those who served in the Revolutionary war by directing the secretary of war to issue certificates to the claimants for the amount to which he should find each entitled, and authorizing the loan officers of the different states to which the respective claimants belonged, to execute deeds. [10]

This plan could not be put into effect, and the ordinance was repealed in 1788. [11] In the meantime, however, [12] Congress endeavored to deal more directly with the claimants and attempted to satisfy certificates for military bounty with land from two tracts in the western country:　One, a large tract in southern Illinois; the other, beginning at the northwest corner of the seven ranges in the Ohio River Survey and running south to the Ohio Company's land, and extending west far enough to include one million acres, in the counties of Washington, Noble,

(9)　9 Wheaton, 459; 22 U. S. S. C. R., 137.
(10)　1 L. U. S., 564.　　　　　(11)　1 L. U. S., 569.
(12)　October 22, 1787; 1 L. U. S., 570.

Guernsey, Tuscarawas, Morgan, Muskingum, Coshocton and Holmes. But until the United States became a nation under the Federal constitution, in 1789, there was no national organization with sufficient, inherent power to contract to do anything, and, therefore, no conveyances of title could be made. The ordinances of the Continental Congress were, in effect, but empty promises and bound no one; and the ordinance of 1787, [12] setting aside the two tracts of land with which to satisfy land warrants, was as ineffective as that of 1785. However, with the adoption of the Federal constitution and the election of officers necessary to carry on the government, the United States became an entity capable of effective action; and all the ordinances and resolutions passed by the Continental Congress, and all debts contracted and engagements entered into by it, before the adoption of the Federal Constitution, were made valid by that constitution, [13] and steps were taken as soon as possible thereafter to carry them into effect.

By the act of June 1, 1796, [6] the new congress provided for satisfying army bounty warrants out of the following described tract of land in central Ohio: Beginning at the northwest corner of the seven ranges in the Ohio River Survey, and thence running due south, along their western boundary, fifty miles; thence due west to the Scioto river;

thence up that river to the Greenville treaty line; thence along that line to the Tuscarawas river at the crossing above Fort Laurens; thence up that river to a point due west of the place of beginning; thence east to the place of beginning. As this tract was thus set aside to satisfy the military certificates for land issued by the Continental Congress, acting for the union, it is known as "The United States Military Tract;" and, since it is an independent survey as well, it is also called "The United States Military Survey." It is located in the central part of the state, in Noble, Guernsey, Tuscarawas, Muskingum, Coshocton, Holmes, Licking, Knox, Franklin, Delaware, Morrow and Marion counties, and contains, by estimation, 2,539,110 acres. [14]

Notwithstanding that congress but a few days before, [15] had provided for the survey of all public lands into townships of six miles square, and directed the thirty-six sections, or 640 acre lots, to be numbered by beginning with number one in the northeast corner of the township, the act of June 1, 1796 [6] required the United States Military tract to be subdivided into five miles square tracts, or townships, instead.

Why this plan was adopted, in this one instance only, is not known. However, since, with few ex-

---

(14) Annals of Congress, 1802-3, Page 1329.
(15) May 18, 1796; 2 L. U. S., 533; 1 U. S. S. L., 464.

ceptions, the number of acres to which each soldier was entitled, was some multiple of one hundred, perhaps it may have been deemed that the five miles square township of sixteen thousand acres, or its quarters of four thousand acres each, could be used for such subdivision better than the six miles square township with its thirty-six subdivisions of six hundred and forty acres each. This possibility was found especially convenient later when the fifty quarter townships were subdivided into one hundred acre lots, and the fractional townships, into fifty acre lots. This survey, however, adds one more to the many in Ohio and interferes with the continuance of the Ohio River Survey surrounding it.

These townships, therefore, were made five miles square, contained sixteen thousand acres each, and were numbered north from the south line of the tract which was adopted as their base; while the rows of townships, or ranges, were numbered west from the east line which thereby became their ruling, or governing, meridian.

The townships were subdivided originally into quarter townships of two and one-half miles square, containing four thousand acres each. (6) These quarter townships were numbered from one to four by beginning with the northeast quarter as number one, and numbering consecutively around to the left. They are, therefore, designated as the "first," "second," "third" and "fourth" quarters, respectively, as shown by the following plan:

As no one officer, or soldier, was entitled to as much as an entire quarter township of four thousand acres, the townships were also subdivided into sections, half sections and lots. [16]

Under the act of 1800, [7] the secretary of the treasury was directed "to designate, by lot, in the presence of the secretary of war, fifty quarter townships," and to divide them "upon the respective plats thereof, as returned by the surveyor general, into as many lots, of one hundred acres each, as shall be equal, as nearly as may be to the quantity such quarter township or fraction is stated to contain; each of which lots shall be included, where practicable, between parallel lines, one hundred and sixty perches in length, and one hundred perches in width, and shall be designated by progressive numbers, upon the

(16)   3 L. U. S., 314, 555; 2 U. S. S. L., 14.

plat or survey of every such quarter township and
fraction, respectively.'' This the secretary of the
treasury did upon the plats only, and no survey or
subdivision of such quarter townships into lots was
made until some years thereafter. However, in
many instances, the surveys and the plats could not
be made to agree and a number of fractional lots,
shown on the plats, were entirely crowded out.

Before these lots were surveyed and located,
many of the remaining quarter townships were subdivided into sections and half sections. To carry out
this purpose the townships were subdivided into
twenty-five sections of one mile square each, and
numbered from one to twenty-five, both inclusive,
by beginning with number one in the northeast
corner of the township, and numbering consecutively west for five sections, thence east, etc., after the
manner prescribed by the act of 1796, (15) and ending
with section number twenty-five in the southwest
corner of the township. Each section, in turn
was divided into lots of three hundred and twenty
acres each by a line running north and south through
the middle of the respective sections. These lots
were numbered from one to fifty, both inclusive, by
beginning with lot number one in the northeast
corner of the township and numbering west, thence
east, etc, after the manner of numbering the sections,
to lot number fifty in the southwest corner of the

township. Where less than a full township was so
subdivided, each section and half section, or lot, was
given the same respective number it would have been
given had an entire township been thus subdivided.

While the sections and half sections were numbered continuously from the northeast corner of the
respective townships, yet, in all surveys, the quarter
township lines were required, by the act of 1800, [7]
to be run from the quarter township corners as established by the surveyor general. This act provided
that the "points on each of the boundary lines of
such township, which are at an equal distance from
those two corners of the same township which stand
on the same boundary line, shall be considered to be
corners of the respective quarters of such township;
that the other boundary lines of the said quarter
townships shall be straight lines, run from each
of the last mentioned corners of quarter townships
to the corner of quarter townships on the opposite
boundary line of the same township; and that the
corners marked in the boundary lines of such township to designate the quarters thereof, shall be considered, and are declared to be, the corners of the
quarter townships thereof, although the same may
be found at unequal distances from the respective
corners of such townships: And such townships
shall be divided, by running lines through the same,
from the corners of the quarter townships actually

marked, whether the interior lines thus extended shall be parallel to the exterior lines of the said township or not; and that each of the said quarter townships thus bounded, shall, in every proceeding to be had under the above-mentioned, or this, act, be considered as containing the exact quantity expressed

JEFFERSON TOWNSHIP
GUERNSEY COUNTY

T 3   R 2

in the plat and survey thereof returned by the surveyor general." Therefore, where the township has been subdivided into quarters, the quarter township has thus been made the unit, and any errors must be reconciled within the quarter where found.

This act also provided that if any quarter township, according to the actual survey and plat returned by the surveyor general, was stated to contain more than four thousand acres, the excess should be paid for at the rate of $2.00 per acre; while if it was stated to contain less than four thousand acres, the secretary of the treasury should issue registry certificates for the number of acres remaining unsatisfied, provided that such shortage should exceed fifty acres. By the act of 1804, [17] persons holding certificates for less than one hundred acres were permitted to locate land in such fractional townships as the secretary of the treasury should subdivide into fifty acre lots for that purpose.

A large number of the quarter townships thus selected by the secretary of the treasury, were subdivided into forty lots of one hundred acres each, and numbered from one to forty by beginning with number one in the southeast corner of the quarter and numbering north and south, and north and south and north, to lot number forty in the northwest corner.

(17)   3 L. U. S., 478; 2 U. S. S. L., 155.

Many, however, were subdivided and numbered otherwise.

As an illustration of the several subdivisions of these townships, township number three of range number two, which coincides with the civil township of Jefferson, Guernsey county, is herein given.

The time within which warrants for military services for land in this tract could be satisfied, was extended from time to time, [18] until 1803, [19] when the "unappropriated land," that is land not needed to satisfy land warrants, lying west of the eleventh range not required to satisfy such warrants, were attached to the Chillicothe land district, while those within the eleventh range and east of it, were attached to the Zanesville district. These were sold under general acts of congress and, of course, became "Congress Lands." However, by special acts, warrants were satisfied with land from this, or other tracts as late as 1832. [20]

(18)   3 L. U. S., 260,305, 314, 478; 1 U. S. S. L., 724; 2 U. S. S.
        L., 7, 14, 155.
(19)   3 L. U. S., 554; 2 U. S. S. L.,236.
(20)   7 L. U. S. 312; 8 L. U. S. 677.

CHAPTER 21

THE MORAVIAN TRACTS.

In Tuscarawas county there are three tracts of land containing four thousand acres each, which constitute surveys independent of the United States Military Survey surrounding them. They are known as the "Moravian Tracts," and, by their individuality as separate surveys, they will forever bespeak their association with the earliest efforts to establish settlements within the present bounds of Ohio.

On these tracts, one hundred and fifty years ago, resided the Moravian Indians. These Indians were not a tribe, as their name might suggest, but were Indians converted to Christianity by the missionaries of the Moravian Church, who, since its organization under that name in 1727, had been active in missionary work.

The Moravian Church derived its name from the valley of Moravia lying within a province of that name in the northern part of Austria, where a few families had preserved the traditions of their fathers who had come from Bohemia where they had organized, about the year 1427, a religious society called the "Bohemian Brethren."

The early activities of the Moravian missionaries in America abound in historic incidents. By their quiet, humble labor they gained and kept the

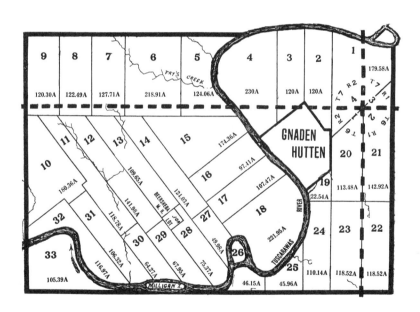

GNADENHUTTEN TRACT

confidence of the Indians and accomplished more, perhaps, than any other organization toward establishing peace with the red man.

Missionaries from the main branch of this church in America, located at Bethlehem, Pennsylvania, visited, in 1761, the Indian villages on the Muskingum river near where the "Great Trail," running east and west, crossed the trail running north and south over the much traveled portage to the Cuyahoga river.   There these missionaries established themselves and thus planted the germs of civilization in the northwest territory.   But on account of the enmity of the Indians living to the northwest, and the jealousy of the French who then regarded Ohio as belonging to them, little progress was made by the missionaries until May 1772, when, with five Indian families from Pennsylvania, they laid out and settled the town of Schoenbrun.   Gnadenhutten was laid out in October of the same year, and Salem in 1780.   It is by these names that the three respective surveys, or tracts of land surrounding these villages are known.

It was also within one of these tracts that the white man disgraced his race by one of the most cruel and treacherous butcheries of a band of confiding red men that history records.   In 1782 depredations, including the killing of some white people, had been committed in Pennsylvania and Virginia.   A

local company of about one hundred men under
Colonel Williamson arrived in Gnadenhutten and assumed these Indians to have been the guilty parties.
With an abiding confidence in their visitors, more
than ninety of these Indians, including women and
children, were induced to congregate in a building
where Col. Williamson and his men slaughtered them
without mercy.

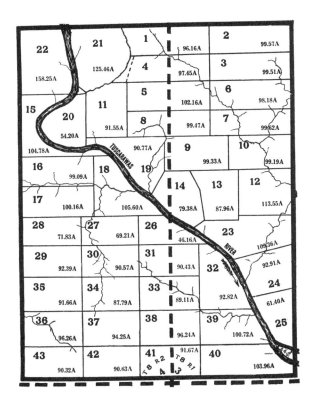

SCHOENBRUN TRACT

When it was learned these Indians were not guilty, but, instead, were christianized and exceedingly friendly, great indignation arose. The act of Williamson and his men was looked upon as an unfortunate outrage upon humanity, and they were vigorously denounced. The remnant of this band of Indians, shocked and frightened by the horrible deed, fled to Canada. Every effort, however, was made to amend the great wrong and a number were induced afterwards to return and resume their good work.

The Continental Congress became active in the matter and, in May of 1785, [1] directed that so much of the lands adjoining each of their towns as the geographer might deem sufficient for them to cultivate, with the buildings and improvements, should be reserved from sale and applied to the sole use of such of these Indians as might return. To aid such application further, congress, in July of 1787, [2] authorized the board of treasury to reserve from sale a quantity of land at each settlement, amounting altogether to ten thousand acres, and vested the title in the Moravian Brethren of Bethlehem, Pennsylvania, or in a society of those brethren, in trust for civilizing the Indians and promoting Christianity.

In September of 1788, congress confirmed [3] its previous ordinances, but modified them by

(1) 1 L. U. S. 568.   (2) 1 L. U. S. 569.   (3) 1 L. U. S. 579.

directing that a town plat, estimated at 666 2-3 acres, be laid out in each tract; that each town and the reserved lands adjoining it, should constitute a tract of four thousand acres; that the geographer should survey the tracts off as speedily as possible and return plats of them to the board of treasury, and that their title should vest in the Society of the United Brethren in trust, for propagating the Gospel among the heathen, as expressed in former ordinances. [3]

June 1, 1796, congress directed the surveyor general to survey off the three tracts of land containing four thousand acres each, at Schoenbrun, Gnadenhutten and Salem, respectively, and that patents should be issued for them to the Society of the United Brethren, in trust, as provided in the ordinance of 1788. [4] This society had previously been created a corporation by Pennsylvania, New Jersey and New York, and in 1810 by Ohio. [12]

After a survey had been made of their outer boundaries a patent was issued, February 24, 1798 [5] conveying these tracts to this society, as trustee, for the use of the Indians. But as white people settled in the surrounding country the habits and character of the Indians changed for the worse. This, together with their intercourse with the San-

(4) 2 L. U. S., 565; 1 U. S. S. L., 490.   (12)   8 L. O. 12.
   (5)   United States Land Records 1, page 38.

dusky Indians who continued to be hostile to the Americans, caused all efforts to re-establish them in their former christian spirit and work, to fail.   As the trust became burdensome to the society and useless to the Indians, the society was unable to accomplish its purposes, and, therefore, decided to abandon further efforts.

The duty of carrying out the trust and caring for the property had placed a serious financial burden upon the society.   By August of 1822 it had expended $43,356.00 in procuring the title, surveying the lands, cutting roads, building mills and making other improvements in connection with the execution of its trust; while it had received but $9,998.58¼, leaving a balance of $32,587.50¾.   Of this sum, $15,840.10¼ had been expended in procuring the title and surveying, and for the payment of $6,654.25 of which the land was still held liable.   (11)

Arrangements were thereupon made, in 1823, to recede the land to the United States.   In March of that year, congress (6) directed the president to take such measures as might be necessary to purchase the title and interest of the Indians in the tracts, and appropriated one thousand dollars to meet the expenses of doing so; and on the 4th day of August, 1823, a deed, or rather a contract, of retrocession

(7)   Tuscarawas County Deed Book 4, page 87.
(11)   These receipts, expenditures and balances are as recited
      in the deed.   (6)   7 L. U. S. 141.

(7) was signed at Gnadenhutten by Lewis Cass, commissioner for the United States, and Lewis De Schweinitz, agent for the society.

But as the Indians were the beneficiaries of the grant, the agreement to recede the lands could not

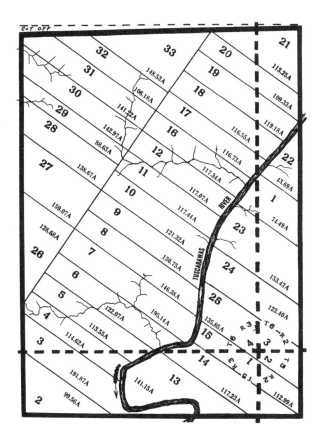

SALEM TRACT

have been legal without their consent. This was
given by an agreement entered into at Detroit,
November 8, 1823, by Lewis Cass on the part of the
United States, and Zacharias or Kootalus, John
Henry, Charles Henry or Killbuck, Francis Henry
Killbuck, John Peter Tobias, John Jacob and Mathias
or Koolots Has Kee, the descendants and representatives of the Indians who had formerly settled upon
the land. The society was to be repaid $6,654.25 out
of the first proceeds of the sale of the land and the
Indians granted an annuity of four hundred dollars.
The deed of retrocession and its supplemental contract were accepted May 26, 1824 by congress [8]
which directed the tracts to be subdivided into suitable lots and sold. [9] They were surveyed in 1825.

The secretary of the treasury was directed by
the act of 1824, [8] to set apart one lot in each of the
three Moravian tracts, not exceeding the one thirty-
sixth part each, for the support of their respective
schools. Accordingly, lot No. 2 of the Gnadenhutten
tract, containing 120 acres, was thus assigned for
the use of schools within that tract; lot No. 11 of
the Salem tract, containing 117.44 acres, for the use
of schools within that tract, while lot No. 25, containing 61.40 acres and lot No. 24 less 37.68 acres, or
55.23 acres off the south side, were assigned for the

(8)   7 L. U. S., 307; 4 U. S. S. L., 56.
(9)   7 L. U. S. 511, 587; 4 U. S. S. L., 185, 237.

use of schools within the Schoenbrun tract. [10]   And in doing so, lot No. 24, which contained 92.91 acres and from which 37.68 acres were deducted, with lot No. 25, were thus assigned.   This left 55.23 acres which has been treated as lot No. 24, while the remainder, 37.68 acres, of this original lot has been merged into lot No. 23 to the north.

[10]   For acts for leasing and selling these school lands, see 38 L. O. 164;   41 L. O. 143; 74 L. O. 429;   97 L. O. 617; 106 L. O. 141;   32 L. O. L. 193.

CHAPTER 22

THE MIAMI RIVER SURVEY.

The tract of land in southwestern Ohio and in southeastern Indiana, lying between the Great Miami river and the Old Indian boundary, or Greenville treaty line, has been subdivided into ranges and townships from the first principal meridian which coincides with the line dividing the two states. The ranges in Ohio are numbered east from that meridian, while those in Indiana are numbered west. The townships in the ranges to the west are numbered north from where each respective range intersects the Ohio river, while the townships in the ranges to the east are numbered north from where each respective range intersects the Great Miami river. Consequently adjacent townships in adjoining ranges seldom have similar numbers.

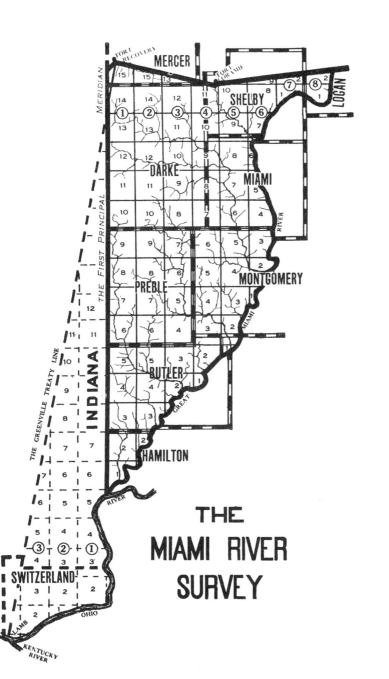

THE
MIAMI RIVER
SURVEY

Two separate surveys of the land in western Ohio are based upon this meridian. To avoid confusion and to make certain the survey of which any subdivision in that section of the state may be a part, distinguishing names for these surveys have been necessary. As the survey to the north, and in which the townships are divided by the forty-first parallel of latitude, is the most extensive, its ranges are very properly referred to as being based upon the first principal meridian. Hence its townships are either north, or south, of range—, east of the first principal meridian. Another name, therefore, was necessarily required for the survey to the south; and, since its townships are numbered from the Great Miami river, it is very properly termed "The Miami River Survey." And the land in this southern survey lying between Ohio and the Indian treaty line should be described as being, for instance, in town 7, range 2 west, of the first principal meridian.

CHAPTER 23

BETWEEN THE MIAMI RIVERS. [1]

All the land lying between the Great and the Little Miami rivers in the southwestern part of the state constitutes an original survey, and, since it is not based upon any meridian of longitude, it is called "Between the Miami Rivers" Survey. Yet while it has been subdivided into townships, ranges and sections upon the rectangular plan, it has been done upon a basis quite different from that employed elsewhere thruout the United States. This is especially so in denominating the six miles square rectangles, townships as progression is made in numbering them to the east or west, and calling them ranges as progression is made north or south, thus reversing the rule universally employed elsewhere and making it the one exception.

This system, or plan, was adopted by Judge Symmes when surveying his purchase off the south end of the tract. Obviously his reason for using

(1) 12 O. L. R., 577, 588; 13 O. L. R., 501.

the term "range" for the rows of townships to the north or to the south was that the two Miami rivers, between which his tract laid, diverged so much to the east of any meridian of longitude that a meridional base could not be had from which to enumerate the rows, or ranges, of townships to the east or to the west, as had been done in the seven ranges; and, as the north line of the tract for which he received a patent was the only boundary line coinciding most nearly with the cardinal points of the compass, that line furnished him the only available base from which to enumerate the rows, or ranges, of townships. Accordingly he adopted it for that purpose and divided the space south to the Ohio river into five rows of which each was six miles in width, except the last, and called them "ranges." These rows, or "ranges," were subdivided into townships, or fractions of townships as the irregularity of the two Miami rivers made it necessary, and numbered from the Great Miami river, which was assumed as the base, east to the Little Miami. The townships were subdivided into thirty-six sections each and numbered by beginning with number one in the southeast corner as required by the land ordinance of 1785 [2] and confirmed by the act of 1796. [3]

Therefore, what are invariably termed ranges elsewhere are denominated "townships" between the

(2)   1 L. U. S., 563.   (3)   2 L. U. S., 533; 1 U. S. S. L., 464.

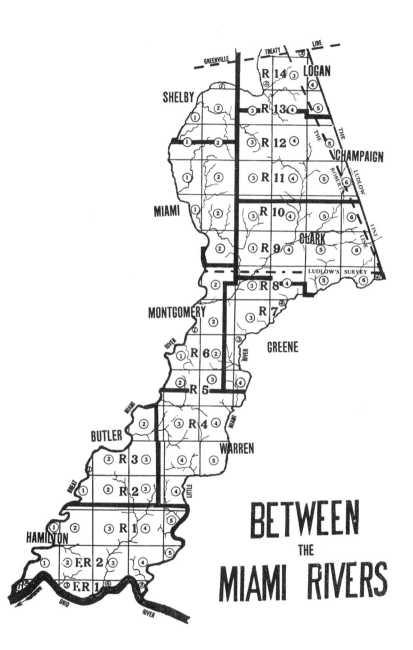

BETWEEN
THE
MIAMI RIVERS

Miami rivers. They are numbered from the Great
Miami river east to the Little Miami, and as progression is made east or west these original surveyed
tracts are termed townships; while the tiers, or rows,
of townships to the north or south are termed
"ranges," and are numbered from the south to the
north. These range numbers, however, as might be
supposed, do not begin from the Ohio river, but
instead, from a point about the width of a township
and one-half north of that river. The intervening
divisions are termed "fractional ranges," and are
numbered one and two, respectively, north from
that river, while those to the north, to the Greenville treaty line, are termed "entire" ranges and begin with number one immediately north of "fractional" range two.

Why Judge Symmes began with "entire" range
number one so far north of the Ohio river, which was
the southern base of his purchase, is not now known.
The understanding, however, is that these two
southern ranges, or, rather, parts of ranges, were
called "fractional range one," and "fractional range
two," because the Ohio river, which forms the
southern boundary of the tract purchased by Judge
Symmes, cuts, or indents, from the south, into each
of the two so called "fractional" ranges; and, therefore, since neither extends six full miles from that
river, they were designated as "fractional" ranges

to distinguish them from the "entire" ranges with which such southern base, or river, did not so interfere.

The balance of the land between the Miami rivers, the Ludlow line and the Greenville treaty line lying north of that purchased by Judge Symmes was subdivided in 1802 into ranges, townships and sections by the surveyor general under the acts of March 2, 1799 and May 10, 1800. [4]   In doing so he had his deputy, Israel Ludlow, survey a line from the source of the Little Miami river to that of the Scioto, since known as the "Ludlow Line," to determine the division between this tract and that reserved by Virginia, [5] and subdivided all to the west of that line and south of the Greenville treaty line, into townships, ranges and sections.   He continued to number the townships east from the Great Miami river, the ranges north from Judge Symmes' tract, and the sections by beginning in the southeast corner as required by the land ordinance of 1785, in all respects as was begun by Judge Symmes, notwithstanding the act of 1796. [3]   This latter act, however, excepted from its application all lands "appropriated for satisfying military land warrants, and for other purposes."   As all this tract to the Greenville treaty

(4)   3 L. U. S., 264, 385; 2 U. S. S. L., 73.   (8)   67 L. O., 17.
(5)   See The Virginia Military Tract.   (7)   15 U. S. S. L., 39.
(6)   1 L. U. S., 497, note; 2 L. U. S., 270; 1 U. S. S. L., 251;
        9 Wheaton, 469; 22 U. S. S. C. R., 137.

line had been set aside prior to 1796, to be used to comply with the terms of the contract with Judge Symmes, [6] it was, of course, excluded from the act of that year and permitted to be subdivided according to the land ordinance of 1785.

A number of islands in the Great Miami river evidently were not considered to have been included in the patents issued by the government.   Accordingly, Congress in 1868, [7] passed an act permitting the persons actually and exclusively occupying these islands to enter them at $2.50 per acre and receive a patent, if proof and application were made within one year; while the legislature of Ohio, in 1870, [8] provided that such occupants, their heirs or assigns, might receive a deed from the state upon making proof to the auditor of state within six months and paying $7.50 per acre.

CHAPTER 24

THE SYMMES PURCHASE

Like Robert Morris and other patriotic men of means, Judge John Cleves Symmes contributed liberally of his private resources to the support of the Continental army under Washington while on its retreat thru New Jersey. Washington gave him certificates of indebtedness for the amount thus contributed; but as the country was bankrupt Judge Symmes still held the claims in 1787, when the proposition of the Ohio Company to buy land in Ohio with army bounty warrants suggested that he do likewise with his certificates of indebtedness.

In the summer of 1786, Benjamin Stites, a friend of Judge Symmes, spent some time at Limestone, now Maysville, Kentucky, when several of his horses were stolen by the Indians. Stites led a party in pursuit across the Ohio river, and up between the Miamis, as far north as the present site of Xenia, but without overtaking the Indians or recovering his horses. He was so impressed, however, with the fertility of the soil and the desirableness of the land for settlement that he returned home sooner than he had intended and enthusiastically told his acquaintances of the possibilities of the country between the Miami rivers, and of his desire to settle upon it. Judge Symmes became much interested in the territory and induced a number of his friends to join him in its purchase. To advertise the project and induce others to become interested, Judge Symmes issued a prospectus in pamphlet form, entitled "Terms of Sale and Settlement of the Miami Lands," setting forth the advantages of the land and a plan by which it could be purchased. [1]

As the plan of the Ohio Company to purchase land, which had just been acted upon by the Continental Congress, appealed to them, Judge Symmes on behalf of himself and associates proposed to that body, in August, 1787, [2] to buy all the land between the two Miami rivers, lying south of the west prolongation of the north line of the tract to be purchased by the Ohio Company, upon the same terms and conditions granted that company, except that one township only, should be assigned for the benefit of an academy. As evidence of good faith they paid into the treasury $82,000.00. At that time no survey of this territory had been made, and, of course,

(1) 12 O. L. R., 577, 588; 13 O. L. R., 501; 5 Arch., 156;
     1 Howe, 746.   (2) 1 L. U. S., 494.

there were no means of knowing how much land this general boundary would include.   It was estimated, however, to be about two million acres, and Judge Symmes, assuming he would get that amount, acted accordingly.

After making the proposition, and without awaiting its acceptance, Judge Symmes, anxious to prepare the land for settlement, immediately began his journey to visit his purchase.   Congress, mis-

SYMMES PURCHASE

taking his zeal, assumed that he intended to obtain
possession of the land and then ignore its rights.
Accordingly a resolution was passed, ordering
Colonel Harmar, then located near Pittsburg, to dis-
possess him, if necessary; that the expenses of such
action be paid out of the money advanced by Judge
Symmes and the balance returned to him.   Two of
his associates were members of that body, and they
made such explanation of Judge Symmes' action as
to satisfy Congress that his intentions were not improper and the resolution was withdrawn. Congress,
therefore, did nothing with the proposition until
October 2, 1787, when it directed the board of treasury to contract with Judge Symmes and his associates for the land, which ever since has been known
as the "Symmes Purchase" or the "Miami Purchase." [3]

Meanwhile a messenger had been dispatched after Judge Symmes and he was informed of the effect
of his hasty action.   Whereupon he gave General
Jonathan Dayton and Daniel Marsh, two of his associates, power of attorney to act for him in all respects and to complete the contract in such manner
and upon such terms as they might deem proper.   He
then continued his journey.

The contract, [4] however, was not made until

(3)   1 L. U. S., 495, note.
(4)   Hamilton County Deed Book v-2, page 57.

October 15, 1788, when the tract of land was described as consisting of but one million acres lying east of
the Great Miami river, and extending only twenty
miles from the mouth of that river as measured by
the meanders of the Ohio.   Sections 16 were reserved for school, 29 for religion, and 8, 11 and 26 for
the future disposition of congress, but no provision
was made for the reservation of land for an academy
or college.

It was impossible to determine the eastern
boundary of a tract of which one side was a line so
irregular as the Great Miami river, especially when
it was further complicated by an uncertain and vague
base of twenty miles measured with the meanders of
the Ohio river, and also when the latter river was
not at right angles with the former.   Besides, such
limitations were not a part of the original proposition made by Judge Symmes and he could not har-
monize them with his understanding of what should
have been provided.   He, therefore, ignored that
part of the contract and proceeded to survey and sell
all the land between the two Miami rivers.

No surveys had been made prior to 1792 determining the north boundary of the land which Judge
Symmes and his associates had contracted to purchase, and it was feared their claims might conflict
with that of the Indians, who, in the treaty of Fort
Harmar, January 9, 1789, [5] had surrendered their

rights to all land lying south of the line subsequently adopted at Greenville. Congress, therefore, April 12, 1792, [6] passed an act altering the contract so as to include all the land lying between the Great and the Little Miami rivers and extending only so far north as to contain one million acres, provided it did not interfere with the boundary line established by the treaty of Fort Harmar.

Since the tract was thus limited, in its east and west boundaries, by the two Miami rivers, it could not, of course, extend farther north than the source of either river. That of the Little Miami was the most southern, and, consequently, its source marked the northern boundary of the tract. To determine the quantity of land, Israel Ludlow surveyed a line, since known as "Ludlow's Survey," from the source of the Little Miami river, due west, through range eight, to the Great Miami, when it was ascertained that less than six hundred thousand acres were included in the contract as thus modified.

Judge Symmes promptly released all claims to any land north of that boundary [7] and Congress, by act of May 5, 1792, [8] authorized the president to execute letters patent to him and his associates and their heirs and assigns in fee simple for such number

(5)   1 L. U. S., 393; 7 U. S. S. L., 28.
(6)   2 L. U. S. 270; 6 U. S. S. L. 7.
(7)   1 L. U. S., 495.   (8)   2 L. U. S., 287; 1 U. S. S. L., 266.

of acres as the amount paid by them under their contract of October 15, 1788, would pay for at two-thirds
of a dollar per acre, including one complete township
of land in trust for the use of an academy according
to the resolution of October 2, 1787, [3] and making
the reservations specified in the contract. The president was authorized also to convey to them so much
of another tract of 106,857 acres as they should pay
for with army bounty warrants according to the
resolutions of Congress of July 23, [9] and October 2,
1787, [3] delivered to the secretary of the treasury
within six months.   All these tracts, however, were
to be located within such boundaries as the president
might judge expedient, and according to the act of
April 12, 1792. [6]

As the tract purchased by Judge Symmes and
his associates was allowed a reduction of one-third
for bad lands, (a privilege permitted in no other
sales than of the two tracts sold to the Ohio Company
of associates,) [10] they received one and one-half
acres of land for each acre of army bounty warrants
delivered.

Certificates of indebtedness and army bounty
warrants for rights to land to the face value of $165,-
693.42, were paid into the treasury, and President
Washington, September 13, 1794, executed a patent
[11] to Judge Symmes and his associates, and con-

(9)   1 L. U. S., 573.   (10)   1 L. U. S., 456.

veyed to him and them, and to his and their heirs and assigns, 248,540 acres of land, which, together with sections sixteen reserved for schools, twenty-nine for religion, one complete township of six miles square for an academy, fifteen acres for Fort Washington, one mile square to be located at or near the mouth of the Great Miami river and sections eight, eleven and twenty-six reserved for the future disposition of Congress, constituted a tract containing in all 311,682 acres, located in Hamilton, Butler and Warren counties. And of the 248,540 acres thus received, 105,683 acres were paid for by $70,455.00 in public securities, paid in 1788, and 142,857 acres with military warrants reckoned to be worth one dollar an acre.

The north boundary of the tract was to be surveyed and located, within five years after the date of the patent, by Judge Symmes and his associates at their expense, but governed, however, by the surveys of the two Miami rivers as certified to the treasury March 24, 1794, by Israel Ludlow. [12] This north boundary line is the north line of the third "entire" range, and is about one and one-half miles north of the city of Lebanon.

Judge Symmes disregarded the eastern limits of the tract as provided in the contract of October 15,

(11)   For copy, see 1 L. U. S., 497; Hamilton county Deed Book S, 203.   (12)   1 L. U. S., 497.
(13)   1 U. S. S. L., 728; 3 L. U. S. 264, 428, 502, 554, 599, 600; 2 U. S. S. L., 112, 179, 236.

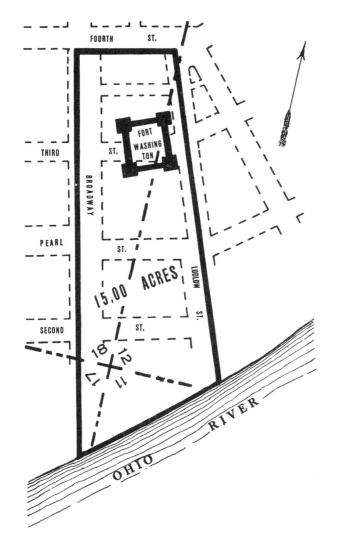

FOURTH ST.

THIRD

BROADWAY

PEARL

ST.

SECOND ST.

FORT WASHINGTON

ST.

15,00 ACRES

LUDLOW ST.

18 12 17 11

OHIO RIVER

FORT WASHINGTON

1788, and also contracted to sell land lying north of the line to which he was able ultimately to buy. His contract was modified, accordingly, several times, but Congress, finally tiring of his conduct, refused him further aid; but, instead, permitted those who had bought land of him beyond the limits of his tract to buy it directly of the government at the rate of two dollars per acre. [13]

The territory between the Miami rivers, used as a passage way by the Indians to the north and the early settlers in Kentucky, had been the scene of so many bloody conflicts that it was termed the "Miami Slaughter House," [1] To protect the settlers on the Symmes tract a detachment of troops from Fort Harmar landed in 1789, on the present site of Cincinnati, built a fort and named it Fort Washington. [14] When selling the land to Judge Symmes, the government reserved fifteen acres surrounding the fort. [15] Abandoning the fort later, Congress, in 1806, directed the secretary of the treasury to subdivide this tract into town-lots, streets and avenues in such manner as he might judge proper, conforming as nearly as possible to the original plan of the town, and that the register of the land office at Cincinnati should sell the lots at public sale. [16]

The residence of Judge Symmes, at North

(15) 1 L. U. S., 495, 497; 2 L. U. S., 270, 287; 1 U. S. S. L., 251, 266.   (14) 3 Arch., 303.
(16) 4 L. U. S., 6; 2 U. S. S. L., 352.   (19) 21 L. O. L., 13.
(17) 9 L. O., 6. (18) 12 L. O. 31; 13 L. O. 33; 19 L. O. 145.

Bend, was burned in 1810, and virtually all the original field notes of the survey of the lands purchased
by himself and associates were destroyed. Thereupon the legislature, in 1811, authorized the record-
ers of Hamilton, Butler and Warren counties, to record such notes pertaining to the land in their
respective counties, as were then possible to obtain. [17] In 1814, the legislature appointed a committee of three persons, one from each of the
counties of Hamilton, Butler and Warren, to collect
all copies possible of the field notes of the original
survey of the Symmes Purchase, and, after being
satisfied of their genuineness, to have them recorded
in the respective counties in which the land to which
the notes might relate, should lie. [18] Again in 1822,
the legislature appointed a committee of three, one
from each of the counties, to "procure, if in their
power, the original terms of sale and settlement of
the Miami lands as published by John Cleves
Symmes at Trenton, in 1787, and also the original
books of entries kept by the register of the Miami
land office in which are entered the locations or entries of lands sold, and the applications and grants
of forfeiture," and to have copies of such as they
might obtain, recorded in each county. [19] The
record of these field notes, or papers, thus recorded,
or duly certified copies of them, are admissible as
evidence in all courts where the original would have
been legal evidence.

CHAPTER 25

MIAMI UNIVERSITY LANDS

The second sale of public lands was made in 1787 to Judge John Cleves Symmes and associates of that lying between the two Miami rivers. But as the amount was estimated to be less than that acquired by the Ohio company, one township only was to be assigned for the benefit of an academy [1]. October 2 of that year congress directed the Board of Treasury "to take order thereon" [2], but in the contract entered into October 15, 1788 [3], no reservation nor promise of land for an academy was made. Later, however, such provision was inserted, and by the act of May 5, 1792 [4], the president was authorized to convey to Judge Symmes and his associates, their heirs and assigns, one complete township in trust for establishing an academy and other public schools

(1) L. U. S. 494.   (2) 12 Journal of Congress, 150.
(3) Hamilton County Deed Book V-2, page 57.
(4) 2 L. U. S. 287; 1 U. S. S. L. 266.

and seminaries of learning, conformably to the order of congress of October 2, 1787. Whereupon, September 13, 1794 [5], President Washington conveyed to Judge Symmes and his associates, 311,682 acres, and declared one complete township of six square miles, located, with the approbation of the territorial governor within five years, as nearly as may be in the center of the tract, to be held in trust for erecting and establishing therein an academy and other public schools and seminaries of learning, and endowing and supporting the same, and for no other use, intent or purpose.

The third township of the first entire range was first selected by Judge Symmes who marked it upon his map as the College township, which he reserved for that purpose till he learned his agents, Marsh and Dayton, had contracted to reduce the amount of land to be purchased and abandon the right to a college township, when he placed the land in this township on sale, and by 1799 he had sold thirty one sections. However, when he learned a township was to be so used, he requested Governor St. Clair to approve the second township of the second fractional range, but as half of it had been sold to Elias Bodinot, this township could not be applied to that purpose.

The territorial legislature, in 1799, instructed

(5)   1 L. U. S. 497;   Hamilton County Deed Book s, page 203.

its delegate in congress to endeavor to secure the remaining portion of township three of the first entire range, and thirty-one sections west of the Miami river and outside of the purchase, while the constitutional convention held in Chillicothe in 1802 [6] requested congress to set aside a sufficient number of sections 8, 11 and 26 within the purchase, reserved by congress, to make out one whole township for the use of an academy, instead of one entire township, as originally intended. Accordingly, March 3, 1803 [7] congress directed that so much of any one complete township, within the Cincinnati land district as then remained unsold, together with as many adjoining sections as may have been sold therefrom, so as to make thirty-six sections, located by the legislature before October 1, 1803, be vested in the legislature of Ohio for the purpose of establishing an academy, in lieu of the township granted for that purpose to John Cleves Symmes and associates, provided such lands should revert to the United States if, within five years, a township should have been secured for that purpose within the lands patented to Judge Symmes.

Accordingly, in April of 1803 [8], the legislature accepted the offer and appointed a commission of three to locate and register the land. This commis-

---

(6)   21 L. O. 44.   (8)   1 L. O. 66.
(7)   3 L. U. S. 541; 2 U. S. S. L. 225.

sion, after selecting all of town 5, range 1, except
section 25 and the west halves of sections 11, 14, and
24, in lieu of which, sections 30 and 31 of town 5,
range 2, and the west half of section 6 of town 4,
range 2, were selected, containing in all 23,321.68
acres, entered the same, September 1, 1803, with the
register of the Cincinnati land office   And upon
the report of the register to the land department,
such lands were segregated from further disposi-

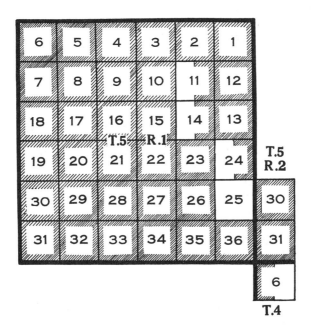

MIAMI UNIVERSITY LANDS

tion. This selection was approved by the legislature in December following [10].

The college was established as the Miami University by the act of February 17, 1809 [11] which created "The president and trustees of the Miami University," a corporation, and provided that all deeds and instruments signed, sealed and delivered by the treasurer, in their corporate name by their order, should be considered as its deed and act. This act vested the lands in that corporation and their successors forever, for the sole use, benefit and support of the university, with full power and authority to subdivide and lease the same in tracts of not less than eighty acres nor more than one hundred and sixty, for ninety-nine years, renewable forever, subject to a valuation every fifteen years, but which revaluation was repealed by the act of 1810 [12]. It was also provided that the land should be offered at public auction for not less than two dollars per acre on which the lessees, except incorporated churches [13], should pay six per cent. per annum, and enjoy all rights as if held in fee simple which, after 1837 [14], descended to their heirs.

Three commissions were appointed [11] to meet in Lebanon in June of 1809 and, if possible, to locate the university within the Symmes purchase. One

(10)   The original report or a copy of it can not be found.
(11)   7 L. O. 184.   (13)   45 L. O. L. 85.
(12)   8 L. O. 94.   (14)   35 L. O. L. 303.

member of this committee being sick, the other two acted, and recommended that the university be located on the western side of Lebanon. However, deeming the institution would best serve its purpose if located upon the land already accepted, the legislature in 1810 [12] directed the trustees to lay out a town by the name of Oxford on the lands selected, and thereby located the university within the bounds of such lands.

In 1837 [14] the trustees were authorized to grant leases for the undisposed and reverted lands in such tracts as they might deem best, and to proportion the rent to be paid, while the act of 1862 [15] permitted the lessees themselves to proportion the rent to be paid by each.

The selection of these lands for the use of the academy deprived the township of section 16 for the use of schools. In lieu thereof, congress in 1839 [16] authorized the township trustees to select land elsewhere. Accordingly there were selected for that purpose the north half of section 23, town 6, south, range 4, east, in St. Marys township, Auglaize county; the northeast quarter of section 25, town 3, north, range 3, east, in Emerald township, Paulding county, and the division of the south half of section 19, lying west of the river, in town 3, north, range 4, east, in Auglaize township, Paulding county.

(15)   59 L. O. 125. (16)   9 L. U. S. 1057;   6 U. S. S. L. 773.

CHAPTER 26

THE MICHIGAN SURVEY.

A strip of land in the extreme northwest corner of Ohio, about seven miles in width, north and south, by about seventy-five miles in length, east and west, is a part of a tract of land composing all of Michigan subdivided from one meridian and one base line and is known as "The Michigan Survey."

The extension of the Michigan survey into Ohio was the result of the contending claims of Ohio and Michigan as to the location of the line separating those states; Ohio claimed to its present boundary, while Michigan claimed south to the south line of the Michigan survey. The cause of this controversy had its origin in the ordinance of 1787, when it was provided that "if Congress shall hereafter find it expedient, they shall have authority to form one or two states in that part of the said territory which lies north of an east and west line drawn through the southerly bend or extreme of Lake Michigan." [1]

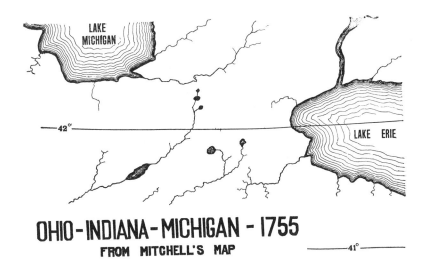

OHIO-INDIANA-MICHIGAN - 1755
FROM MITCHELL'S MAP

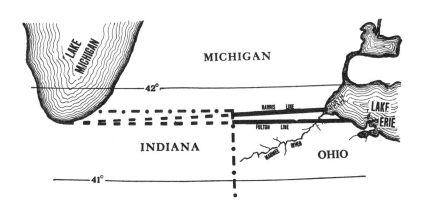

OHIO-INDIANA-MICHIGAN - 1836

At this time the topography of this country was little known, and definite maps were not to be had. A map made, in 1755, by John Mitchell, of Virginia, was then considered the most reliable. It was copied extensively by other map makers, and used by congress when planning legislation for the western territory. Mitchell's map indicated "the southerly bend or extreme of Lake Michigan" to be at a latitude north of Lake Erie, and, consequently, it was assumed that a due east line from such "southerly bend or extreme of Lake Michigan" would intersect Lake Erie, north of its western extremity.

The act of 1802, enabling Ohio to become a state, defined its north boundary to be "an east and west line drawn through the southerly extreme of Lake Michigan, running east until it shall intersect Lake Erie." [2] However, while the constitutional convention was in session, the accuracy of the maps was doubted, and question arose as to what point on Lake Erie a line east from the southern extremity of Lake Michigan would strike. Therefore, since all maps, then known, indicated that such line would strike north of the western extremity of Lake Erie, and feeling that the new state should include such western extremity, that convention provided in the constitution that "if the southerly bend or extreme of Lake Michigan should extend so far south, that a

(1) 1 L. U. S., 475.

line drawn due east from it should not intersect Lake Erie east of the mouth of the Miami river of the Lake, then with the assent of congress, the northern boundary of this state shall be established by, and extend to, a direct line running from the southern extremity of Lake Michigan to the most northerly cape of the Miami Bay." [3] In 1803, Congress approved the constitution and admitted Ohio into the union without determining its northern boundary. [4]

Ohio, however, was not content to allow the location of such boundary line to remain in doubt, and from 1807 to 1811, the legislature passed several resolutions requesting congress to determine the matter. [5] Accordingly, in May of 1812, the surveyor general was directed to survey and mark "so much of the boundary line as runs from the southerly extreme of lake Michigan to lake Erie, particularly noting the place where the said line intersects the margin of said lake," and to return a plat of it to congress. [6] But on account of the hostilities of the Indians and the war with Great Britain, arrangements to make the survey were not made until the fall of 1816 when William Harris was employed to do so. Mr. Harris, acting under the interpretation of its location as given by the constitution of Ohio, sur-

(2)   3 L. U. S., 496; 2 U. S. S. L., 173.
(3)   Section 6, Article 7; 18 L. O. L., 151.
(4)   3 L. U. S. 524; 2 U. S. S. L. 201.
(5)   5 L. O., 143; 7 L. O., 225; 10 L. O., 191.
(6)   4 L. U. S., 434; 2 U. S. S. L., 74.

veyed and located, in June and July of 1817, the boundary line as running from a willow tree eleven inches in diameter, on the north cape of the Maumee bay, south 87° 42' west, directly toward the southern extremity of Lake Michigan, until it intersected the line between Ohio and Indiana; and which line, as thus established has been repeatedly affirmed by the Ohio legislature. [7]

Upon learning the result of this survey, Governor Cass of Michigan protested, claimed the line should have been surveyed due east from the southern bend of Lake Michigan, as stated in the ordinance of 1787, [1] and prevailed upon President Monroe to direct a survey of the line to be made in that manner.   John A. Fulton was engaged to make the survey and, in 1818, located a line running east from the southern bend of Lake Michigan.

While plats of both surveys were transmitted to congress, in 1820, that body affirmed neither, and took no action in the matter until 1832, when the president was directed to ascertain the latitudes and longitudes of, "the southerly extreme of Lake Michigan; the point on the Miami of the Lake, which is due east therefrom; the most northerly cape of the Miami bay; the most southerly point in the northern boundary line of the United States in Lake Erie and

(7)   16 L. O. 205; 18 L. O. L. 151; 24 L. O. 97; 29 L. O. L. 257; 33 L. O. L. 446; 33 L. O. 2d session, 3; 107 L. O. 776.

THE MICHIGAN SURVEY

(IN OHIO)

the points at which a direct line drawn from the southerly extreme of Lake Michigan to the most southerly point in said northern boundary line of the United States, will intersect the Miami river and bay." [8]

The controversy between Ohio and the territory of Michigan over this intervening strip, led to the "Michigan War." In March of 1835, Governor Mason of Michigan sent twelve hundred troops to Toledo, while Governor Lucas of Ohio sent six hundred to occupy Perrysburg, with ten thousand in reserve. President Jackson removed Governor Mason from office and established a truce until congress could take action.

Meanwhile Michigan endeavored to gain admission into the union, but, claiming territory to the line running due east from the southern extremity of Lake Michigan, according to the ordinance of 1787, was opposed by Ohio. As Ohio had electorial votes and Michigan, being a territory, had none, the application of Michigan assumed political significance, and it was said that "everybody courted Ohio." Besides, the claim of Michigan likewise affected Indiana, and, perhaps, Illinois, and those states sided with Ohio in opposition to the admission of Michigan.

Finally, in 1836, a compromise was effected and Michigan was given some nine thousand square miles

(8)   8 L. U. S., 705.

north of Lake Michigan for the territory of less than one thousand square miles taken by Indiana, and by Ohio between the Harris and the Fulton lines. The bill pending for the admission of Michigan and that establishing the boundary line between that state and Ohio were united, Michigan was admitted as a state, and "a direct line drawn from the southern extremity of Lake Michigan, to the most northerly cape of the Maumee (Miami) bay," as surveyed by Harris, was established as the boundary line between those states. [9]

The Harris line, running obliquely through the land already subdivided as part of the Michigan survey, of course, ignored all lines and ran through the sections. Sixty-six miles of this line, extending from the Indiana line east for eleven townships, were resurveyed and relocated in 1837, and the remaining four miles in the ninth township of the eighth range were resurveyed and relocated in 1842. In 1915 the entire line was resurveyed and relocated and marked with seventy-one large granite posts set in beds of concrete, by a joint commission of the two states. [10]

(9)   9 L. U. S., 376, 391; 5 U. S. S. L., 49, 56; 33 L. O. L., 92, 437, 446; 19 O. R., 239; 20 O. R., 283.
(10)   See "The Ohio-Michigan Boundary," by Professor C. E. Sherman of the Ohio State University.

CHAPTER 27

THE TWELVE MILES SQUARE RESERVE.

The first fortification built within the state of Ohio by white people was "Fort Miami," established in 1680 by Frontenac, the French Governor of Canada on the west bank of the Maumee river, then called the "Miami of the Lake." It was used as a military trading post by the French but a short time and then abandoned for a location farther within the Indian country. The fort was not rebuilt nor occupied again until 1785 when it was taken possession of by the British and held by them until the Indian treaty of 1795. The British came into possession of it again during the war of 1812, and, at the close of that war it fell into the hands of the United States, which soon abandoned it as a military post.

The military occupation of this fort, situated so advantageously in the heart of the Indian country,

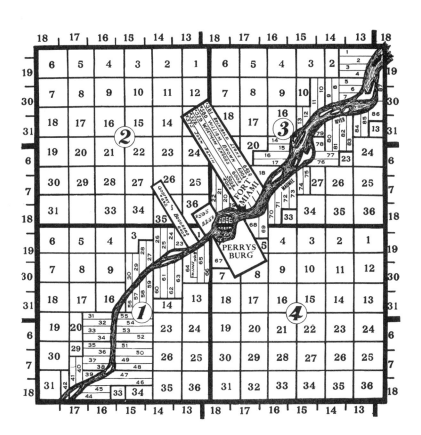

TWELVE MILES SQUARE RESERVE

was considered of such strategic importance that the United States, when concluding the Greenville treaty acquired the Indian title to "one piece of land twelve miles square" surrounding the fort. [1] This tract is located in Wood and Lucas counties, between which it is equally divided by the Maumee river, and has been the scene of much that is historically interesting. Within its limits many battles have been fought with the Indians as well as also between the white men themselves. Near this fort and within the reserve General Wayne fought the decisive battle of "Fallen Timbers," defeated the Indians and brought about the treaty of Greenville.

During the alternate occupations of this part of the country by the French and the English many white persons settled near the fort which afforded them protection. When the United States acquired the reserve, it was desired to give these occupants titles to the lands they had settled upon, and also to provide for the sale of the balance of the tract. It became necessary, therefore, to subdivide it into tracts suitable to meet these requirements. That all should be treated justly, Congress, in 1805, [2] provided that any person claiming any part of such land under legal grants derived from the French or the British governments, by virtue of actual posses-

(1) 1 L. U. S., 398; 7 U. S. S. L., 49.
(2) 3 L. U. S., 596, 670; 2 U. S. S. L., 277, 343.

sion and improvement, or for any other account whatever, should file with the register of the land office at Detroit by November 1, 1805, a statement of the nature and extent of his claim together with a plat of the tract claimed, and also any grant, order of survey, deed, conveyance or other written evidence. The register and the receiver of public moneys of that land office were constituted commissioners to pass upon the claims and report their findings to the secretary of the treasury.

In 1807, [3] Congress confirmed the report of these commissioners and directed that every person in the actual possession of any tract of land, in his own right, and settled, occupied and improved by him prior to the first day of July, 1796, or by some other person under whom he claimed the right to its occupancy or possession, should be confirmed in his title as an estate of inheritance in fee simple, and be entitled to a patent for it in the manner provided by law for the other lands of the United States.

In compliance with the acts of 1804, [4] and 1805, [5] deputy surveyor Elias Glover, in the latter year, made a partial survey of the tract and subdivided it into four townships of six miles square each. The southwest township was designated number one, the

(3)   4 L. U. S., 109; 2 U. S. S. L., 437.
(4)   3 L. U. S., 596; 2 U. S. S. L., 277.
(5)   3 L. U. S., 670; 2 U. S. S. L., 343.

northwest number two, the northeast number three and the southeast number four. The tract contains no ranges and is denominated by townships only; and, being an original survey, it is known as "The Twelve Miles Square Reserve."

Each township was subdivided into thirty-six mile square lots, or sections. The sections were numbered from one to thirty-six by beginning in the northeast corner of the township and numbering west, etc., as provided by the act of 1796, [6] except that part occupied by the settlers under the French or British, and the sections bordering along the river. Under the act of 1816, [7] Joseph Wampler surveyed the north and the east boundaries and subdivided the sections adjoining the river into tracts approximating 160 acres each. These were numbered from one to ninety-three and were termed "River Tracts"; while the parts of sections not used for river tracts were termed "Fractional Sections." The boundaries of the private claims were surveyed, in 1817, by deputy surveyor, S. Carpenter. And in 1819 the legislature directed the auditor to obtain from the surveyor general a plat of all private grants of land and the time when they were granted. [16]

By the act of Congress of 1816, [7] section six-

---

(6)   2 L. U. S., 533; 1 U. S. S. L., 464.
(7)   6 L. U. S., 121; 3 U. S. S. L., 319; 23 L. O. 33; 43 L. O. L.,
        433.   (16)   18 L. O. L. 145.

teen in each township was reserved for the benefit of schools within the township. Many special acts of the legislature, however, have been passed affecting these sections.

In 1835, [8] section sixteen in township one was directed to be subdivided into forty and eighty acre lots, appraised and sold at public sale by the auditor of Wood county, who should certify such proceedings to the auditor of state when deeds would be given as provided by the act of 1827. [9] The act of 1835, however, erroneously designated township three instead of township one, and was corrected in 1836, [10] Meanwhile several lots in township one had been sold before the error was discovered. To correct such error the purchasers of lots Nos. 1, 2, 3 and 9 of section 16 in that township, reconveyed them to the state; [11] while the treasurer of Wood county was directed to bid off in the name of the state, such lots in that section as might be offered for sale under decree of the Lucas county court. [12]

Under the act of 1840, the auditor of Lucas county was authorized to sell section sixteen in township two, at public sale, in half quarter sections, and, upon sale, to execute and deliver deeds to the purchasers. [13]

(8)   33 L. O. L., 206.   (10)   34 L. O. L., 152.
(9)   25 L. O., 56.   (12)   43 L. O. L., 176.
(11) 42 L. O. L., 99; 43 L. O. L., 66.

In 1841, the auditor of Lucas county was directed to sell section sixteen in township three, at public
sale, in half quarter sections and certify the sales to
the auditor of state when deeds were to be made as
provided by the act of 1827 [9]; while the commissioners of that county were permitted to select two
half quarter sections upon which they had erected a
county poor house, at the average price at which the
balance of the section should sell. [14]

CHAPTER 28

THE TWO MILES SQUARE RESERVE.

One piece of land two miles square at the lower rapids of the Sandusky river was ceded by the Indians to the United States by the Greenville treaty, [1] and has since been known as "The Two Miles Square Reserve." It is located at Fremont in the central part of Sandusky county, in townships four and five, north, of the fifteenth range east of the first principal meridian.

This tract came into prominence during the war of 1812 when Fort Stephenson built within it on the west bank of the river, was successfully defended by Colonel George Croghan and a garrison of but two hundred men against five hundred British and eight hundred Indians under General Proctor. Colonel Croghan was rewarded by promotion and given much praise, especially by the people of Chillicothe who presented him an elegant sword.

(1)   1 L. U. S., 398; 7 U. S. S. L., 49.

A town was laid out on the east bank of the river
and named "Croghanville" in honor of Colonel
Croghan. It was incorporated Lower Sandusky, in
1829, by the legislature [7], and in 1848 that name
was changed by court procedure to Fremont.

While the reserve is but a small part of all the
land in Ohio, it is, nevertheless, an original survey
and is subdivided upon a plan independent of that
used in the subdivision of the surrounding land. It
has neither townships nor ranges. It was originally
subdivided in 1807, by William Ewing, under the act
of 1805, [2] into four sections which were numbered
from one to four by beginning with number one in
the northeast corner and numbering around to the
left, as the quarter townships are numbered in the
United States military tract; while Joseph Wampler,
in 1816, in compliance with the act of that year, [3]
resurveyed the exterior lines, laid off three hundred
and ten inlots and sixty-three out-lots for the town
of Croghanville, and set off two "Public Reserves" of
one quarter section each. He also divided the island
in section number one into two equal parts, and subdivided the balance of the reserve into twenty-two
"Fractional Sections," having one front on the river,
and containing as nearly as possible, eighty acres
each. None of the subdivisions included the bed of

(2)   3 L. U. S., 670; 3 U. S. S. L., 343.   (7)   27 L. O. L. 83.
(3)   6 L. U. S., 101; 3 U. S. S. L., 308; 23 L. O., 33; 43 L. O. L.,
      433   (4)   16 U. S. S. L. 230.

the river, which, however, was relinquished to the
city of Fremont in 1870. [4] The lots and fractional
sections were directed to be sold at public auction by
the register of the land office at Wooster, provided,
however, that none of the inlots should be sold for
less than $20.00, the outlots for less than $5.00 per
acre, or the fractional sections for less than $2.00

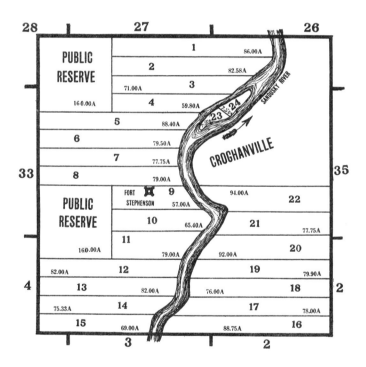

TWO MILES SQUARE RESERVE

per acre; and that such as may not have been sold within seven days, were to be disposed of at private sale by the register of that office, according to the provisions for the sale of other public lands.

The secretary of the treasury, under authority of the act of 1816, [3] selected inlots numbered 163, 165, 167, 169, 171, 173, 175, 177 and 179, and outlots numbered 10 and 11 in Croghanville for the benefit of the schools within the reserve; [5] and the auditor of Sandusky county was authorized to sell them by special acts of the legislature. [6]

(5)   L. L. O., 161.
(6)   31 L. O. L., 32; 32 L. O. L., 325.

CHAPTER 29

MISCELLANEOUS SURVEYS.

One section of land containing six hundred and forty acres on the Sandusky river, laid off in a square form and including his improvements, was given to Horonu, or the Cherokee Boy, a Wyandot chief, by the treaty of 1817. [1] This land is located in Wyandot county in town one, south, range fourteen east of the first principal meridian. Horonu conveyed one quarter of the section, containing 160 acres, to James Whitaker, and the sale was confirmed by the president. Horonu died in March, 1826, and devised the remaining three quarters of the section of land to Sooharress, or Isaac Williams and Squeendehtee, who were his nearest kin. By the treaty of 1842 this remainder was to be sold by the President of the United States and the net proceeds paid to the devisees. [2]

(1)   6 L. U. S., 709, 723; 7 U. S. S. L., 160, 178.
(2)   10 L. U. S., 950; 11 U. S. S. L., 581.

Jean Bapt. Richardville, principal chief of the Miami nation of Indians, was granted several tracts of land by the treaty of 1818. [3] One of these consisted of "two sections on the twenty-seven mile creek where the road from St. Mary's to Fort Wayne crosses it, being one section on each side of said creek," and for which President Monroe issued a patent, March 21, 1823. [13]

This tract, as thus conveyed, did not correspond with any two sections as originally surveyed, but, instead, was a tract eighty chains, east and west, by one hundred and sixty chains, north and south, one part of which was in township three, south, of range one east of the first principal meridian, in the southwestern part of Van Wert county, Ohio, and the other in township twenty-seven, north, of range fifteen east of the second principal meridian, in Adams county, Indiana. However, all the tract was merged into and became parts of the sections into which the respective townships were subdivided, except the northeast quarter.

———

The United States, by the treaty with the Miami Nation of Indians, in 1818, [3] granted to Peter Labadie one section of land lying south of the St. Mary's river in townships three and four, south, of

(3) 6 L. U. S., 728; 7 U. S. S. L., 118.
(13) Van Wert County Deed Book 74, page 327.

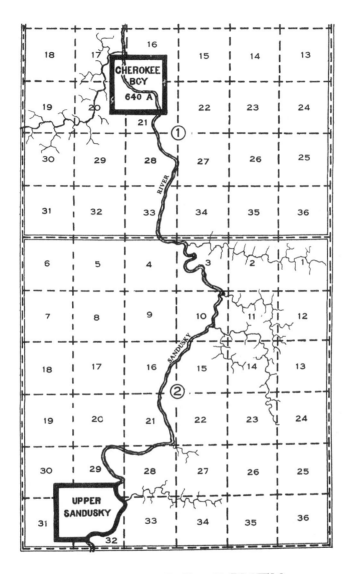

TOWNS 1,2, SOUTH
RANGE 14 EAST
OF
THE FIRST PRINCIPAL MERIDIAN

range one east of the first principal meridian. Part of this tract is in Van Wert county and part in Mercer.

———

By the treaty with the Miami Nation of Indians, in 1818, [3] Charley, a Miami chief, was given one section of land which was located in townships four, south, in ranges one and two east of the first principal meridian. It lies south of the St. Mary's river in the north part of Mercer county.

———

Black Loon Crescent is the name of a survey on the St. Mary's river, in the north part of Mercer county, of two sections of land in the northwest corner of town four, south, of range two east of the first principal meridian. It was granted to Wemetche (Pemetche) or the Crescent, by the treaty of 1818 with the Miami Nation of Indians. [3]

———

For some years prior to the war of 1812, several friendly Indians had their lodges on the south bank of the St. Mary's river, near the site of the Indian village of "Oldtown," in Dublin township, Mercer county, and in the fourth township, south, of the second range east of the first principal meridian. For a number of years, Anthony Shane, a halfbreed Ottawa Indian, did much business as a trader at this place which became known as "Shane's Crossing."

Mr. Shane rendered such valuable services to the United States during that war that Congress, in 1815, granted him three hundred and twenty acres of land surrounding his improvements, on the south side of the St. Mary's river. (4)   By the treaty of 1817, Mr. Shane was also given six hundred and forty acres on the opposite side of the river. (1)

By the treaty with the Miami Nation of Indians, in 1818, the United States granted to Louis Godfroy six sections of land on the north side of the St. Mary's river in the north part of Mercer county, (3) and in the north part of township four, south, of range two east of the first principal meridian.

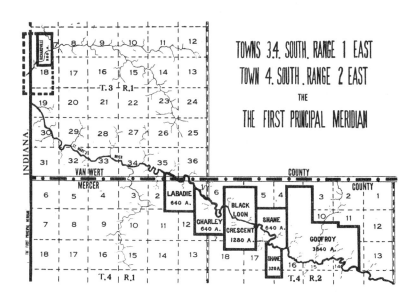

TOWNS 3.4. SOUTH. RANGE 1 EAST

TOWN 4. SOUTH. RANGE 2 EAST

THE

THE FIRST PRINCIPAL MERIDIAN

In 1786, a body of Kentuckians under General Benjamin Logan destroyed a number of Indian towns within the present bounds of Logan and Champaign counties. Among the prisoners taken to Kentucky was a Shawnee Indian lad, Spamaga-labe. He became a member of the family of the commander and was afterwards known by the name of Logan to which the prefix of captain became attached. However, he was permitted to return to his own people and eventually became a chief. He remained friendly to the Americans and fought with them in the war of 1812, when he lost his life leading an expedition into the camp of the enemy. [5] For his services the United States, by the treaty of of 1817, granted to his children six hundred and forty acres of land on the east side of the Auglaize river in town four, south, of range five east of the first principal meridian, and in the north part of Auglaize county. [1] The restrictions on the title were removed by Congress in 1881. [6]

———

In 1836, the secretary of the treasury was authorized to cause to be issued to Henry Stoddard, assignee of Nicholas Smith, assignee of Francis Dochoquet, a patent for 320 acres of land in sections 30 and 31 in township five, south, in range six

(4)   4 L. U. S., 807; 6 U. S. S. L., 149.
(5)   2 Howe, 100, 101, 102.   (6)   21 U. S. S. L., 511.

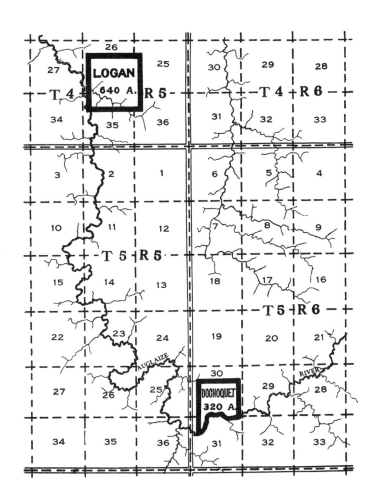

TOWNS 4,5, SOUTH, RANGE 5 EAST
TOWNS 4,5, SOUTH, RANGE 6 EAST
OF
THE FIRST PRINCIPAL MERIDIAN

east of the first principal meridian, in accordance with a grant to the chiefs of the Shawnee nation of Indians. [7]

————

James McPherson, a native of Carlisle, Pennsylvania, who had been taken prisoner by the Indians at the mouth of the Great Miami river and had since continued to live with them, was granted, by the treaty of 1817, one section of land of 640 acres, which he located at the intersection of the Roberts line with that of the Greenville treaty, in Logan county in town number seven, south, of range number nine east of the first principal meridian. [1] By the treaty of 1831, Mr. McPherson was also granted the further amount of 320 acres, which he was permitted to locate adjoining that given him by the former treaty. [8]

————

By the treaty of 1817 there was granted to Nancy Stewart, daughter of a Shawnee chief, Blue Jacket, one section of land on the Great Miami river, adjoining the Greenville treaty line, in the northwest part of Logan county. [1] Four hundred and eighty acres of this amount was located on the east side of the river and one hundred and sixty acres on the west side, in town seven, south, of range eight east of the first principal meridian.

(7) 8 L. U. S., 1087; 9 L. U. S., 397; 6 U. S. S. L., 639; 7 U. S. S. L., 355.	(8) 8 L. U. S., 1081; 7 U. S. S. L., 351

At the request of the chiefs of a mixed band of Seneca and Shawnee Indians, Henry H. McPherson, an adopted son of the band, was granted by the treaty of 1831, [8] a half section of land containing three hundred and twenty acres. This tract, together with a half section granted him, March 20, 1821, by the chiefs, constituted an entire section which he located in the northeast part of Shelby county on the Greenville treaty line in the seventh township, south, of the seventh range east of the first principal meridian.

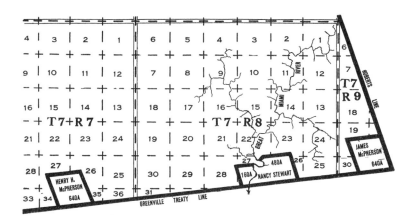

TOWNSHIPS 7, SOUTH
RANGES 7, 8, 9, EAST
OF
THE FIRST PRINCIPAL MERIDIAN

John Vanmeter was among the many white persons taken prisoner by the Wyandots. He married a Seneca woman and continued to live among the Indians. By the treaty of 1817, Vanmeter and his wife's three brothers, were granted one thousand acres, beginning north 45 degrees west, one hundred and forty poles from his house and running "thence south three hundred and twenty poles, thence and from the beginning, east, for quantity." [1] This tract is located in the southern part of Seneca county, in town one, north, of range fifteen east of the first principal meridian.

John R. Walker was the son of Catherine Walker, a Wyandot woman. He was wounded at the battle of Mauguagon (Maguaga), [9] in August, 1812, while in the service of the United States under Colonel Miller who was unsuccessfully attacked by the British under General Proctor and the Indians under Tecumseh. For his services in that battle and also because his mother was a Wyandot Indian, Walker and his mother were each given one section of land by the treaty of 1817. These two sections adjoined east and west and constituted one tract of 1,280 acres in town one, north, of range fourteen east of the first principal meridian, in Seneca county. The tract was described as beginning "at the northwest corner of the tract granted to John Vanmeter and his wife's

(9) About fourteen miles south of Detroit, Michigan.

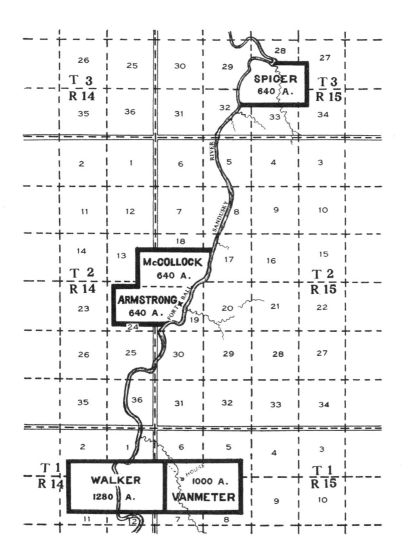

TOWNS 1,2,3, NORTH, RANGE 14 EAST
TOWNS 1,2,3, NORTH, RANGE 15 EAST
OF
THE FIRST PRINCIPAL MERIDIAN

brothers, and running with the line of that tract, south 320 poles; thence and from the beginning, west, for quantity." [1]

———

By the treaty of 1817, the United States granted to Robert Armstrong, who had been taken prisoner by the Indians and had married a Wyandot woman, six hundred and forty acres of land "on the west side of the Sandusky river, beginning at a place called Camp Ball, and running up the river, with its meanders, one hundred and sixty poles, and, from the beginning, down the river, with its meanders, one hundred and sixty poles, and from the extremity of these lines west for quantity." [1]

There was also granted, by that treaty, to the quarter blood Wyandot children of William McCollock, who was killed near Mauguagon (Maguaga) in August, 1812, six hundred and forty acres "on the west side of the Sandusky river, adjoining the lower line of the tract granted to Robert Armstrong, and extending in the same manner with and from the river." [1] These two tracts constitute one survey and are located in Seneca county in townships two, north, of ranges fourteen and fifteen east of the first principal meridian.

———

William Spicer had been taken prisoner by the Indians, married a Seneca woman and continued to

live among the Indians. By the treaty of 1817, Mr.
Spicer was given six hundred and forty acres "beginning on the east bank of the Sandusky river, 40
poles below the lower corner of said Spicer's corn
field, thence, up the river on the east side, with the
meanders thereof, one mile, thence, and from the
beginning, east, for a quantity." [1] This tract is
located in the north part of Seneca county in town

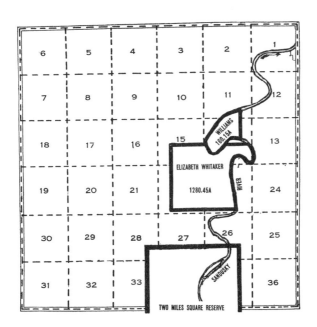

TOWN 5, NORTH,
RANGE 15 EAST
OF
THE FIRST PRINCIPAL MERIDIAN

three, north, range fifteen east of the first principal
meridian.

Elizabeth Whitaker, a white woman, was taken
prisoner by the Wyandot Indians and continued to
live with them after she was free to return to her
people. At the request of the Indians, the United
States, by the treaty of 1817, granted her twelve
hundred and eighty acres of land, on the west side
of the Sandusky river, in a square form, as nearly
as the meanders of the river might permit, and to
run an equal distance above and below the house in
which she lived. [1] This tract is located in the north
central part of Sandusky county, in town five, north,
of range fifteen east of the first principal meridian.

Isaac Williams, a half-blood Wyandot, married
a white woman who had been taken prisoner by the
Indians and had ever since lived among them. After
the death of her husband, the United States by the
treaty of 1817, gave the widow and her two children,
Joseph and Rachel, one hundred and sixty acres of
land at a place called Negro Point in the north part
of Sandusky county, in town five, north, of range
fifteen east of the first principal meridian. [1]

Sawendebans, otherwise known as Yellow Hair,
or Peter Minor, an adopted son of Tondaganie, or
the Dog, was given, by the treaty of 1817, six hun-

dred and forty acres of land in a square form on the
north side of the Maumee river at Wolf's Rapids, [1]
and for which he was given a patent, November 20,
1827.   His children were given one-half section of
land adjoining the north side of the former grant,
by the treaty of 1831. [10]   These two tracts form one
survey of 960 acres in Lucas county in townships
five and six, north, of range nine east of the first
principal meridian.

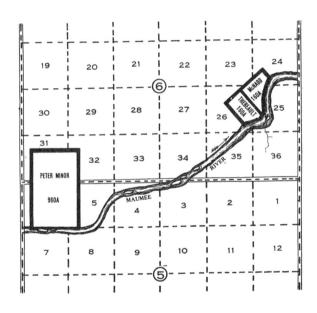

**TOWNS 5,6, NORTH, RANGE 9 EAST
OF
THE FIRST PRINCIPAL MERIDIAN**

Hiram Thebeault, a half-blooded Ottawa Indian, by the treaty of 1831, was given a quarter section of land at the Bear Rapids of the Maumee river in Lucas county, in town six, north, of range nine east of the first principal meridian. William McNabb, another half-blooded Ottawa Indian, was given, by the same treaty, a like quantity of land adjoining that granted to Hiram Thebeault. (10)

By the treaty with the Ottawa Indians, in 1833, the following grants of land about the mouth of the Maumee river in the ninth township, south, of the eighth range east of the Michigan meridian, in Lucas county, were made: Three hundred and twenty acres at the mouth of the river, including Presque Isle, to Autokee, a chief; eight hundred acres to Jacques, Robert, Peter, Antoine, Francis and Alexis Navarre; one hundred and sixty acres, on which stood his father's old cabin, to Waysayon, the son of Tushquaguan; eighty acres, including, if practicable, her cabin and field, to Petau; eighty acres higher up the little creek, to Cheno, a chief; eighty acres to Joseph Le Cavalier Ranjard, in trust for himself and the legal representatives of Albert Ranjard, deceased, who had purchased the land of the Indians, paid them three hundred dollars and had received no equivalent; one hundred and sixty acres fronting

(10) 8 L. U. S., 1093; 7 U. S. S. L., 359.

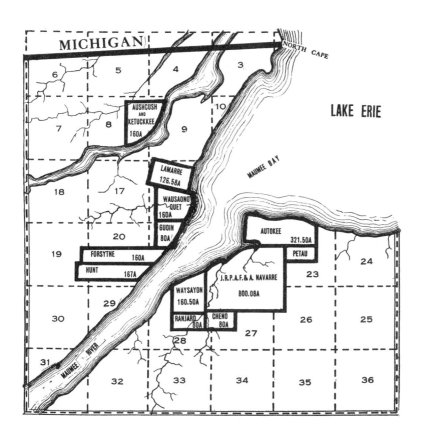

**TOWN 9, SOUTH
RANGE 8, EAST
OF
THE MICHIGAN MERIDIAN**

on the bay and including his improvements, on Pike creek, to Wausaonoquet, a chief; eighty acres adjoining the south side of the last tract, to Leon Guoin and his wife during their joint lives and the life of the survivor, and to their children in fee; one hundred and sixty acres fronting on the north side of Ottawa creek, above where Aushcush lived, to chiefs Aushcush and Ketuckkee; one hundred and sixty acres on each side of the turnpike road where Halfway creek crossed it, and one hundred and sixty acres fronting on the river and including the former residence of Kenewauba, to Robert A. Forsythe, and one hundred and sixty acres fronting on the river immediately above and adjoining the last tract, and one hundred and sixty acres adjoining on the turnpike road, to John E. Hunt. As Autokee, Waysayon, Petau, Cheno, Wausaonoquet, Aushcush and Ketuckkee were Indians, the lands granted them could not be alienated without the approval of the President of the United States. [11]

To encourage settlement, and to protect occupants, "either under legal grants derived from the French or British governments, or by virtue of actual possession and improvement, or from any other account whatever," Congress provided that all such persons could make application to the register of

[11]   8 L. U. S., 1093, 1178; 7 U. S. S. L., 359, 420.

the land office of the district and receive a patent
for the land, upon producing satisfactory evidence
of occupancy, or other rights. (12) Under these provisions, Andre Lamarre, July 3, 1812, received a
grant for 126.58 acres situated on the Maumee Bay
in Lucas county, in section 16, in town nine, south,
of range eight east of the Michigan meridian, and
more particularly described as follows: "Beginning
at a post standing on the border of the Miami Bay
on the northerly side of a small run, thence North
81 degrees West, 43.50 chains to a post, thence North
9 degrees East, 29.10 chains to a post, thence South

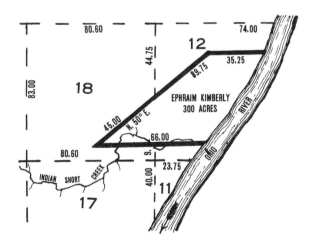

EPHRAIM KIMBERLY'S SURVEY

TOWN **4**   *RANGE* **2**

81 degrees East, 43.50 chains to a post standing on the border of the Miami Bay, thence along the border of said Bay South 9 degrees West 29.10 chains to the place of beginning.''

By the act of 1843 [14] the surveyor general was directed to lay off a portion of land, not exceeding 640 acres and including the town of Upper Sandusky, lying in town 2, south, range 14, east of the First Principal meridian survey, and since in Crane township, Wyandot county, into town lots, streets and avenues and into out lots, in such manner and of such dimensions as he might judge proper.

While the government was endeavoring to survey the land in Ohio and provide land to satisfy warrants issued for services in the American army, Ephraim Kimberly, a holder of such warrants, settled upon and improved three hundred acres near Indian Short Creek, now in sections 12 and 18, town 4, range 2 of The Ohio River survey, and in Warren township, Jefferson county.   And being thus occupied before the surrounding lands were surveyed under the rectangular plan, its lines do not correspond with those of lands surrounding it. It therefore became an independent survey for which the president in 1794 [17] was authorized and empowered to issue a patent.

(12) 3 L. U. S, 596; 670; 4 L. U. S., 109, 185, 412; 2 U. S. S. L.,
(17)   2 L. U. S. 389; 6 U. S. S. L. 14.
343, 437, 502, 710.   (14) 10 L. U. S. 470;   5 U. S. S. L. 624.

CHAPTER 30

THE TURNPIKE LANDS

Altho the Indians, by the treaty of Brownstown, in 1808, granted to the United States a tract of land one hundred and twenty feet wide for a roadway from Fremont southwardly to the Greenville treaty line, [1] the general government never provided for its establishment. [2] Instead, however, congress, in 1827, appropriated to the state of Ohio for the purpose of making a road from Columbus to Sandusky city, "the one half of a quantity of land equal to two sections, on the western side of said road, and most contiguous thereto, to be bounded by sectional lines, from one end of said road to the other, wheresoever the same may remain unsold, to be selected by the Commissioner of the General Land Office the whole length of said road thru the lands of the United States, reserving to the United States each alternate

(1)   1 L. U. S., 398, 417; 7 U. S. S. L., 49, 112.
(2)   4 L. U. S. 364; 2 U. S. S. L., 608; 18 L. O. L., 148; 41 L. O. L.. 251.

section." And also the right at any time to transport over such road any mail stage, troops or property of the United States, free of toll. [3]

In lieu of these lands, and to describe those appropriated instead more definitely, congress, in 1828, granted to the state of Ohio, "forty-nine sections of land to be located in the Delaware Land District, in the following manner, to-wit: Every alternate section through which the road may run, and the section next adjoining thereto on the west, so far as the said sections remain unsold, and, if any part of the said sections shall have been disposed of, then a quantity equal thereto shall be selected under the direction of the Commissioner of the General Land Office, from the vacant lands in the sections adjoining on the west of those appropriated." [4]

The road was constructed under the act of 1817 regulating turnpike companies, [5] by The Columbus and Sandusky Turnpike Company, incorporated, in 1826, with a capital of one hundred thousand dollars in shares of $100 each. [6] The road was completed two years later when toll-gates were established. Its estimated cost was $81,680, but its actual cost was $74,736, including the bridges which were few and small. The road was the first commercial connection between the capital city and the lake in

(3) 7 L. U. S., 602; 4 U. S. S. L., 242.   (5) 15 L. O., 39.
(4) 8 L. U. S., 35; 4 U. S. S L., 263.   (6) 24 L. O. L., 66.

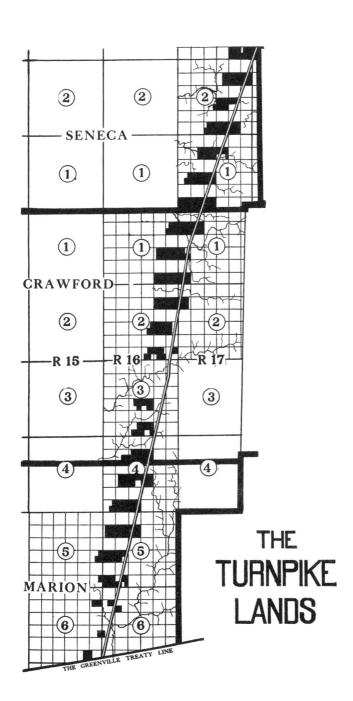

THE
TURNPIKE
LANDS

SENECA

CRAWFORD

R 15 — R 16 — R 17

MARION

THE GREENVILLE TREATY LINE

the establishment of which both the federal and state governments were interested. Its building was attended with graft. Little or no stone was used, and it was practically a dirt road, hardly passable except during the summer season. Such vigorous protests continued to arise all along the line that the legislature in 1843 [8] cancelled the company's charter, leaving it without authority to collect toll.

The land thus granted, amounting to 31,596.09 acres, was divided into twenty-eight tracts of which the largest contained 1920 acres,and was located in Marion, Crawford and Seneca counties. In 1828, the legislature declared this land to be for the use and benefit of The Columbus and Sandusky Turnpike Company for the purpose of building the road, and authorized that company to sell the land and the governor to execute deeds to the purchasers. [7]

[7]   26 L. O., 74; 27 L. O., 60; 33 L. O. L., 440.
[8]   41 L. O. L. 104.

CHAPTER 31

THE MAUMEE ROAD LANDS.

From the time of its settlement in 1683, Detroit was the headquarters of the influence of the white man over considerable territory. France used it as a center of governmental activity until the treaty of 1763, England until that of 1783 and the United States from 1796 until improved facilities for communication enabled the national government to transact business more directly from Washington. For a number of years Detroit was, therefore, the seat of territorial government where a military post and a land office were maintained and much important business was transacted.

But to reach Detroit from the east, it was necessary to pass along the southern side and around the western end of Lake Erie. Much of this country was swampy and almost impassable for teams for the greater part of the year. However, a dependable roadway thru it was early deemed a necessity. This necessity was so obvious that, in 1803, when admitting Ohio into the union, congress directed the secretary of the treasury to pay three per cent. of the net proceeds of the land in Ohio belonging to the United States, sold after June 30, 1802, to such persons as the legislature should authorize to receive them, to be used in laying out, opening and making roads within the state. [1] Consequently, by the Brownstown treaty of 1808, the United States obtained the release of the Indian claim to "a tract of land for a road, of one hundred and twenty feet wide, from the foot of the rapids of the river Miami of Lake Erie to the western line of the Connecticut Reserve, and all the land within one mile of said road, on each side thereof, for the purpose of establishing settlements along the same." [2]

In 1811, congress authorized the president to appoint three commissioners to explore, survey and mark the road which should be sixty feet wide, and appropriated six thousand dollars to defray the expenses of such preliminary work. [3] In 1816, the president was authorized to alter the course of the road so that it might pass thru the reservation at Fremont, or not exceeding three miles north of it [4]

The war of 1812, much of which was carried on

(1)   3 L. U. S., 541; 2 U. S. S. L., 225.
(2)   1 L. U. S., 417; 7 U. S. S. L., 112.
(3)   4 L. U. S., 364; 2 U. S. S. L., 608.
(4)   6 L. U. S., 61; 3 U. S. S. L., 285.

in northwestern Ohio, emphasized the necessity of
this road. The national government, however, took
no action in the matter, the state was unable to do so
itself and the project did not appeal to individuals.
Nothing, therefore, was done until 1820 when the
legislature requested congress to use the money appropriated in 1811, in exploring, surveying and opening either this road, or the one running south from
Fremont to the Greenville treaty line, or both, as
contemplated by that act. [5]

Thereupon congress, in 1823, authorized the
state of Ohio "to lay out, open and construct a road
from the Lower Rapids of the Miami of Lake Erie,
to the western boundary of the Connecticut Western

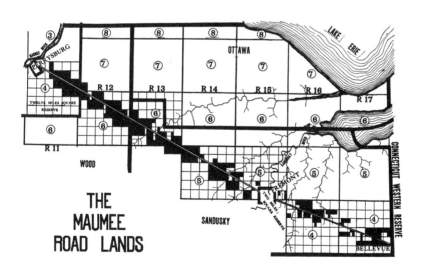

THE
MAUMEE
ROAD LANDS

Reserve, in such manner as the legislature of said state may by law provide,'' and granted to the state "a tract of land, one hundred and twenty feet wide, whereon to locate the same, together with a quantity of land equal to one mile on each side thereof and adjoining thereto, to be bounded by sectional lines as run by the United States, to commence at the Miami Rapids, and terminate at the western boundary of the Connecticut Western Reserve, with full power and authority to sell and convey the same;'' and that the right of the state to the land should be complete whenever the legislature accepted the duty of building the road. [6] The legislature promptly accepted the trust, [7] and, in 1825, appropriated twenty-five thousand dollars to be used in constructing the road. [8] The legislature also provided for the sale of the land and that the governor should execute deeds to the purchasers. [9]

To confirm the title to these lands in the state of Ohio which had complied with the conditions upon which they had been appropriated, congress, in 1838, granted to it "all right or title of the United States, acquired by the treaty of Brownstown, in a certain road from the foot of the rapids of the Miami of the Lake to the western line of the Connecticut Western Reserve. [10]

(5) 18 L. O. L., 148; 19 L. O., 205.
(6) 7 L. U. S., 118; 3 U. S. S. L., 727.
(9) 22 L. O. L., 128; 24 L. O., 64.   (7) 21 L. O. L., 55.
(10) 9 L. U. S., 888; 5 U. S. S. L.. 296.   (8) 23 L. O., 33.

The road thus provided for extended from the Maumee river at Perrysburg in Wood county, directly to Fremont in Sandusky county, and from there, directly to Bellevue in the southeast corner of Sandusky county on the west line of the Connecticut Reserve, a distance of about forty-six miles. The lands thus appropriated, known as the "Maumee Road Lands," constituted a tract about two miles wide, being about one mile on each side of the road, in Wood and Sandusky counties, and amounted to about sixty thousand acres.

CHAPTER 32

THE CANAL LANDS.

As Ohio increased in population transportation facilities became increasingly important, and while the natural bodies of water and streams were used as avenues of traffic, they could accommodate but a limited portion of the inhabitants. To reach those in the interior of the state artificial waterways, or canals, were conceived. The first time the building of canals in Ohio was brought to attention in a public manner was, in 1818, in the inaugural address of Governor Brown who has been referred to as the "Father of the Canals."

In 1820, the legislature provided for the appointment of a committee to locate a route for a canal between Lake Erie and the Ohio river, and applied to congress for a donation and also for a grant of land to aid in the building of a canal upon such route as might be found the most suitable. It was requested that the donation be not less than two miles wide along the route, and that the grant be from one to two million acres, at not to exceed $1.25 per acre. [1]

Congress, thereupon, by the acts of 1828 [2] and 1830, [3] granted to the state, to aid it in extending the canal from Dayton to Lake Erie, a quantity of land equal to one half of five sections in width on each side of the canal between Dayton and the Maumee river, so far as it should be located through the public lands, reserving, however, to the United States each alternate section unsold.

Congress also granted to the state five hundred thousand acres to be selected from any lands belonging to the United States within Ohio, to aid the state to pay the debt it had contracted in the construction of canals. The state, under the authority of the legislature, was given the power to sell and convey in fee simple the whole or any part of these lands, provided that the canals should be public highways, the United States should be permitted to use them free of charge and that the legislature of Ohio should express the assent of the state to the several provisions and conditions of the act granting the lands, which was done in December of that year. [4]

And while several canals connecting the Ohio river with Lake Erie were contemplated, but two

(1)   18 L. O., 147.   (2)   8 L. U. S., 118; 4 U. S. S. L., 305.
(4)   27 L. O., 16.   (3)   8 L. U. S., 282; 4 U. S. S. L., 393.

main lines were completed: The "Miami and Erie Canal" along the western part of the state from Cincinnati to Toledo, and the "Ohio Canal" through the middle part from Portsmouth to Cleveland. Each had a number of branches of which some were begun or constructed by private capital and purchased by the state. The most important of these branches was the Hocking Canal, built for the transportation of coal and salt from that valley.

The proceeds of the first grant were applied to the construction of the Miami Canal, while those of the latter grant were applied to the construction of the Ohio Canal .

In 1827, congress granted to the state of Indiana, for the purpose of building a canal from the Wabash river to Lake Erie, a quantity of land equal to one half of five sections in width on each side of such proposed canal, but reserved to the United States each alternate section. [5] However, in the act of 1828, granting land to the state of Ohio [2] for the construction of the Miami Canal, congress also authorized Indiana to release to Ohio, upon such terms as those states should agree, all the right and interest granted to the former state by the act of 1827, [5] to any lands thus granted it within the limits of Ohio. This agreement was effected in 1834. [6] Whereupon

(5)   7 L. U. S., 585; 4 U. S. S. L., 236.   (6)   32 L. O. L., 308, 439.
(7)   9 L. U. S., 110, 829; 4 U. S. S. L., 716; 5 U. S. S. L., 261.

congress authorized the state of Ohio to select a quantity of land in Ohio along that route, to be used in the construction of the canal. [7] These lands are known as the Wabash and Erie canal lands.

The legislature provided in 1829, for the sale of the lands thus granted, in half quarter sections to the highest bidder and that the governor should execute deeds to the purchasers. [8] To encourage the sale and settlement of these lands, a deduction of thirty-three per cent. from the appraised value was allowed, after 1847, to the purchaser of any tract not exceeding one hundred and sixty acres, who would make affidavit of his intention to reside permanently upon the land and improve it. [9]

In 1866, the auditor of state was authorized to sell the canal lands then remaining unsold, for the best price he could obtain, [10] and, in 1872, the board of public works was required to ascertain and locate all unsold canal lands and cause an appraisement of them to be returned to the auditor of state. [11]

The selection of all the lands made by the state of Ohio for canal purposes, under the acts of March 2, 1827, [5] and of May 24, 1828 [2] was confirmed by congress in 1855, [12]. And any defects in the title

(8)   27 L. O. 55;   28 L. O. 59;   40 L. O. 72.
(9)   45 L. O., 31.   (11)   69 L. O., 194.
(10)   63 L. O., 140.   (12)   10 U. S. S. L.. 634.

of the purchasers of such lands, previously bought from the state of Ohio, were quieted by the act of 1856. (13)

The lands thus acquired by the state of Ohio to aid in the construction of canals, were located in the northwestern part of the state. They amounted to 1,230,521 acres and were divided into three classes: One for the Miami Canal, one for the Ohio Canal and one for the Wabash and Erie.

(13)   53 L. O. 197.

CHAPTER 33

SWAMP LANDS

In 1850, the national government granted all the swamp and overflowed lands remaining unsold after the 28th day of September of that year, to the respective states in which such lands were situated. [1] Ohio received 26,252 acres, the most of which were located in the northwestern part of the state in the region known as the "Black Swamps," and consisted of land unfit for settlement until it had been reclaimed by drainage. Much of such land in Ohio constituted the old "black swamp" of pioneer days. Since then the most of this land has been drained and has become equally as productive as the most fertile in the state.

If, for any reason, any swamp lands were sold by the national government after September 28, 1850, and before March 2, 1855, the purchase money was

[1]   9 U. S. S. L., 519.

paid to the state entitled to such land, or other lands were given it instead. However, if within ninety days after the latter date, the state failed to return to the general land office, a list of such lands so sold by the national government, the state was not entitled to other lands in the place of those so sold, nor to the proceeds for which such lands may have been sold. [2] In 1857, Congress confirmed to each state, respectively, all lands selected as swamp and overflowed lands and reported to the general land office prior to March 3, 1857. [3] However, by reason of previous sales, and especially the selection of the canal lands by alternate sections, much land in Ohio that otherwise would have been classed as "swamp lands," did not pass to the state as such.

Any land unfit for cultivation without drainage was considered swamp land, while overflowed lands were those which were subject to periodical overflows and required levees or embankments to keep out water to render them suitable for cultivation. The test as to whether certain public lands were swamp or overflowed lands ,was whether or not they could be successfully, not profitably, cultivated in grain or other staple products by reason of the overflow.

The Secretary of the Interior transmitted to the governor of each state containing swamp or over-

(2)   10 U. S. S. L., 634.   (3)   11 U. S. S. L., 251.

flowed lands, a list and plats of the legal subdivisions of all such lands within the state; and in making out these lists and plats the legal subdivisions of which the greater parts were wet and unfit for cultivation, were classed as swamp and overflowed lands. After the selections had thus been made, the Secretary of the Interior, at the request of the governor of any state, caused patents to be issued to such state conveying to it those lands in fee simple, subject, however, to the application of so much of the proceeds of the sale as might be necessary to reclaim these lands by means of drains or levees. The legislature, in 1852, directed the governor to procure patents to the state for the swamp and overflow lands within Ohio, and file a certified list and diagram of them with the auditor of state who should record such list in substantial form. (10)

In 1851, the legislature provided that the net proceeds received from the sale of swamp lands should be appropriated to the general fund for the support of common schools and the interest distributed to the several counties in proportion to the number of white male inhabitants above the age of twenty-one years. (4) However, in 1892, section thirty-six in town five, north, of range one east of the first

<hr />

(4)   49 L. O., 40; G. C., 7577. This act was modified, in 1883, by omitting the word "white," to comply with the amendment to the federal constitution entitling colored people to equal school rights. 80 L. O., 39; G. C., 7578.   (5)   89 L. O., 232.

(10)   50 L. O. L. 44; 51 L. O. 547.   (11)   108 L. O. 630.

principal meridian, in Paulding county, was directed to be sold and the proceeds, after paying $6,150.00 to the county for draining the land, were to be credited to the Miami and Erie canal fund. [5]

By the act of 1853, the commissioners of each county containing swamp or overflowed lands, were to determine the mode of draining such lands and to contract for their drainage which was to be paid for by the lands themselves at their appraised value. Upon the completion of the work, deeds were to be issued by the governor of the state; and any such land remaining thus undisposed of, was to be sold by the county auditor, at its appraised value, to any one who would agree to reside upon the land and improve it. [6] In 1919 it was made the duty of the attorney general to investigate the title of swamp and overflow lands and recover such as yet belonged to the state. [11]

The canal commission was authorized, in 1891, to survey such swamp and overflowed lands as had not been surveyed, and required to file plats of them with the auditor of state. [7] In 1894, that commission was also authorized to sell whatever of these lands it deemed could be sold to the advantage of the state. [8] Virtually all the swamp and overflowed lands in Ohio have been sold, and the net proceeds,

(6)   51 L. O., 357.   (7)   88 L. O., 936.   (8)   91 L. O., 229.
(9)   Report of Auditor of State for 1913, page 72.

amounting to $25,121.09, known as the "Swamp Lands Indemnity Fund," are carried as one of the items of the irreducible debt of the state on which the interest to January 1, 1914, amounted to $41,819.36. [9]

CHAPTER 34

MISCELLANEOUS GRANTS.

Washington always had faith in the possibilities of the Ohio valley. In the darkest hours of the revolution, he expressed himself as believing that if the fates of war should go against the colonists they could retire west of the Allegheny mountains, found an empire and live in safety.

General Washington, like all others who served in the Revolutionary war, was entitled to land warrants for services rendered in that war. He was also entitled to land warrants from Virginia for services rendered in the French and Indian war. He accepted none for himself in either case. However, he purchased a few warrants from others. Among these was one for three thousand acres issued by Lord Dunmore, Governor of Virginia, to Captain John Rootes, a naval officer, under the proclamation of King George III, of 1763, [1] for services rendered at the capture of Louisbourg, and one for one hundred acres issued under resolutions of the Continental Congress, to Thomas Cope for services rendered in the Revolutionary war. Washington located these warrants, in 1788, upon 3,031 acres in Clermont and Hamilton counties and obtained survey No. 1650 for 839 acres, No. 1765 for 1,235 acres and No. 1775 for 977 acres.

However, by failing to comply with the technicalities of the law by which warrants issued under such proclamation could be used to acquire land northwest of the Ohio river, Washington was unable to obtain the title to these surveys; and patents were issued, in 1806, instead to the devisees of General John Nevill for the first and second surveys and to Major Henry Massie for the third.

The executors of Washington endeavored to recover this land, but, failing in that, they sought instead to recover its value thru Congress. Congress was appealed to many times, by both the executors and the heirs of Washington even as recently as 1910, but without success. [2]

———

Of the many foreigners who offered their services to the colonies during the Revolutionary war, none were more popular than General La Fayette; and, while he acquired no land in Ohio, yet he came

(1)   1 L. U. S., 443.   (2)   19 Arch., 304.

so nearly doing so that the history of the proceedings by which he was given lands elsewhere may not be out of place in the history of Ohio lands.

General La Fayette, at an early age, was left with a great fortune. He became so interested in the success of the colonies that, in 1777, he fitted out a ship, came to America and offered his services to Congress without pay or command. He soon became a favorite and was rapidly advanced until he became a major general. After the war he returned to France where, in the troublous period following, he lost his fortune.

In grateful recognition of his services, Congress passed many acts for his relief. In 1803, it gave him land warrants for 11,520 acres, which he could have located on any land in Ohio then owned by the United States. [3] He did not do so, however, and, in the following year, Congress permitted him to locate that quantity of land in the territory of Orleans. [4]

In 1824, Congress directed the President to invite La Fayette to the United States as the guest of the nation, and assigned a ship to bring him to this country. [5] He remained eleven months and was everywhere received with the highest honors, and Ohio did her part to entertain the "Nation's

(3)   3 L. U. S., 554, 626; 2 U. S. S. L., 236, 303.
(4)   3 L. U. S., 629; 4 L. U. S., 54, 360; 10 L. U. S., 676; 2 U. S. S. L., 303, 617; 5 U. S. S. L., 729.   (5)   7 L. U. S., 332.

guest." [6] In December of that year Congress gave him two hundred thousand dollars and a township of land to be located by the President, in any of the unappropriated lands in the United States. [7]

Since the history of the title to real estate is sometimes romantic as well as prosaic it may be interesting to know that five shares of land of 1173.37 acres each, in the Ohio Company's Purchase, in southeastern Ohio, were once owned by Paul Jones of Revolutionary naval fame. These shares include sections and fractions four, eighteen, twenty-four, thirty and thirty-six in the fifth township of the thirteenth range of the Ohio River Survey, which coincides with the civil township of Canaan, in Athens county.

The career of Paul Jones, whose proper name was John Paul, is full of romance and adventure. He was born in Scotland in 1747 and went to sea at the age of twelve. He soon became an able sailor, and while on a voyage home, when both the captain and mate had died, he brought the ship in so skillfully that its owners appointed him captain. And to Paul Jones is credited the fact that he was the first to fly the American flag over a naval vessel.

In 1773, he settled in Virginia, where an older brother resided, and made his home with an influen-

(6)   24 L. O., 101.   (7)   7 L. U. S., 333; 6 U. S. S. L., 320.

tial family by the name of Jones. Through the influence of the Jones family he was appointed a lieutenant in the Continental navy, and, in gratitude, assumed the name of Jones. He rose rapidly in the ranks and soon became a commodore with a fleet of five vessels. His skill, dash and daring soon became famous and did much to establish the colonies as a nation among nations. But his most signal adventure, which is read with interest by old and young, was his battle on the "Poor Richard" with two British men-of-war off the coast of Scotland in 1779 . During this battle he ran his own ship, then in a sinking condition, alongside the British frigate, "Serapis," lashed them together, and captured the latter vessel to which he transferred his own men as the Poor Richard went down.

Jones retained the land in Athens county till his death.   He never married, and, dying intestate, the title passed to Mary Ann Lowden, one of the sisters of "Admiral John Paul Jones, alias John Paul, deceased," and to several nieces and nephews, of Dumfries, Scotland.   Under power of attorney they sold this land, in 1818, for five thousand dollars. [8]

Thaddeus Kosciusko, the Polish patriot, was so imbued with the spirit of liberty that he came to America with the French fleet, joined the colonists in their fight for freedom and displayed so much

(8)   Athens County Deed Book 4, pages 4, 12, 71.

military ability that he soon became a brigadier general. His account for services amounted to $12,-280.54, for which he was given a certificate, which he lost. [9] Congress, however, afterwards recognized his claim for that amount. [10]

As part of the land to which he was entitled under warrants issued to those who served in the Revolutionary war, [11] General Kosciusko selected five one hundred acre lots in the second quarter of the second township in the nineteenth range of the United States Military Survey, for which President Adams issued him a patent in April, 1800. [12]

These lots constituted one tract, were located on the east side of the Scioto river, near the Delaware county line, in Perry township, Franklin county, and possess additional historical interest from the fact that Leatherlips, a Wyandot chief, was executed there in 1810 by members of his own tribe for being too friendly with the whites.

Frederick William Baron de Steuben was born in Prussia and trained to military life with all the strictness of Prussian discipline. During the Revolutionary war he tendered his services to the col-

(9) American State Papers. Claims. Page 207.
(10) 3 L. U. S., 25.
(11) See The United States Military Tract.
(12) Franklin County Deed Book 21, page 447.

onies, became drillmaster of the American army and did much for its efficiency. [13] In appreciation of his services, the general assembly of Virginia, in 1780, granted him fifteen thousand acres of land, [14] while the United States, in 1790, bestowed upon him an annuity of $2,500.00 [15]

Under the acts of Congress granting land for military services, [11] his devisees, Benjamin Walker and William North, were given, in 1806, a patent, signed by President Jefferson, for two tracts of land, one for eight hundred acres in the first quarter and one for three hundred acres in the third quarter in the second township of the eighth range of the United States Military Survey which is in Muskingum township, Muskingum county. [16]

The community plan of owning and operating land was put into practice in the north part of Tuscarawas county by about two hundred Germans who belonged to a religious sect called Separatists and who had sought homes in this country that they might enjoy religious freedom. Their agent and leader, Joseph M. Bimeler, in 1818, purchased 5,500 acres in the tenth townships of the first and second ranges of the United States Military Survey. They located their buildings in one place and called the

(13) American State Papers. Claims. Page 14.
(14) L. L. O., 116.   (15) 2 L. U. S., 107.
(16) Muskingum County Deed Book 143, Page 360.

village Zoar. In 1846 they owned nine thousand acres, operated a saw mill, a woolen mill, two flouring mills and two furnaces, and had considerable money otherwise invested.

These people continued to prosper until the death of Bimeler in 1853, since when their success remained undiminished for some years and then began to decline until 1898, when it was decided to partition the land. A deed was accordingly executed September 20, 1898. [17]

Isaac Zane was born on the south branch of the Potomac river in Virginia about the year 1753, and died in 1816, at Zanesfield in Logan county, Ohio, where he had bought eighteen hundred acres of land and had lived since shortly after the Greenville treaty of 1795. Zanesfield, named in honor of Mr. Zane, was first called "Zane's Town," and was formerly the site of a Wyandot Indian village.

When about nine years of age, Mr. Zane, who was the youngest of the five Zane brothers who did so much to open Ohio for settlement, was taken prisoner by the Wyandot Indians and carried to Detroit where he grew to manhood with his captors. He declined to leave them or to return to his home, or even to his white friends, but continued to live with

[17] Tuscarawas County Deed Book 129, Page 1; 2 Howe, 700; 8 Arch., 1.

the Indians and eventually married a Canadian woman, of whose parents, one was French and the other a Wyandot Indian.

Mr. Zane took no part in the Revolutionary war, but, nevertheless, performed many acts of kindness in behalf of his white friends, and used his influence for peace with the Indians at a time when their friendship was so essential. His successful efforts in inducing the Indians to remain peaceable were worth much more to the cause of freedom than any personal services he might have rendered within the ranks.

On account of his friendly relation with the Indians and his great influence with them, Mr. Zane was chosen, in 1785, to serve as a guide to one of the commissioners delegated by the Continental Congress to treat with the Indians.

To reward him for his various services, Congress, in 1802, [18] granted Mr. Zane "his heirs and assigns, in fee simple, three sections of land of one mile square each," which he was allowed to select in as many locations. Two of these sections, however, were to be held by him in trust for the use and benefit of his children who should be living at the time of his death, and of the heirs of any children, deceased, and their heirs, respectively, as tenants in common.

(18) 3 L. U. S., 468; 6 U. S. S. L., 46.

During the war of 1812, the government for a time feared the friendly Indians might be induced by the Canadians, who remained loyal to England, to take up arms against the Americans. To guard against any possible outbreak, several hundred of these Indians were placed in Zane's blockhouse where they could be watched more easily and where they would be under the influence of Mr. Zane. When subsequent events dispelled that fear, the Indians were allowed their liberty.

Sections fifteen and fourteen in township five, east, and section two in township four, east, all in range twelve "Between the Miami Rivers," and now in the civil townships of Salem and Concord, respectively, in Champaign county, were selected. A patent was issued August 28, 1806, to Mr. Zane conveying to him section fifteen in fee, and also sections fourteen and two, "in trust, nevertheless, * * * to and for the use and benefit of the children of said Isaac Zane who shall be living at the time of his death, and of the heirs of any child or children, deceased, and their heirs respectively, to hold as tenants in common."

Two records of the patent are to be found in Champaign county. One in deed book C, at page 296, and the other in deed book S, at page 15. In the first record, sections fifteen and fourteen are erroneously recorded as being located in township four.

CHAPTER 35

SCHOOL LANDS.

The endowment of the means of education with land by our general government was first given official endorsement in 1785 when the Continental Congress reserved "lot number sixteen of every township for the maintenance of public schools," in the ordinance providing for the survey of the historic seven ranges in southeastern Ohio. [1] And in the creation of the territory of Oregon in 1848, and in the states admitted into the union since, [27] two sections, 16 and 36, have been reserved for that purpose.

This ordinance, however, did not, within itself, apply any land to the cause of education. Two reasons are obvious: One is that the Continental Congress was without power or authority to carry any of its obligations into effect; and the other, that, as there were then no settlements in Ohio, there was no grantee in existence to accept a grant had one been

(27)   9 U. S. S. L. 323.   (1)   1 L. U. S., 563.

THE TWO MILES SQUARE RESERVE

THE CONNECTICUT WESTERN RESERVE

ORIGINAL SURVEYED TOWNSHIPS

THE UNITED STATES MILITARY TRACT

THE MORAVIAN TRACTS

THE VIRGINIA MILITARY TRACT

ORIGINAL SURVEYED TOWNSHIPS

OHIO

RIVER

THE FRENCH GRANTS

GENERAL   CLASSES
OF
SCHOOL   LANDS

intended. This reservation of lot number sixteen, therefore, merely withheld it from sale and did not in any way attempt to pass title in the land. However, with such obligation thus quasi officially instituted, our federal government subsequently assumed the duty of carrying it out in good faith by attempting to grant to the cause of education the one thirty-sixth part of all public lands.

Who first conceived the plan of thus supporting the cause of education, history does not record, but as that purpose was entertained by the colonists quite generally, every endeavor possible was put forth to promote the movement. Besides, the vast expanse of territory then owned by the colonies suggested the advisability of using a part to promote so good a cause as an inducement to the settlement of the remainder. So the Continental Congress, therefore, was influenced, undoubtedly, to set aside a portion of the land for that purpose that the balance might be sold more readily, altho that body may not have desired, especially, to promote education at public expense. However, whatever its intentions may have been, such action by that congress virtually committed the federal government and the various state legislatures to the very wise policy of providing the means that have since assured the permanent establishment and maintenance of education.

Having adopted the township of thirty-six square miles as the unit for the community plan then probably first suggested, it was but logical that one such square mile, or the one thirty-sixth part of the whole, should be set aside for the benefit of education; and that it might be as centrally located as possible in the plan adopted for sub-dividing townships, section sixteen was selected.

Circumstances and conditions determining the establishment of settlements in Ohio, and the absence of perfected plans for subdividing the land and carrying them into effect, interfered materially with the appropriation of land for the support of schools and prevented its being made with uniformity. Besides, as Virginia had reserved the right to dispose of all the land lying between the Scioto and the Little Miami rivers, and Connecticut was conceded her claim to a large tract in the northeast corner of the state, no land within them could be assigned by the general government for the support of their respective schools. So lands elsewhere, owned by the United States, were necessarily selected for these tracts for that purpose.

Moreover, since the United States Military tract was subdivided into townships of twenty-five square miles, it is obvious that to have selected one square mile in each township for the support of schools would have appropriated too large a proportion;

while the irregular quantities and the separate and unusual manner of subdividing the lands in the Donation tract, the French grants, the Moravian tracts and the Two Miles Square reserve, prevented their classification with other tracts. Separate plans, therefore, were required to provide these tracts with school land.

Five general plans for the assignment of lands for the support of schools in Ohio, were, consequently, necessarily adopted: One for the Virginia Military tract; one for the Connecticut Western reserve; one for the United States Military tract; one for the French grants, the Moravian tracts, the Two Miles square reserve, the donation tract, the refugee tract and other miscellaneous grants, and one for the several respective original surveyed townships of thirty-six square miles each.

These lands, therefore, are divided into five general classes:

1. School lands belonging to the Virginia Military tract.
2. School lands belonging to the Connecticut Western reserve.
3. School lands belonging to the United States Military tract.
4. School lands belonging to miscellaneous grants.
5. School lands belonging to the respective original surveyed townships.

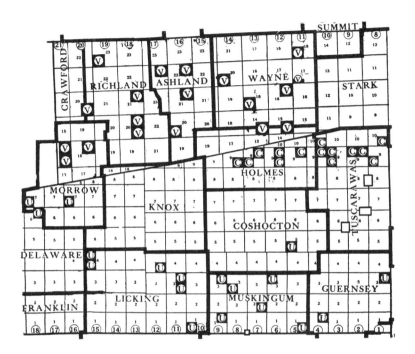

SCHOOL LANDS

FOR

Ⓥ THE VIRGINIA MILITARY TRACT_____105,600 ACRES

Ⓤ THE UNITED STATES MILITARY TRACT____72,000 ACRES

Ⓒ THE CONNECTICUT WESTERN RESERVE____56,000 ACRES
    (EAST OF THE GREENVILLE TREATY LINE)

1. To the Virginia Military tract was given for the support of its schools by the act of 1803, [2] an amount equal to one thirty-sixth part of the whole, to be selected by the legislature out of the unlocated land within the tract . However, as it soon appeared that Virginia would require all the land in such tract to satisfy outstanding army bounty warrants, Congress proposed, in 1807, [3] to give elsewhere, instead, eighteen quarter townships and three sections of land amounting to one hundred and five thousand six hundred acres, to be selected, by lot, by the secretary of the treasury. To this the legislature consented [4] and thereupon, in 1808, Albert Gallatin, then secretary of the treasury, [5] located the tracts in Wayne, Holmes, Ashland, Richland, Crawford and Morrow counties.

2. To the Connecticut Western reserve for the support of schools within it east of the Greenville treaty line, was given, by the same act, [2] fifty-six thousand acres located in Holmes and Tuscarawas counties But since the Indians retained possession of the land in that part of the reserve lying west of the Cuyahoga river, until after the treaty of 1805, [6] no attempt was made for several years to provide it with land for the support of schools; and, as congress failed to take the initiative to provide it with

(2)   3 L. U. S. 541; 2 U. S. S. L., 225.   (4)   6 L. O., 125.
(3)   4 L. U. S., 93; 2 U. S. S. L., 424.   (5)   L. L. O., 159.
      (6)   1 L. U. S., 409; 7 U. S. S. L., 87.

land for that purpose, the legislature repeatedly petitioned that body to do so. [7] Congress, however, took no action in the matter until 1834, [8] when it directed that a quantity of land, which, together with that already granted for that purpose, would equal one thirty-sixth part of the whole reserve, should be reserved in sections, half sections or quarter sections. Thereupon the secretary of the treasury selected this additional land in Williams, Defiance, Paulding, Putnam, Henry and Van Wert counties, to the amount of 37,724.16 acres, [9] which, together with that selected under the act of 1803, [2] amounted to a total of 93,724.16 acres.

3. To the United States Military tract for the support of schools within that tract, there was given by congress, in 1803, [2] seventy-two thousand acres located in Guernsey, Coshocton, Muskingum, Licking, Morrow and Delaware counties.

4. To the Donation tract, the Two Miles Square reserve, the Moravian tracts and the French grants, there were assigned for the support of their respective schools, lands within them, or in contiguous territory, by the acts of 1803, [2] 1816, [10] 1824 [11] and 1826, [12] respectively.

[7] 25 L. O. L., 115; 26 L. O. L., 175; 27 L. O. L., 170; 31 L. O. L., 259.

[8] 9 L. U. S., 39; 4 U. S. S. L., 679.

[9] 47 L. O. L., 381; 48 L. O. L., 727.

5. To each original surveyed township of thirty-six square miles there was also given, by the act of 1803, section sixteen, where possible, and where that section had been otherwise disposed of, the secretary of the treasury was directed to select a like amount out of any unappropriated lands in the most contiguous townships. [2]

By reason of neglect in the passage of acts for the sale of several tracts of land, or, because of expediency in some instances, the appropriation of section sixteen within them for schools was not made; and the land for the maintenance of schools in many tracts, and even in original surveyed townships, was, therefore, necessarily selected elsewhere.

Moreover, the irregularity of boundary lines of original surveys, particularly along rivers, caused many townships to contain less than thirty-six full sections. To care for such townships, Congress, in 1826, [12] provided that each fractional township containing more land than three quarters of an entire township, should be given one section of land for the support of its schools; that each township containing more than one half and not more than three quarters of a township, should be given three quar-

(10)   6 L. U. S., 101; 3 U. S. S. L., 308.
(11)   7 L. U. S., 307; 4 U. S. S. L. 56.
(12)   7 L. U. S., 491; 4 U. S. S. L., 179.

ters of a section; that each township containing more
than one quarter, and not more than one half of a
township, should be given one half section, and that
each township containing more than one entire section and not more than one quarter of a township,
should be given one quarter of a section.   Congress also provided that this land should be selected by the secretary of the treasury out of any
unappropriated public land within the land district
in which the township for which it should be selected
was situated.

The attempt to provide townships which did, or
could, not have their own section sixteen, with land
elsewhere, could not be carried out with any degree
of uniformity, since the government, in the meantime, had sold much of its land.   Therefore, many
tracts of school land are located necessarily some distance from those which they respectively benefit.
Sometimes they are in two or more detached tracts
many miles apart, as well as many miles from the
territory to which they belong.   For instance, a part
of section 8 in town 4, of range 12, and of section 26
in town 3, of range 13, in Meigs county, and a part
of section 8 in town 5, of range 12, in Athens county,
were set aside for the support of schools in township
3, of range 11, in Meigs county, and from which section sixteen is cut off by the Ohio river. [13]

(13)   38 L. O. L., 211; 43 L. O. L., 38; 58 L. O., 162.

In some cases land scrip has been given by the general government for the support of schools in lieu of section sixteen which had been otherwise disposed of. For instance, a part of section sixteen in the fourth township, south, of the second range east of the first principle meridian, which coincides with the civil township of Dublin, in Mercer county, had been granted to Anthony Shane and Louis Godfroy; and congress, in 1842, authorized the secretary of the treasury to issue to the trustees of that township land scrip to the amount of $311.08 for the part of that section granted to Mr. Shane, and $426.62 for the part granted to Mr. Godfroy, and directed that such scrip should be applied to the use of the schools of that township in the same manner as that section, or the proceeds of its sale, or its rents, would have been held and applied, had the land not been granted to Shane and Godfroy. [14]

Thus, from time to time, by general, or special, acts, Congress endeavored to set aside one thirty-sixth part of all the land in Ohio for the support of schools; and, as the state contains about 26,073,000 acres, there should have been about 724,266 acres so applied instead of but 704,488 acres actually appropriated. Many tracts, therefore, have no land assigned them for that purpose, several being found in that part of the Michigan survey lying between

[14] 9 L. U. S., 812; 10 L. U. S., 275; 6 U. S. S. L., 726, 862.

the Harris and the Fulton lines, in Lucas, Fulton and Williams counties; [15] while each of ten townships in the Ohio Company's second purchase, in Morgan, Athens, Hocking and Vinton counties, has two sections for the support of its schools: One, section sixteen, given it by the Ohio Company, and the other, in contiguous territory, by the United States under the act of 1803. [2]

For a number of years, the school lands were leased for terms varying from one year to ninety-nine years renewable forever, under general laws passed by the legislature. Many leases were also made under special acts applying to particular tracts, often to but parts of a section. These leases were executed, generally, by three trustees of the original surveyed township. Sometimes the county commissioners did so, while in some instances other provisions were made instead. [16]

It was the duty of local officers to collect and distribute the rent and to care for the property. This duty, however, was performed so indifferently and carelessly and so many abuses crept in, that the management of the school lands soon became quite unsatisfactory. Besides, few persons cared to lease land and jeopardize their improvements by having

(15) 48 L. O. L., 728.

(16) In 1808, the town council of Marietta was authorized to subdivide and lease section 16 in town 2 of range 8 for ninety-nine years renewable forever. 8 L. O., 96.

them at the mercy of a revaluation of the land when
other land in the vicinity could be purchased outright for one or two dollars per acre. It was another demonstration that land ownership is the best
basis of social and economic contentment and stability of government. Even the legislature, in 1824,
when appealing to Congress for permission to sell
these lands, was constrained to say "that the great
body of those who constitute the strength and basis
of every government, and who are to be considered
as the friends of good order and public improvement
are among those who are the owners as well as oc-
cupiers of the soil." [17] The school lands, therefore,
produced comparatively little revenue and gave so
little promise of doing any better that their sale was
decided upon.

Altho the title to the land in Ohio, appropriated and set aside by the United States for the use
of schools, was considered to have vested in the legislature in fee simple, by the enabling act of 1802, [18]
the ordinance and resolution of the Ohio constitutional convention of November 29, 1802, [19] the constitution of Ohio, the act admitting the state into
the union [20] and the act of March 3, 1803, [2] assigning land for the support of its schools, yet it was
doubted if the state thereby acquired the power of

(17)   22 L. O. L., 153.   (20)   3 L. U. S., 524.
(18)   3 L. U. S., 496; 2 U. S. S. L., 173.

sale, or could convey the fee in the land to others. Therefore, the legislature, in 1824, petitioned congress to vest it with that power. [17]   Whereupon, congress, in 1826, authorized the legislature to sell and convey all the school lands in fee simple, but required it first to obtain the consent of the inhabitants to their sale; [21] to invest the money in some productive fund and apply the proceeds to the use of the schools within the respective districts, or townships, for which the lands were originally reserved. [22]

And although the impression prevailed at that time that the state did not possess the power to sell the school, ministerial, salt, university and other lands entrusted to its legislature by various acts of congress, and even that the legal, or fee simple, title might yet be retained by the United States, the supreme courts of Ohio and of the United States later held such title to have passed to the state by such acts themselves which were considered the equivalent of patents. [29]

The title to sections sixteen in the Ohio Company's second purchase, however, is of a different

(19)   21 L. O., 44.

(21)   In 1828, the legislature determined that the inhabitants of many counties had voted to sell their school lands. 26 L. O., 4.

(22)   7 L. U. S., 434; 4 U. S. S. L., 138; 16 O. S. R., 11; 31 O. S. R., 301.

(29)   10 O. 233; 16 Peters, 281; 52 O. S. 586; 47 Florida 307; 95 U. S. 551; 121 U. S. 448; 142 U. S. 241.

character, since those sections were not appropriated to the use of schools by the United States.

Intending that all their land should have the benefit of one thirty-sixth part for the support of schools, and no reservations having been made for that purpose by the United States in the grant of the second purchase, [23] the trustees of the Ohio Company of Associates, January 7, 1796, appropriated section sixteen in each of the ten townships in that purchase for such purpose, and directed the inhabitants to lease such land for periods not exceeding seven years each.

Following the action of Congress, many general laws [24] were passed by the legislature providing for the sale of school lands· Many special acts were also enacted, each sometimes providing for the sale of but a single tract; in some instances, for but a small part of a section. Sales of school land have, therefore, since been made until but about 20,573 acres remained unsold at the end of the fiscal year of (June 30) 1918.

Upon the sale of any school land being made, a certificate, upon the final payment of the purchase price, was given the purchaser who presented it to the auditor of state. That officer prepared the deed which the governor signed. After recording the

(23)   See the Ohio Company.

deed the auditor of state delivered the original to the purchaser. The state, however, kept no record of deeds executed prior to 1833. But if no deed is found of record or otherwise, and any evidence is found that one should have been made, "the governor shall execute a deed therefor in the name of the original purchaser." [30] While deeds for school lands not made in strict conformity to law are confirmed. [31]

Many special acts have also been passed authorizing other officials than the governor to execute deeds for school land. In many instances the county auditor has been so empowered instead; [25] and in such cases no record of the deeds has been kept by the state.

The income from the school land in general classes, one, two, three and four, derived from rent, or from the interest on the proceeds of the sale of the land, is divided pro rata among the inhabitants of each respective tract; while that derived from the lands in class five, applying to each original surveyed township, is divided among the inhabitants of the respective townships for which the tracts were assigned. However, in keeping account, the state has combined the funds received from the sale of

(24)   25 L. O., 56, 103; 26 L. O., 23; 28 L. O. L., 18; 29 L. O. L., 90; 49 L. O. L.   232.

(30)   54 L. O. 12;   79 L. O. 136.
(31)   53 L. O. 63;   99 L. O. 359.

the lands in the fourth class with those of the fifth class, and has, therefore, kept the record of the respective amounts received from the sale of school lands in four separate entries, which, at the end of the fiscal year of 1917, were as follows:

1. Virginia Military School Fund......$ 197,068.07
2. Western Reserve School Fund.......   257,499.21
3. United States Military School Fund.......   120,272.12
4. Section 16 School Fund 3,539,296.50

     Total ....$ 4,114,135.90

This fund, designated the "common school fund," constitutes a part of the irreducible debt of the state, on which it pays annually six per cent interest [26] to the respective districts, or original surveyed townships, for the benefit of which the funds were received. That part of the interest on the fund to which any district in general classes one, two, three or four is entitled, together with the rent from any such land remaining unsold, is apportioned to such respective districts by the auditor of state upon the basis of the enumeration of youth of school age residing within the district; [26] while that to which an original surveyed township in class five is en-

(25)   30 L. O. L., 344; 31 L. O. L., 93; 38 L. O. L., 177; 53 L. O., 63.

titled, is apportioned to it by the auditor of the county in which the township is situated. (26)

The lack of ownership of the land in the Connecticut Western reserve by the federal government; the right of Virginia to locate all the land in the Virginia Military tract; the many special acts of Congress for the sale of particular tracts of land; the subdivision of the United States Military tract into townships five miles square; the failure to reserve sections sixteen thruout the state; the provision for fractional townships, and the many special acts of the legislature for leasing, selling and conveying the land, have all contributed to create a condition little understood, and have caused the school lands in Ohio to become an unsolved problem to many. However, their solution may be simplified if their history is considered, especially chronologically. Therefore, if it is ascertained what led to the early settlements; where they were made, and why; how the title to the land was acquired, and, particularly, how the land was subdivided, and why, much of what may appear to be but confusion will readily dissolve itself into a more clear comprehension of the school lands in Ohio.

(26)   G. C., 7580; 107 L. O., 357.

CHAPTER 36

MINISTERIAL LANDS.

Notwithstanding the fact that Ohio's earliest settlers were descendants of the Puritans whose landing upon Plymouth Rock, in 1620, began the establishment of an ideal government under which, as one of its fundamental principles of success, was the separation of the Church and State, yet we have in Ohio, as nowhere else in the United States, the anomaly of that union. And strange and inconsistent as it may seem, this union was first conceived and brought about by the descendants of these Puritans who had fled their native land almost two centuries before, to escape persecution resulting from such combination. It was, therefore, in the New England States that the plan originated of endowing the church with land and making the state the trustee of the endowment.

With "religion, morality and knowledge," as their guiding rule of life, it is easy to understand that

MINISTERIAL LANDS IN OHIO

the descendants of these sturdy and devout pioneers would naturally endeavor to foster and support the development of education, and guarantee the freedom of religious worship "according to the dictates of one's own conscience." To this end, education and religion were each, therefore, endowed with the one thirty-sixth part of the land to be settled.

Who first conceived the idea of thus endowing the cause of religion with land, is not now known. The earliest suggestion of which any record is had, is that contained in a letter written in June of 1783, by General Rufus Putnam to General Washington, asking his aid to prevail upon the Continental Congress to redeem its land warrants given the revolutionary soldiers, by providing them with land "between the Ohio river and Lake Erie"; and when he recommended that the land be divided into "townships of six miles square, allowing to each township three thousand and forty acres for the ministry, schools, waste land, rivers, ponds and highways." Washington referred this letter to congress with his approval and urged that the request be granted as early as possible.

By reason of the circumstances leading to the creation of the new government, and the time necessary to acquire the Indian and the Colonial titles to these lands, congress was unable to consider appropriating land for the maintenance of churches

until the land ordinance of 1785 [1] was proposed;
and in the second report of which the committee
recommended that section twenty-nine in each township be set aside "for the support of religion." This
part of the report was rejected by a vote of seventeen
to six.   More definite action, however, was taken by
congress, in 1787, when Reverend Manasseh Cutler,
representing a number of New England people in
their contemplated purchase of land in southeastern
Ohio, known as the "Ohio Company's Purchase," insisted that such an endowment should be provided
for as one of the conditions on which that company
would make the purchase.

Dr. Cutler had had charge of parishes for many
years and was of the opinion that the religious interests of the people of any locality, especially in a newly settled country, could best be served by a clergy-
man residing within the community; that some
means should be provided to assure a dependable
fund for his support, and that land would be the most
permanent.   It was, therefore, through Dr. Cutler,
and in connection with the purchase of land by the
Ohio Company, that a resolution was adopted by the
Continental Congress, July 23, 1787, providing that
"the lot No. 29 in each township or fractional part of
a township, be given perpetually for the purposes of
religion." [2]

(1) 1 L. U. S., 563.   (2) 1 L. U. S., 573; L. H. O. U., 39.

Consequently sections twenty-nine were reserved for that purpose in the one million, five hundred thousand acre tract contracted for October 27,
1787, [3] by Dr. Cutler and Winthrop Sargent as
agents for the Ohio Company of Associates.   As
that company decided to take but half the land contracted for, a patent was issued in 1792, for that
amount which is known as the Ohio Company's first
purchase; and in each township of which, except the
two townships set aside for the Ohio University, [4]
section twenty-nine was reserved for the purposes
of religion as provided in the contract. [5]

Reservation of section twenty-nine "for the purposes of religion" was also made by the United
States, in 1794, in the grant to Judge John Cleves
Symmes and his associates for 311,682 acres lying
between the Miami rivers in the southwestern part
of the state. [6]   These two were the only grants
made by Congress for the support of religion. Many
others were applied for, but all were refused except
that in 1811 to the Baptist Society at Salem, Mississippi, which the president vetoed "because it com-
prised a principle and precedent for the appropriation of funds of the United States for the use and

(3)   L. H. O. U., 43.

(4)   See the Ohio University Lands.

(5)   2 L. U. S., 276; 1 U. S. S. L., 8; Washington County
      Deed Book 1, page 115.

(6)   See the Symmes Purchase; 1 L. U. S., 458, 494, 497;
      2 L. U. S., 287; 1 U. S. S. L., 266.

support of religious societies contrary to the article of the Constitution which declares that Congress shall make no law respecting a religious establishment."

As congress had reserved nothing for the purposes of religion in the grant of the second purchase to the Ohio Company of Associates, those associates, true to their original design, made the application themselves. Thereupon, by resolution of January 7, 1796, the trustees of that company assigned section twenty-nine in each of the ten townships in that purchase "for the purposes of religion within the townships respectively," and provided that the land should be leased by the inhabitants for a term not exceeding seven years at any one period.

The legislature of the state was designated to be the trustee of sections twenty-nine in the Ohio Company's first purchase and in the Symmes tract by the ordinances, contracts and acts of congress providing for the sale of those two tracts; while that body was authorized to act as trustee for those sections in the townships in the Ohio Company's second purchase, by the resolution of the trustees of that company, of January 7, 1796. [7]

The plan of setting aside section twenty-nine "for the purposes of religion" was not long con-

[7] See the Ohio Company.

tinued by the government which did so only in the Ohio Company's first purchase in Washington, Athens, Meigs, Gallia and Lawrence counties, and in the grant to Judge Symmes in Hamilton, Butler and Warren counties; while the Ohio Company appropriated section twenty-nine for that purpose in its second purchase in Morgan, Athens, Hocking and Vinton counties. Consequently, "Ministerial lands," as these lands have since been termed, are found nowhere in the United States, except within these three parts of the state of Ohio. They total about 43,500 acres of which but about 3,143 acres remained unsold at the end of the fiscal year of 1918.

For a number of years the ministerial lands were leased for farming purposes for terms varying from seven years to ninety-nine years renewable forever, for the annual rental of six per cent upon their appraised value, under laws, both general and special, passed by the legislature. The leases were executed generally by the three trustees of the original surveyed township to which the land belonged, and who also collected and distributed the rent and cared for the property. Sometimes other provisions were made for doing so, instead. [8]

As the ministerial lands were managed by the same officials who had charge of the school lands, abuses similar to those which prevailed in the man-

(8) 2 Sess. 1 G. A. T., 8; 3 L. O., 200; 4 L. O., 33.

agement of the latter, also crept into the management of the ministerial lands, and it was decided to
sell them.   But as the title to sections twenty-nine in
the Ohio Company's first purchase and in the
Symmes tract had been retained by the United
States, it was necessary for the state of Ohio to acquire the fee to the land and the power to sell.   Consequently, in 1827, the legislature requested congress
to authorize the state of Ohio to dispose of these
lands and invest the proceeds in some permanent
fund. (9)   Accordingly, in 1833, congress authorized
the legislature to sell and convey sections twenty-
nine reserved and appropriated by congress for the
support of religion within those two tracts, and to
invest the money arising from their sale in some productive fund of which the proceeds should be applied
annually to the support of religion within the several
townships for which the lands were originally reserved, provided that no part of such land should be
sold without the consent of the lessee and of the inhabitants of the township to which it belonged. (10)

Thereupon, in 1834, the legislature provided, by
a general act, for the sale of sections twenty-nine in
the Ohio Company's first purchase. (11)   Special acts
have also been passed since for the sale of many of
those sections within that tract, in a number of in-

(9)   25 L. O. L., 112.
(10)   8 L. U. S., 770; 4 U. S. S. L., 618.
(11)   32 L. O. L. 356; 51 L. O. 536.

stances for the sale of but part of a section. No general act, however, was passed for the sale of sections twenty-nine in the Symmes Purchase, but, instead, special acts were passed from time to time for the sale of each section. Where any of the land was held under lease, provision was made for the lessee to surrender his lease and obtain the fee instead. Upon the sale of any ministerial land being made, or the lessee surrendering his lease and purchasing the fee, the governor executed a deed to the purchaser. After being recorded by the auditor of state, the deed was delivered to the grantee. However, no record was kept of deeds issued prior to 1836.

The money paid on account of sales of ministerial lands, amounting, at the end of the fiscal year of 1918 ,to $150,216.00, constitutes the "ministerial trust fund," [12] and is a part of the irreducible debt of the state on which it pays annually six per cent interest to the denominations of religious societies having members residing within the township entitled to the fund, without regard to the township in which any such society regularly assembles for public worship. This amount, together with the rental received from the unsold ministerial lands, known as the "ministerial trust rental fund," is distributed to agents of the several societies in proportion to their membership. [13]

(12)   G. C. 3239; 107 L. O., 357.
(13)   G. C. 3205, 3206; 107 L. O., 357; 2 O. R., 108; 6. O. R., 445; 11 O. R., 24; 7 O. S. R., 58.

INDEX

A

Page

B

C

D

E

F

G

H

I

J

K

L

M

N

O

P

R

S

T

THE DEVELOPMENT OF PUBLIC LAND IN THE UNITED STATES

An Arno Press Collection

Bartley, Ernest R. **The Tidelands Oil Controversy.** 1953

Bayard, Charles J. **The Development of the Public Land Policy, 1783-1820, With Special Reference to Indiana** (Doctoral Dissertation, Indiana University, 1956). 1979

Bledsoe, S[amuel] T[homas]. **Indian Land Laws.** 1909

Copp, Henry N[orris]. **Manual for the Use of Prospectors on the Mineral Lands of the United States.** 1897

Copp, Henry N[orris]. **Public Land Laws.** 1875

Copp, Henry N[orris]. **United States Mineral Lands.** 1882

Dana, Samuel Trask and Myron Krueger. **California Lands.** 1958

Davison, Stanley R. **The Leadership of the Reclamation Movement, 1875-1902** (Doctoral Dissertation, University of California, Berkeley, 1952). 1979

Gould, Clarence P. **The Land System in Maryland, 1720-1765.** 1913

Ise, John. **Our National Park Policy.** 1961

Johnson, V. Webster and Raleigh Barlowe. **Land Problems and Policies.** 1954

Martz, Clyde O. **Cases and Materials on the Law of Natural Resources.** 1951

Malone, Joseph J. **Pine Trees and Politics.** 1964

Montgomery, Mary and Marion Clawson. **History of Legislation and Policy Formation of the Central Valley Project.** 1946

O'Callaghan, Jerry A. **The Disposition of the Public Domain in Oregon.** 1960

Peters, William E. **Ohio Lands and Their History.** 1930

Rae, John B. **The Development of Railway Land Subsidy Policy in the United States** (Doctoral Dissertation, Brown University, 1936). 1979

Shambaugh, Benjamin F[ranklin]. **Constitution and Records of the Claim Association of Johnson County, Iowa.** 1894

Smathers, George H. **The History of Land Titles in Western North Carolina.** 1938

Stewart, Lowell O. **Public Land Surveys.** 1935

Tatter, Henry W. **The Preferential Treatment of the Actual Settler in the Primary Disposition of the Vacant Lands in the United States** (Doctoral Dissertation, Northwestern University, 1933). 1979

Taylor, Paul S. **Essays on Land, Water, and the Law in California.** 1979

U.S. House of Representatives. **The Existing Laws of the United States of a General and Permanent Character, and Relating to the Survey and Disposition of the Public Domain, December 1, 1880.** 1884

U.S. House of Representatives. **Laws of the United States:** Of a Temporary Character, and Exhibiting the Entire Legislation of Congress Upon Which the Public Land Titles Have Depended. Two vols. 1881

U.S. Senate. **A National Plan for American Forestry.** Two vols. 1933

U.S. Senate. **The Western Range.** 1936

Wiel, Samuel C. **Water Rights in the Western States.** Two vols. 1911

Winter, Charles E. **Four Hundred Million Acres.** 1932

Wirth, Fremont P. **The Discovery and Exploitation of the Minnesota Iron Lands.** 1937